An Introduction to Climate Change Economics and Policy

Felix R. FitzRoy and Elissaios Papyrakis

publishing for a sustainable future

London • Sterling, VA

First published by Earthscan in the UK and USA in 2010

ISBN   978-1-84407-809-7 hardback
          978-1-84407-810-3 paperback

Typeset by MapSet Ltd, Gateshead, UK
Cover design by Susanne Harris

For a full list of publications please contact:

Earthscan
Dunstan House
14a St Cross St
London, EC1N 8XA, UK
Tel: +44 (0)20 7841 1930
Fax: +44 (0)20 7242 1474
Email: earthinfo@earthscan.co.uk
Web: **www.earthscan.co.uk**

22883 Quicksilver Drive, Sterling, VA 20166-2012, USA

Earthscan publishes in association with the International Institute for Environment
and Development

A catalogue record for this book is available from the British Library

Library of Congress Cataloging-in-Publication Data

FitzRoy, Felix.
  An introduction to climate change economics and policy / Felix R. FitzRoy and
Elissaios Papyrakis.
    p. cm.
  Includes bibliographical references and index.
  ISBN 978-1-84407-809-7 (hardback) — ISBN 978-1-84407-810-3 (pbk.) 1.
Climatic changes—Economic aspects. 2. Economic policy. I. Papyrakis, Elissaios.
II. Title.
  QC903.F58 2009 2010
   363.738'74—dc22

                                         2009021281

At Earthscan we strive to minimize our environmental impacts and carbon footprint
through reducing waste, recycling and offsetting our CO_2 emissions, including those
created through publication of this book. For more details of our environmental
policy, see www.earthscan.co.uk.

This book was printed in the UK by TJ International,
an ISO 14001 accredited company. The paper used
is FSC certified and the inks are vegetable based.

Mixed Sources
Product group from well-managed
forests and other controlled sources
www.fsc.org Cert no. SGS-COC-2482
© 1996 Forest Stewardship Council

We dedicate this book to:
Renate, Olga, Jamie,
Katia, Maira, Manolis and Kostis

Contents

Preface

There is now an overall scientific consensus that Earth is warming as a consequence of reckless human activity. What still remains contentious is the appropriate response to climate change. In recent years, the political and public debate on how we should respond to the threat has intensified. How should we divide investment between mitigation and adaptation? Should we give priority to renewable technologies, the development of carbon capture and storage, or halting deforestation? How much of our income should we sacrifice to prevent further warming for the sake of the poor and future generations? Without doubt, there is an increasing interest in economic and policy aspects of climate change, which is reflected in the rapidly rising number of scientific publications, informal reports, newspaper articles and public debates. In 2009, 'climate change' attracted approximately 50 million hits with Google, more than 'inflation' and 'unemployment'. Increasing interest is certainly encouraging, but the flood of information can easily become daunting and overwhelming for the average reader.

While there are many good and accessible introductions to climate science and to the policy debates, they usually include much more detail than the average interested but non-specialist reader is willing or able to assimilate. With this book, we offer readers a short, uncluttered introduction to the *key* scientific developments on climate change, the most threatening consequences and the most appropriate policies in response. We avoid less relevant detail and technical terminology, but rather analyse current issues in a simple, systematic way that does not require prior knowledge of the problems. Anyone with an interest in the most vital environmental and development issues should benefit from reading the book, and quickly become familiar with the recent evidence on global warming – and what we should do about it – without having to follow complicated jargon, numerous acronyms and a mass of statistics.

We do cover a wide range of topics, some of which have been neglected in discussions of climate change. In particular, we emphasize the role of global agriculture, already facing severe problems of erosion and water shortages, since climate change will amplify existing risks and challenges in the sector. Long before rising sea levels flood the world's coastal cities, prolonged drought in major food-producing areas could lead to starvation for the poorest populations and large-scale loss of life. Such catastrophes are not included in economic cost–benefit analysis that only relates future consumption of survivors to current investment in reducing emissions. In addition to the ethical obligation of the rich countries that are responsible for most past emissions, we emphasize the local and short-term benefits to all countries from conservation agriculture, reforestation and energy saving. All mitigation policies incur political costs of persuasion and redistribution, but in contrast to widely held views, many generate net economic benefits, as well as insurance against the incalculable human costs of truly disastrous climate change under continued growth of greenhouse gas emissions.

Some of the material here has been included in courses at various levels at the Universities of St Andrews, Edinburgh and East Anglia for a number of years. This includes a first-year, interdisciplinary introduction to sustainable development at St Andrews, undergraduate and postgraduate environmental economics options at St Andrews and Edinburgh, and the Master's programme in climate change and international development at the University of East Anglia. We hope the book will also be particularly useful for undergraduate students in environmental sciences, economics, geography and development who want a simple introduction to the current debate on climate change issues and policies. It should also be helpful to more advanced students and academics, as we put more emphasis on the interdisciplinary nature of the problems considered than is usual, and throughout all chapters provide notes and references to more advanced readings on specific aspects of climate change and policy.

Acknowledgements

Several people have played a decisive role in shaping this book. Colleagues, friends, and former students from various institutions and countries have been generous with their time, reading drafts of our chapters and providing insights and feedback, including Frank Ackerman, Natalia Alvarez, Konstantinos Angelopoulos, Jeroen van den Bergh, Declan Conway, Tim Daw, Roger Few, Jennifer Franz, Reyer Gerlagh, Elisa Lanzi, Eric Neumayer, Peter Newell, Nicola Searle, Max Steinhardt, Geoff Tansey, David Ulph, Hans-Peter Weikard and Ernst von Weizsäcker. We are especially grateful to Roger Perman of Strathclyde University, Glasgow, who reviewed the whole manuscript and provided detailed comments. Special thanks also to our students, who were taught parts of this material at various levels and generously provided feedback on the book's content. None of them are to blame for opinions expressed or any remaining errors.

We were particularly privileged to work with Earthscan, who provided continuous support and detailed comments for both the content of the manuscript as well as the overall presentation, production and marketing. We received extremely useful input from our editor Rob West, who oversaw the whole process. Claire Lamont assisted us in designing the book cover and provided help and guidance whenever called upon. Gudrun Freese looked after marketing, and Hamish Ironside managed the complexities of copy-editing. At St Andrews, Nikos Terzopoulos expertly organized our manuscript into final format.

Last but not least, our deepest thanks go to our immediate family and friends, who patiently read drafts of the book, without having any particular expertise either in economics or in climate change issues. Their feedback was important in shaping the style of the book. With their help, we produced a book that we hope is accessible to a broad audience. They contributed to every single stage of our ambitious endeavour to synthesize the rapidly expanding literature on the economics and policy of climate change, just by being there for us and responding critically to our preoccupations. This book would simply not be the same without the presence of our children, nieces and nephews, who continuously reminded us that this is a book for the benefit of future generations. We therefore thank Tina Caba, Ali Caba, Ozan Caba, Elif Caba, Renate FitzRoy, Jamie FitzRoy, Olga FitzRoy, Andries Kamminga, Manolis Papyrakis, Kostis Papyrakis, Katia Stavroulaki and Maira Stavroulaki.

1

Introduction

Climate Change and the Political Landscape

Climate change has moved rapidly up the political agenda as the scientific evidence has become better known. The perils of extreme weather conditions, such as the disaster of Hurricane Katrina in New Orleans in 2005 and the more deadly, record European heatwave of 2003, attracted widespread public attention. Following the success of his documentary *An Inconvenient Truth*, former US Vice-President Al Gore was awarded the Nobel Peace Prize, jointly with the Intergovernmental Panel on Climate Change (IPCC) for their Fourth Assessment Report early in 2007. This contained stark warnings on the threat of global warming and the urgency of mitigation measures to reduce greenhouse gas (GHG) emissions, but was not entirely up to date. Newer scientific predictions have become considerably more pessimistic, with Arctic sea ice and snow cover in particular receding far more rapidly than expected, which in turn will accelerate warming and sea-level rise.

Another milestone in the discussion of climate change was the first official government review of its economic effects, led by British economist Lord Nicholas Stern and known as the Stern Review, in 2006. The estimated costs of global warming from continued business as usual were much larger than previously claimed – however, what Stern called 'strong policies' and targets for mitigation still imply very high risks of catastrophic warming that could destroy civilization and agriculture as we know it over much of the planet. Stern thinks the very worst possible outcome could be the loss of 20 per cent of future global economic output, which would still be much greater than current output, because he assumes that economic growth will continue unabated. He does not consider the possibility of collapsing agriculture and economies under runaway warming, or the real risk of mass starvation facing the world's poorest people. However, as the first study of this kind by a government team, the work attracted widespread publicity – as well as criticism, mainly for the wrong reasons, from other economists and, more soundly, from environmentalists. Stern's analysis has influenced government targets, but they, too, remain seriously inadequate. Thus the official UK target, in the Climate Change Act of 2008, is an 80 per cent reduction of emissions only by 2050 (which is much too late according to the latest science), and little in the way of concrete policy measures has been announced since.

After European Union governments had also announced (weak) targets for reducing GHG emissions, a United Nations conference in Bali in December 2007 reached agreement in principle on the need for a successor to the now largely defunct Kyoto Protocol, in spite of fierce opposition by the US Bush Administration's representatives. Serious negotiation was postponed to the next UN climate conference at Copenhagen in December 2009, when cooperation from new US President Barack Obama is expected, with plans for a US carbon cap-and-trade system and other energy-saving policies. After poor management of the EU emissions trading system (ETS) since its launch in 2005, there is now the prospect of US leadership for improved regional or national cap-and-trade systems, which might pave the way to global carbon pricing.

The sheer flood of commentary and information on the science, policy and economics of climate change has left many people unclear or confused on key questions – just how great and how urgent is the threat from climate change, and what will it cost to take appropriate action? For many years, confusion has been deliberately spread by lobbyists for the fossil fuel industries (some of whom had previously worked in a similar capacity for tobacco companies) and a few eccentrics who ignored the real science. Confusion has been fostered by the media everywhere, including public service broadcasters such as the BBC, which until recently gave more-or-less equal coverage to warnings by serious scientists and to denials by lobbyists. Systematic public education on these vital questions has been neglected in most countries.

Much has also been written on policy for reducing GHG emissions from various perspectives. Economists have usually ignored the possibility of large-scale loss of life under catastrophic climate change if present policies are continued with 'business as usual'. They also exaggerate the costs of mitigation by neglecting the additional health and efficiency benefits from energy saving, conservation agriculture and a greener economy. However, there are always political costs of change. Increasing efficiency by shifting taxes from labour to pollution, and switching subsidies from fossil fuels and industrial agriculture to sustainable alternatives, does generate strong opposition from the losers and their government supporters.

Structure of the Book

Any book on the economics and policy of climate change needs to be rooted in the science of climate change and what it implies for how we react or should react as a global society. Chapter 2 provides a brief, non-technical overview of the consensus on the basic science of climate change. It explains the role of greenhouse gases and carbon sinks, as well as the key feedback mechanisms that are likely to accelerate the pace of climate change and carry the risk of runaway warming, such as methane emissions from thawing permafrost and decreased surface albedo or reflectivity as ice and snow cover recede.

Most writers on the consequences of climate change acknowledge that the world's poorest countries will bear the greatest burden of water shortages and falling food supply. However, most discussions of *policy* response to climate change pay little or no attention to agriculture, which is of particular importance for the livelihoods of billions of poor households in the developing world (while accounting for tiny fractions of output and employment in developed countries). Chapter 3 examines the prospects for agriculture in a changing climate, summarizing extensive evidence that modern agriculture is *already* under severe threat from the very same methods that have dramatically raised yields – as well as water and energy requirements – over the past 50 years. The predicted rising temperatures and worsening droughts in major food-producing regions which are already hot and arid are likely to have devastating consequences for agriculture, with global impact. Each additional temperature rise of one degree Centigrade during the hot growing seasons of many southern agricultural areas is predicted to reduce grain yields by at least 10 per cent. Just a small decline in the world output of wheat, in the face of growing demand, doubled its price in 2007. The further, rapid rise of grain and oil prices was only halted by the financial crash and global recession of 2008. Really large-scale crop failures resulting from future warming and water shortages in developing areas would cause prices of staple foods to rise many times over and lead to mass starvation among the world's poorest people.

Historically, famines have always been local or regional, and there has never been a global food shortage, but the combination of declining water reserves, increasing temperatures and growing population in the developing countries means that agricultural catastrophe, probably accompanied by global conflict, becomes the most immediate threat from continued climate change. Surprisingly perhaps, simple well-tried techniques of conservation, or no-till agriculture and large-scale reforestation, could substantially reduce this threat. As well as lowering the GHG emissions from modern agriculture, these methods reverse currently accelerating carbon loss from eroding soils and actually capture atmospheric carbon in accumulating organic material. Input costs are reduced, and sustainable yields increased in the long run, so abatement of GHG emissions can be combined with the co-benefits of more efficient and sustainable farming. Further mitigation measures are, of course, urgently required, as even the most robust agriculture will ultimately be decimated if runaway warming is triggered by growing fossil fuel consumption.

Chapter 4 looks at the links between economic growth, wellbeing and the environment. A major theme of our approach is that the costs of climate change mitigation have been exaggerated under the influence of fossil fuel lobbying and the prevailing ideology of ever-increasing material consumption and economic growth, whatever the real environmental costs. One reason is that many policies to reduce emissions will have substantial additional or co-benefits, in the form of reduced pollution and better human and animal health in the short to medium term. A second point is that possibly slower economic growth due to mitigation policies is not really a 'cost' in the advanced economies. In fact, 30 years of careful survey research by social scientists show clearly that in rich countries, subjective wellbeing does not increase with average real incomes in the long run (though short-term economic fluctuation certainly influences welfare). The reason is partly the erosion of 'social capital' and human relations that is often the price of material growth and partly the fact that subjective wellbeing depends on relative rather than absolute income when basic needs have been met. Recent surveys suggest that even in China, where fast growth and poverty reduction have been absolute priorities, rapidly increasing inequality has been accompanied by declining happiness and life satisfaction.

It follows that even if mitigation policies to reduce emissions also slow down the rate of material growth in rich countries, this does not imply a future cost in terms of reduced subjective wellbeing. In poor countries, which are the main focus of Chapter 5, economic growth can bring real benefits to all, though most of the benefits are usually appropriated by a wealthy minority. Sustainable development and distributional justice, without the environmental degradation and growing inequality that have hitherto always accompanied early industrialization, should thus become a major goal of international policy. The developed economies are responsible for most of the existing stock of GHGs in the atmosphere, and most discussion of policies for abatement has focused on these countries. But the largest developing countries, China and India, are now among the fastest-growing polluters (and economies), and China has actually caught up with the US in total emissions. We will therefore consider policies for reducing GHG emissions in both developing and developed countries, as well as the related issues of aid, trade and globalization in relation to the environment and sustainable development.

In Chapter 6 we argue that the ethical principles of justice provide an essential foundation for policies to protect unborn generations, and the poorest countries, from climate change, though this aspect has been neglected by many economists. Related issues arise in connection with persistently inadequate aid for these nations, in the face of growing threats to agriculture and water supply, and rules of international trade which mainly benefit the rich countries. Increasing aid for the world's poorest peoples can be an integral part of effective mitigation. With 20 per cent of carbon emissions from (mostly tropical) deforestation, carbon credits for forest preservation would combine aid to poorer countries with one of the most cost-effective forms of abatement. Perhaps the most cost-effective but politically fraught policy reform would be the removal of several hundred billions of dollars of annual subsidies from the two biggest recipients in the Organisation for Economic Co-operation and Development (OECD) – destructive industrial agriculture and fossil fuels. A small fraction of this would accelerate the already rapid rate of technical progress in renewable energy, and the still glacial pace of adoption in most areas, as well as encouraging the essential switch to conservation agriculture.

Turning to international agreements in Chapter 7, we evaluate the Kyoto Protocol and its mechanisms as a means to reduce global emissions. With few incentives for mitigation, and the absence of sanctions against the worst polluters such as China and the US, we argue that Kyoto has largely been a failure in the fight against climate change. Emissions trading in the EU has been equally unsuccessful in its first phase, with free distribution of carbon allowances or permits to the biggest emitters, who have used their market power to raise prices and generate huge windfall profits. Permit prices have fluctuated, but generally remained too low to provide an adequate incentive for investment in alternative or decentralized energy generation. While more permits should be auctioned in future stages of the EU ETS, there is strong industry lobbying for exceptions, which are, of course, easier to justify during the current economic downturn.

Chapter 8 reviews the economic instruments and incentives for reducing GHG emissions. Although carbon taxes have many theoretical advantages, new US President Obama has made a commitment to a comprehensive carbon cap-and-trade system. Applied 'upstream' to all producers and importers of fossil fuels, this could improve considerably on the European system, which only covers large industrial emitters, and perhaps be politically more acceptable than new taxes, though likely to be delayed by the recession. As in the EU, an initial free allocation, with a limited but growing share of auctioned permits, will reduce industry opposition, and in the long run could approach an ideal carbon tax. This long-overdue initiative by the US may encourage other countries to follow, so that international, and ultimately global, carbon trading could result. On the other hand, there is very little prospect at the moment of starting with one of the far-reaching, 'top–down' global agreements on carbon trading that have often been proposed before there is more experience with functioning national or regional systems.

Most economic analysis of climate change and mitigation, as we explain in Chapter 9, has seriously underestimated the risks of runaway warming under current policies, or 'business as usual', and resulting catastrophic effects on third world agriculture. At the same time, the costs of switching to sustainable conservation farming and alternative energy supply have been exaggerated by agribusiness and fossil fuel industries. Economic growth is simply assumed to continue unabated for the next century or two, and the very worst impact of climate change has been compared by Lord Stern to the Great Depression of the 1930s, though he still thinks this 'worst case' is very unlikely. This means that our descendants, who will be many times richer than we are, might lose at most 20 per cent of their incomes. How many lives might be lost is not generally considered.

We shall argue that this position is based on fundamental misunderstanding of the latest climate and environmental science, as well as neglect of the basic ethical issues. Really catastrophic outcomes of runaway warming are not only possible but even likely if GHG emissions are not reduced much more rapidly than under Stern's – and all government – targets to date. The global conflict potential of large-scale starvation in the poorest regions, and the collapse of fragile but nuclear-armed states, will threaten prosperity and security even in the most affluent countries. Prudence and concern for the welfare of our children justify major investment in mitigation as insurance against these risks. In the developed countries we have the additional ethical responsibility for having produced most of the GHGs in the atmosphere today. The biggest developing nations are now catching up as polluters, while devastating their environments and the health of their citizens, increasing the likelihood of globally catastrophic climate impact in the future. These countries are repeating all the mistakes made by the West in earlier industrialization, with little public awareness of the prime threat to their own populations. A refocusing of trade and aid policies to promote 'cleaner', sustainable development thus becomes all the more urgent.

In our concluding Chapter 10 we show that the current economic crisis offers huge opportunities for 'green fiscal policy', government spending on energy-saving projects that would also reduce unemployment, particularly in construction sectors that have been hardest hit by collapsing housing bubbles. These opportunities have been largely missed, with only a very small share of green projects in the stimulus packages of the major economies. In our discussion of policy responses to climate change and environmental degradation we emphasize the ethical and distributional issues to complement the economic, cost–benefit aspects that usually dominate the discussion. We find that substantial mitigation can be achieved with measures that actually improve health and welfare, and that most of the perceived costs of the necessary drastic emissions reduction are political and distributional. However, there are also real psychological costs of changing familiar habits, even when more environmentally friendly behaviour also brings personal benefits in the long run. So we come back to the crucial issue of public education about the magnitude of the threats facing us all and, more optimistically, about the feasibility and multiple benefits of effective 'insurance' policy – which summarize the two main aims or themes of this book.

Basic Science of Climate Change

New findings by climate scientists are reported ever more frequently in the media, as public interest in the prospects of climate change has grown dramatically in the recent past for a number of reasons. The long-standing consensus among almost all scientists on the human causes of current rapid global warming and its huge threat for life on Earth has been widely disseminated by former US Vice-President Al Gore in his 2006 book and Oscar-winning documentary *An Inconvenient Truth*. Early in 2007, the IPCC summarized the scientific consensus in its Fourth Assessment Report, and shortly afterwards the EU announced commitments to reduce emissions of greenhouse gases by increasing the share of renewable energy. The IPCC and Al Gore then shared the 2007 Nobel Peace Prize in recognition of the importance of their work for the future of humanity. At about the same time, the Stern Review commissioned by the British Government provided estimates of huge expected economic costs of global warming and emphasized the urgent need for major investment in mitigation.[1]

Some political commitments and much discussion at a series of EU and UN conferences have followed the publicity. Late in 2008, the global economic crisis took centre stage, but new US President Barack Obama, in striking contrast to his predecessor, has announced plans for a carbon cap-and-trade system and other initiatives to reduce emissions by 80 per cent by 2050. In December 2009, the UN climate change conference in Copenhagen is scheduled to negotiate a successor to the ill-fated Kyoto agreement. As we shall show, all targets that have been announced so far are woefully inadequate in the light of the science that we review here.

Unfortunately, there remains much confusion among the general public about the key facts and implications of climate change. This is partly due to the veritable flood of media reports on climate change, including the science, policy discussion and possibly related-weather phenomena. At the same time, ever more frequent, usually vague and often misleading statements by leading politicians make it difficult for the layperson to see the wood for the trees. More fundamentally, however, the long-standing campaign by the fossil fuel lobbies to systematically confuse and misinform public opinion has been regularly and uncritically reported by the media and raised honest doubts among some who are unfamiliar with the evidence.

In this chapter we start with a brief summary of key facts from the geological history of the Earth's climate – the 'palaeoclimate' – that are particularly relevant for predicting how our climate is likely to react to various future scenarios of human activity. We then turn to the evidence on current climate change and the actual predictions of the complex computer models of the global climate system that have reached close agreement on many important issues. The absurdity of the claims made by climate change deniers will be exposed on the way, and for the benefit of readers unfamiliar with their tactics we will present some background to the most egregious examples.

A Very Short History of Climate

For as far back as temperatures can be estimated from geological evidence, the Earth's climate has undergone major fluctuations. These have ranged from the extremes of 'Snowball Earth' when most of the planet was probably covered with ice around 600 million years ago, to more frequent and extended 'hothouse' periods of global tropical climate with no polar ice. The most detailed records come from ice cores drilled out of the ice caps that cover Greenland and Antarctica. The annual snowfall that has built up the ice sheets to a thickness of several kilometres also traps microscopic air bubbles from the atmosphere, and these can be analysed for their content of carbon dioxide, methane and other greenhouse gases. These gases (and also water vapour) absorb infrared, or long-wave, heat radiation from the Earth's surface better than other components of the atmosphere such as oxygen and nitrogen, and thus warm the atmosphere as their name 'greenhouse gases' implies. The ratio of oxygen isotopes in the ice cores also provides a precise record of the prevailing temperature when the snow fell.

The ice core records now go back 800,000 years and reveal a remarkable pattern of cold periods that lasted about 100,000 years, with warmer spells of variable length in between. Other evidence shows extensive coverage of northern regions by ice sheets up to four kilometres thick during the cold periods, which are commonly referred to as 'ice ages'. Our current warm 'interglacial' spell – called the Holocene – has lasted about 11,000 years and enabled the development of human culture in benign climates.

Ice ages were probably triggered by small changes in the Earth's axis of rotation, and orbit around the sun, that alter the distribution and intensity of solar radiation, particularly in the polar regions. A slight initial cooling then began to remove CO_2 from the atmosphere, probably through biological activity in the oceans, which amplified the cooling effect. At the same time, expanding ice and snow cover reflected more of the incoming radiation back into space – a process known as the 'ice albedo effect'. These positive 'feedbacks' were ultimately the main reason for much lower temperatures persisting throughout the ice age, with the albedo effect responsible for two-thirds of the cooling. Just what started the warming process that ended the ice ages is less clear, but the same feedbacks operated in reverse to increase greenhouse gases and reduce albedo as the ice cover receded and temperatures rose. While sea levels were about 120 metres lower than at present during the greatest extent of ice, melting then accelerated to a dramatic pace, raising the sea level by about a metre every 20 years for four centuries around 14,000 years ago.

This is an ominous portent for our near-term future, with rapidly accelerating loss of Greenland ice observed in the last few years, though this development was ignored by the IPCC in its 2007 Assessment Report, which foresees only slow melting and sea-level rise over the next century. However, this forecast (like the rest of the report) is based on research that had already been published, after often lengthy peer review, when it was being prepared in 2005–2006. Thus the 2007 IPCC report summarizes research that was already several years old and thus obviously did not consider the most recent observations pointing to a possible break-up and collapse of the ice caps, rather than a slow melting from the top down. The need for consensus among the hundreds of scientists involved, from many different countries, also means that the IPCC reports are quite conservative documents and is another reason why they do not always represent the frontiers of current climate science.

During the last ice age, the quantity of carbon dioxide in the atmosphere was about 190 parts per million by volume (ppm). This increased over a few millennia to about 280ppm in the current interglacial, an amount that remained stable until industrialization, but has now increased by more than a third to about 390ppm.[2] Global mean temperature has increased by nearly 0.8°C over the past 150 years.

Records from the ice cores also reveal rapid, short-term temperature oscillations of several degrees between the two polar regions throughout the ice ages. A likely candidate for explaining this instability is the ocean current that transports warm, salty surface water from the South Atlantic to the North Atlantic between Iceland and Greenland, where it cools and sinks, returning south as a deep, cold ocean current. This Atlantic 'meridional overturning circulation' (also called 'thermohaline circulation' and sometimes, incorrectly, 'the Gulf Stream') is responsible for north-western Europe's relatively mild climate. The circulation probably stopped abruptly at the end of the last ice age, about 12,800 years ago, as a giant freshwater lake left by the receding ice sheet over North America suddenly flooded into the North Atlantic, diluting the salty surface current sufficiently to prevent it sinking. The break lasted for 1200 years and plunged Europe into a local ice age called the Younger Dryas, though it probably had little effect in much of the southern hemisphere. Interruption or slowing of the circulation at regular intervals before this may well have caused the observed swings of temperature between the poles, though the reasons remain unclear. A major slowdown or interruption of the Atlantic circulation is now thought by most scientists to be unlikely in the medium-term future.

There was another similar, though less severe, 'mini ice age' starting about 8200 years ago but only lasting a few centuries, but then the climate settled into the current stable, warm period known as the Holocene, with only minor fluctuations. The last of these was the 'little ice age', a cool spell that was depicted by the great Flemish and other artists of the 17th and early 18th centuries in their paintings of skaters and revellers on frozen rivers, scenes that became increasingly rare with subsequent warming. Prior to that, the 'medieval warm period', when Viking settlers could grow crops in southern Greenland, as their descendants have recently started to do again, has attracted some attention. However the consensus is that current global mean temperatures are definitely higher than at the medieval maximum, though of course the latter can only be estimated indirectly from evidence such as tree rings, and individual results for particular regions are subject to some uncertainty.

An interesting question, then, is what caused these fluctuations when atmospheric greenhouse gases were quite stable. One likely factor in relatively small historical temperature variations is fluctuating solar activity, which follows cycles in the number of sunspots. For most of the 20th century there was a close correlation between solar activity and global mean temperature, but the most accurate measurements to date, by Mike Lockwood of Oxford University and Claus Fröhlich from the Davos Observatory in Switzerland, show the opposite development since 1985.[3] During these last two decades of most rapid warming, all solar indicators have been *declining*, which provides conclusive confirmation of what earlier observations had already suggested, that recent warming would have been even greater without solar effects.

This important scientific advance also puts the final nail in the coffin of the 'denial industry', or 'contrarians', who contest various aspects of climate science with false or misleading claims, many of which were recently broadcast in a notorious TV programme.[4] The latest climate models also show that the effect of solar activity was fairly small over the last 100 years, with most of the warming explained by rising concentrations of greenhouse gases. The slight cooling observed in the 1950s and 1960s is also explained by the same models as a result of sulphates and dust, or 'aerosols', in the atmosphere; these reflect more radiation than they absorb and thus have a cooling effect. A further decline in solar activity is possible, though speculative, and could briefly slow down the warming process. A diminishing North Atlantic circulation could have a similar but stronger local effect in Western Europe, though this is now considered unlikely by most experts.

There is an erroneous popular view that evidence for climate sensitivity to natural 'forcing', such as orbital or solar variation, in some way undermines the importance of current anthropogenic greenhouse gas emissions for future climate change. This quite illogical conclusion is close to the opposite of the truth. Greater sensitivity of the complex climate system to one kind of forcing influence and associated feedbacks is actually more likely to imply greater sensitivity to other influences. All the evidence we have suggests that the climate has a tendency to switch quite rapidly from one relatively stable 'equilibrium' state to another (such as from ice ages to interglacials). These switches have been driven by very small changes in the distribution or intensity of solar radiation, which are then amplified by various and complex feedback processes. One of these – the carbon cycle feedback – is also directly affected by modern agriculture, while thawing Arctic permafrost and Siberian peat deposits represent major additional sources of greenhouse gases that have not yet been quantified and incorporated into standard climate models.

To obtain more direct lessons for our future, we have to go further back into the past. Before the last ice age, during the Eemian interglacial period around 125,000 years ago, global mean temperatures were about one degree warmer than today, with even higher temperatures close to the poles and less ice cover, so that sea levels were about five metres higher than now. Since about the same amount of additional warming is now expected as the oceans catch up with the atmosphere, even with no further rise in atmospheric greenhouse gases, this suggests a threat of sea-level rise much greater than predicted by the IPCC, as we discuss in detail below.

The threat appears even greater if we go back much further to the Pliocene era, 3 million years ago, just before the start of the sequence of ice ages and interglacials that has continued ever since.[5] The global temperature was then around three degrees warmer than at present, with probably somewhat more carbon dioxide in the atmosphere (between 350ppm and 450ppm). There seem to have been no glaciers in the northern hemisphere and less ice in the Antarctic, while sea levels were 20–25m higher than today. While reduced albedo, differences in the Earth's orbit and orientation (and perhaps in solar activity too) played a role in causing the higher temperatures during these prehistoric epochs, the overriding lesson is that dramatic rises in sea level are likely with quite modest increases in global temperature. As we explain next, there is strong, recent evidence that this process has already begun, but because quantitative modelling is still in its infancy (and perhaps also due to the constraints of forming a conservative consensus) the latest IPCC report has ignored this evidence.

Climate Change Today

Signs of warming have become increasingly evident even to casual observation in recent years. Winters are shorter and milder, snow and ice cover and glaciers are everywhere receding, and, as in previous episodes, warming is much faster in the Arctic. Here, sea ice in summer has been receding recently much faster than predicted by climate models, probably due to changing winds and ocean currents, while the remaining ice has become much thinner and hence more fragile. The IPCC predicted an ice-free Arctic in late summer by the end of the century, but forecasts have fallen to a decade or two. This trend, together with reduced and shorter snow cover on land, means less solar radiation is reflected and warming is accelerated over most of the northern permafrost region.

It also used to be thought that warmer climate would cause the ice caps of Greenland and Antarctica to melt slowly, from the top down, and take millennia to complete. This view was still the basis for the IPCC predictions that there will not be a significant rise in sea levels this century. However, the dramatic increase in sea levels at the end of the last ice age described above casts doubt on this view, and recent observations also suggest a much more alarming development. Both the ice caps appear to be quite fragile, with deep cracks and crevasses now opening up on the surface of Greenland, allowing surface meltwater to plunge right down to the bedrock on which the ice cap rests. This water then lubricates the flow of glaciers into the sea and accelerates the rate of loss of coastal icebergs.

The West Antarctic ice sheet is still more vulnerable, as it rests on submerged islands rather than mainland. Although Antarctic temperatures have so far risen much less than in the Arctic, ice loss there has also accelerated. Most climate models do not incorporate any break-up or collapse of the ice sheets, so the optimistic predictions of the IPCC seem to be as fragile as the ice sheets now appear. While no one knows if, or by how much, current ice loss will accelerate, further warming can only increase the likelihood of collapsing ice sheets and a repeat of the rapid sea-level rise that occurred around 14,000 years ago. Leading climate scientist James Hansen has recently warned, 'Huge sea level rises are coming – unless we act now.'[6] At the same time, it is not only polar ice that is receding: glaciers (and winter snow cover) all over the world are also shrinking rapidly, including those in the Himalayas that maintain water supply for about a billion people in the densely populated surrounding regions.

At the moment atmospheric carbon dioxide is increasing by about 2.5ppm per year. In terms of carbon content, human activity is adding more than 10 billion metric tonnes of carbon annually to the atmosphere, of which about half, or 5 billion tonnes, is absorbed by the natural environment of the oceans, plant life and so on; the other half remains in the atmosphere. The total stock of carbon in the atmosphere of about 800 billion tonnes is thus increasing by less than one per cent per year. This may seem to be only a modest increase, but is nonetheless alarming because our climate is so close to the threshold beyond which runaway warming and large-scale agricultural collapse become very likely. Anthropogenic carbon emissions are still increasing by about three per cent annually. This is due to growing use of coal in the rapidly developing and most energy-wasteful countries, and these trends have dominated any gradually improving overall energy efficiency.

The capacity of natural 'sinks' to absorb carbon is also likely to decline with further warming, a tendency that will be exacerbated as the oceans, which are the largest sink, catch up with higher atmospheric temperatures. The increasing concentration of carbon dioxide in the atmosphere is causing the oceans to become more acidic, which in turn inhibits the micro-organisms (phytoplankton) that remove carbon from the air, as well as destroying coral reefs and other biodiversity. Globally, soil contains more organic carbon than atmosphere and vegetation combined, and under favourable conditions such as low-till cultivation and cover cropping (discussed in Chapter 3) can accumulate or sequester large amounts of carbon. However, modern industrial agriculture and overgrazing are causing widespread soil erosion in many parts of the world, which leads to loss of humus and further carbon dioxide emissions. The oxidization of organic matter is also accelerated by higher temperatures.

Deforestation contributes roughly 20 per cent of current anthropogenic carbon emissions, mostly by burning. In addition to carbon dioxide, burning any kind of biomass produces clouds of smoke, particles of soot and sulphates, or aerosols, which has created a persistent atmospheric brown cloud (ABC) or haze over much of South and East Asia and parts of the Amazon basin. As well as rural cooking with biomass, growing use of dirty, high-sulphur coal is also a major contributor to haze and smog in rapidly industrializing China and India. This aerosol haze obstructs solar radiation and thus has a cooling effect opposed to the greenhouse effect of carbon dioxide, as well as reducing plant photosynthesis and thus slowing growth. However, the black carbon or soot component of haze absorbs radiation and thus has a strong warming effect in the lower atmosphere, as well as reducing the reflectivity – and thus accelerating melting – of ice and snow where it is deposited, particularly in the Himalayan region.[7] Globally, aerosols still have a very substantial overall cooling influence on surface temperatures, but in contrast to greenhouse gases, soot and other aerosols are quickly washed out of the air by rainfall, so must be constantly replenished to maintain their effects.

Biomass burning is a major contributor to anthropogenic carbon emissions, though some of this is absorbed by fresh growth.[8] It includes the burning of forest and savannah, as well as the use of biomass for cooking by 3 billion people in much of the developing world. 'Indoor' air pollution from the latter (and other solid fuel such as coal) has been identified by the World Health Organization as a greater overall health hazard than 'outdoor' urban air pollution, though both are responsible for millions of annual deaths and much ill health in the developing countries. As discussed in detail in Chapter 9, stopping deforestation, large-scale reforestation and replacing biomass burning with the cheap, simple solar cookers already available would be among the most cost-effective policies to make a major impact on both GHG emissions and health in affected countries. However, it is often forgotten that the elimination of ABCs and aerosol pollution would have an immediate warming effect as well, perhaps equivalent to 50–80ppm of CO_2, simply because of the removal of the net cooling or dimming caused by aerosols currently.

Future Prospects

The warming effects of atmospheric water vapour, carbon dioxide, methane and other greenhouse gases have been well known since the 19th century. In a remarkable study in 1896, the Swedish scientist Svante Arrhenius calculated the effects of a doubling of atmospheric carbon dioxide, using fundamentally the same approach as modern climate models (though with less computing power!) and reaching a similar conclusion: that a four to six degree global temperature rise was to be expected. Since the oceans take much longer to warm up than the atmosphere, we know that warming will continue for many years even if there were no further increase in the stock of greenhouse gases in the atmosphere. Snow and ice will continue to recede, reducing albedo and also enhancing warming, until a new equilibrium is reached with smaller ice sheets and higher sea levels.

The albedo effect is just one of the many positive feedbacks that amplify the primary influence of anthropogenic GHG emissions. Another important feedback that is attracting increasing attention, but which has not yet been incorporated into most climate models, is the carbon feedback. Increasing emissions from eroding soils have already been mentioned, but another potentially major source is the currently permanently frozen Arctic tundra region of Siberia, Canada and Alaska. As the ground continues to thaw under the rapidly warming northern climate, organic matter such as peat begins to decompose, releasing carbon dioxide or the much more powerful GHG methane from anaerobic decomposition in waterlogged, marshy areas. The tundra is believed to contain perhaps twice as much carbon as the atmosphere, and emissions of methane have been accelerating at various locations, while subsidence of roads and buildings is a serious problem in many northern settlements.

In low latitudes, tropical rainforest is currently an important carbon sink, but rising temperatures are likely to transform these crucial areas into carbon emitters. Worldwide, the rainforest contains nearly as much carbon as the atmosphere and it will become increasingly vulnerable to drought and natural fires. There is thus a real threat of large-scale feedbacks from the tropics as well as from the tundra.

As with the uncertainty about the future rate of collapse of the polar ice sheets, there are no firm estimates of how rapidly permafrost will thaw or how future carbon emissions from the tundra and land use will develop. These feedbacks are thus excluded from quantitative climate models and are not considered by the IPCC in their predictions based on numerical models of well-understood climate processes.[9] Nevertheless, it is clear that the risk of a major carbon/methane feedback can only increase with further warming. There are also huge deposits of frozen methane hydrates (or clathrates) – perhaps trillions of tonnes containing several times as much carbon as the atmosphere – under marine sediment on the seabeds of many continental shelves, which could be released by sufficient warming of the oceans.

The likely fate of the Earth, if continued warming under business as usual were to trigger large-scale carbon and methane feedbacks, is illustrated by one of the hottest periods in our distant past – called the Palaeocene-Eocene thermal maximum (PETM) – 55 million years ago. Possibly caused by a gigantic release of methane from undersea deposits similar to those that exist today, temperatures rose to 5–10 degrees above current levels, with atmospheric carbon dioxide at 1000ppm or more. Environmental writer Mark Lynas gives a graphic description of a world with mass extinctions, 'ice-free poles and extremes of wet and dry ... a world very much like the one we are heading into this century'.[10] Climate scientist David Archer remarks that the amount of carbon released into the atmosphere that caused the PETM was comparable to total reserves of coal today:

> *The potential for planetary devastation posed by the methane hydrate reservoir therefore seems comparable to the destructive potential from nuclear winter or from a comet or asteroid impact.*

While this and other extreme warming episodes from our geological history probably took thousands of years to reach maximum temperatures, we are currently approaching the much-discussed threshold or danger point of two degrees above pre-industrial temperatures much faster than during any known natural episode of global climate change.

What Climate Models Tell Us

In order to provide some quantitative indications of how much future warming is likely to be generated by various scenarios of growing or declining emissions over time, scientists use complex computerized simulations of the global climate system, interacting with alternative policies such as business as usual or cutting emissions by, say, five per cent annually. Where consequences of warming, such as carbon feedback or the collapse of the ice sheets, are not well enough understood to be quantified, scientists have to make some subjective judgements on just how probable the various possible outcomes are. Cloud formation in a warmer climate with more atmospheric water vapour is another big area of uncertainty that affects climate predictions, because different types of cloud have warming or cooling effects. These assumptions can then be incorporated into a climate model to generate, for example, probabilities for a range of global mean temperature forecasts by the end of the century. Long-term predictions are thus generally in the form of a range of outcomes, where the extreme values are relatively unlikely and the outcomes close to the mean, in the middle of the range, are considered the most probable.

This approach yields interesting and alarming insights that go beyond simply listing possible outcomes in qualitative or descriptive terms. The key 'quantitative' prediction, on which a wide consensus has been reached, is that any increase in global temperature to more than about two degrees above pre-industrial levels very rapidly increases the risks of 'runaway warming'. This means generating irreversible carbon and other feedbacks that are likely to cause another two degrees, or perhaps much more, of additional warming, melting at least the West Antarctic and Greenland ice sheets. According to the evidence from the Pliocene era, two degrees would raise sea levels by about 20 metres, inundating the world's coastal cities and much of the most fertile agricultural land. An increase of four degrees might raise sea levels by around 50 metres, changing the world's geography and displacing extensive coastal populations, with many other catastrophic effects. The two-degree limit is thus a conventional threshold or 'tipping point', beyond which climate disaster looms with ever greater probability. Of course, there are very substantial dangers even below this threshold, but it has been officially adopted by the EU as its key climate change target, though unfortunately without the policies needed to achieve it.

It is fairly obvious that we need to know how the concentration of carbon dioxide will affect the probability of exceeding the two-degree limit in order to specify appropriate policies for staying below this target. Even with no further increase in atmospheric carbon dioxide, a total warming of at least 1.5 degrees – and possibly considerably more – is already in the pipeline, due to delayed warming of the oceans and albedo feedbacks. We must also remember that existing natural carbon sinks are likely to weaken with rising temperatures, so emissions will have to start falling dramatically in a very few years to keep safely below the limit.

Just how difficult this is likely to be is shown more precisely by climate modelling simulations published by the Institute for Public Policy Research.[11] With an ambitious policy of mitigation, global emissions would soon start to decrease rapidly, by around five per cent a year, declining by about 80 per cent by 2050 (this is equivalent to the British target and much more ambitious than most global 'targets'). Under this policy, carbon dioxide reaches a maximum of about 410ppm (which declines to 355ppm by 2100), but there is still a substantial chance – between 10 and 25 per cent – of exceeding the two-degree limit.[12] This model also makes the completely unrealistic assumption that methane emissions will decline to half the present rate, rather than continue to rise substantially from thawing peat bogs as Arctic permafrost retreats, so is already outdated and much too optimistic. As Arctic ice retreats much faster than predicted, forecasts have become more pessimistic, and, as noted in Chapter 9, even holding the present concentration of greenhouse gases constant is likely to result in the two-degree threshold being ultimately exceeded. Much of the Arctic area has already warmed by about three degrees, which may even be sufficient to generate runaway warming from accelerating methane emissions unless the world rapidly reduces net emissions to zero or less (by sequestering carbon, as discussed in the next chapter).

Any serious mitigation policy would have to stop destructive and unsustainable deforestation and biomass burning, which would be one of the most cost-effective policies, as we discuss in more detail in Chapter 9. To protect the health of their urban populations, developing countries will sooner or later have to take steps to reduce current dramatic levels of local air pollution from coal burning and motor vehicles, particularly in the biggest cities (this kind of clean-up, which western countries partially accomplished decades ago, is much easier than reducing carbon dioxide emissions). Aerosols are quickly washed out of the atmosphere by rainfall, in contrast to very long-lasting carbon dioxide, so these measures would promptly eliminate much of the aerosol cooling, and hence have a *warming* effect likely to be equivalent to up to perhaps 80ppm of carbon dioxide. Recall that this is the amount of carbon dioxide that would be added to the atmosphere by about 30 years of current emissions (and unchanged natural sinks). However, there is much uncertainty about the precise magnitude of aerosol cooling. This is due to a combination of direct effects such as smog reflecting sunlight, and indirect influence on cloud formation, as well as some atmospheric warming due to the black soot component. The range of uncertainty includes the possibility of substantially greater cooling, as well as higher estimates of warming in the lower atmosphere from soot.

Also important is the role of the other greenhouse gases, particularly methane. At the moment, their warming effect is probably equivalent to the aerosol cooling. Methane emissions have declined in recent years, but as Arctic permafrost areas continue to thaw, decomposing peat bogs could become a major source of accelerating carbon and methane emissions. In addition, declining ice and snow cover will have a substantial warming effect as less sunlight is reflected. In the light of all these factors, prudent risk aversion thus suggests that atmospheric carbon must be rapidly reduced to a level substantially *below* the current 390ppm to avoid serious danger of climate catastrophe. Based on palaeoclimate evidence, Hansen has also recently argued for a carbon dioxide target level of at most 350ppm. Of course, the ultimate objective is to stabilize the climate (rather than any particular quantity of GHGs) and to prevent any further rise in global mean temperature. To achieve this, simulations show that net emissions would have to rapidly approach zero, so that natural sinks could reduce atmospheric GHGs.[13]

The risk of exceeding the two-degree threshold rises dramatically under the much less ambitious targets proposed by Nicholas Stern (in his Review and later writings), who considers a target range for stabilizing greenhouse gases equivalent to carbon dioxide concentrations of 450–500ppm.[14] This range, and similar government targets, are almost certain to result in temperatures exceeding the two-degree threshold, and perhaps rising much further. Stern proposes these very high-risk policies because the policy cost of attaining a low risk target is assumed to be 'prohibitive'. As we show in detail in Chapter 9, Stern and most other writers (particularly economists) seriously overestimate the costs of mitigation, while underestimating both the risks and costs of truly catastrophic climate change.[15]

There are various complications that are relevant for mitigation policies. Stabilizing a particular stock of carbon dioxide (with or without including the other greenhouse gases) in the atmosphere is frequently considered, but is not necessarily the most appropriate policy focus, because warming depends on aerosols, cloud formation and albedo, as well as greenhouse gases and other factors. Any path of emissions reduction will have uncertain effects on the accumulation of greenhouse gases (and hence their ultimate quantity in the atmosphere), because the behaviour of natural sinks and carbon and other feedbacks is difficult to predict. Delaying the achievement of a particular target, or overshooting the target level, will thus require a subsequently more rapid rate of emissions reduction, which is likely to be more costly, while loss of human life and biodiversity in the meantime becomes irreversible.

Ocean currents are another major area of uncertainty. Some models suggest that the Atlantic circulation could slow down or even cease if a large enough influx of fresh water from melting Greenland and Arctic ice sufficiently diluted the salty surface flow, so that it no longer sank as it cooled. Though a complete interruption of the circulation is regarded as unlikely in the medium term, such a repeat of the many apparent past interruptions of the circulation indicated by ice core data could one day become a serious additional destabilizing factor, though with effects that are unlikely to resemble the science fiction film scenario in *The Day after Tomorrow*. However, a more plausible weakening of the circulation could still have serious effects on the global weather system, in particular disruption of the Asian monsoon. This, in turn, would endanger the food supply for around 2 billion inhabitants of the region.

While much climate modelling is concerned with predicting mean global temperature under various assumptions, models can already explain the considerable regional variations in warming that have been observed in recent years. Thus parts of the Arctic have seen temperature increases of three or four degrees over the last three decades, with much less warming in the tropics. Most climate modellers are agreed that hot and dry continental interiors are likely to become hotter and drier, with more frequent droughts, posing a serious threat to water supplies and agriculture in many developing countries and also the whole Mediterranean region.

Total rainfall is expected to increase, with more water vapour in a warmer atmosphere. However, much of the increased precipitation is expected to be in the form of heavy rainstorms that increase the risk of flooding and erosion, while rapid runoff means that intense rainfall is less effective in replenishing groundwater and reservoirs. Extreme events of all kinds, such as storms, floods, heatwaves and droughts, are already becoming more frequent and severe, and this trend will almost certainly continue. If the concentration of greenhouse gases does not soon begin to decline rapidly, the world described by climate modellers at mid or end of century will be parched and scorched throughout much of its once most populous areas. Canada and Siberia may have milder winters, but extremely hot and dry summers, and just how many of the future world's refugees these northern regions with their poor soils will be able to feed remains doubtful. The threat to world food supply is already severe for a number of reasons, even before climate change impacts kick in, as we discuss in detail in Chapter 3.

In his book *Global Fever*, William Calvin details a long history of recurrent major droughts over much of the western US, lasting for decades. Much of the western and southern US has been suffering from drought for the last ten years. According to climate models, more devastating droughts, with far worse consequences than the Dust Bowl of the 1930s, are likely within the present century. The forecast is that the 10 per cent of the Earth's land surface suffering from severe drought today will double by mid century and again to 40 per cent by 2100.[16] This is all the more serious because sources of water for the irrigation of modern high-yielding crop varieties, such as groundwater and 'fossil water' aquifers, are being rapidly depleted by overuse, as we discuss in subsequent chapters.

Many factors in the complex interactions of the climate system cause short-term fluctuations not only in local weather conditions, but also around long-term trends. Thus the rising trend of global mean temperatures does not imply that every year is warmer than the last. For example, 2007 was the second warmest year since records began, but only very slightly cooler than the hottest year – 2005 – in spite of various temporary cooling influences. It was easily the hottest year in the northern hemisphere, bringing both floods and droughts (and heatwaves), which are likely to become ever more frequent, and the trend is clear from the fact that the eight warmest years all occurred in the last decade. The third warmest year was 1998, and this slight irregularity in the warming trend sometimes generates confusion among those who are ignorant of climate science, who have been mislead by frequently inaccurate media reporting (that often confuses weather with climate), or who have a vested interest in denying the fundamental science and its consequences.

Periodic variations in ocean current circulation and surface temperatures are believed to be the main cause of such short-term irregularities. Some climate modellers are now trying to make predictions on this basis for the next few years, and some suggest that recent rapid Arctic warming could slow down temporarily. This might stabilize surface air temperatures until the fundamental warming trend resumes, faster than before. Such a slowdown or pause in warming would doubtless be used by climate change deniers as 'evidence' for their absurd claims.

Denial

No discussion of climate change for a general readership today is complete without some explicit exposure of the deliberate campaign of confusion and deception that has been orchestrated by fossil fuel lobbies, and the Bush Administration in the US, with considerable media support. This campaign has been aptly called the 'denial industry' by George Monbiot,[17] and includes a few scientists and others who call themselves 'climate sceptics' or 'contrarians', mostly (though not always) funded in some way by fossil fuel interests. Monbiot shows how the tactics used by the tobacco industry in its decades-long campaign to discredit the scientific evidence on the dangers of smoking have been adopted by these climate sceptics. Indeed, some lobbyists have moved seamlessly from one denial industry on to the next.

A recent report by the Boston-based Union of Concerned Scientists shows how ExxonMobil spent nearly $16 million from 1998 to 2005 on funding 'a network of 43 advocacy organizations that seek to confuse the public on global warming science'. According to Alden Meyer, the Union of Concerned Scientists' Director of Strategy and Policy, 'ExxonMobil has manufactured uncertainty about the human causes of global warming just as tobacco companies denied their product caused lung cancer.' James McCarthy (Alexander Agassiz Professor of Biological Oceanography at Harvard University and former Chair of the Intergovernmental Panel on Climate Change's working group on climate change impacts) comments, 'It's shameful that ExxonMobil has sought to obscure the facts for so long when the future of our planet depends on the steps we take now and in the coming years.'[18]

Even the most absurd claims by contrarians are still given media coverage by ill-informed journalists, fuelling further citations and public confusion. Thus, as Monbiot remarks, 'until mid 2005, the BBC seemed incapable of hosting a discussion on climate change without bringing in one of the Exxon-sponsored deniers to claim that it was not taking place'.[19] An international panel of leading climate scientists maintains an invaluable discussion forum for the interested public and journalists on the website www.realclimate.org. New scientific results are clearly explained in non-technical terms, while comments, questions and answers are also posted. Particularly useful for non-experts, the false claims and illogical arguments of the contrarians that still appear in the media are regularly exposed and refuted in detail.

An egregious example of 'climate denial' was a programme called *The Great Global Warming Swindle*, which appeared on the UK's Channel 4 in March 2007. Typical of its many specious claims, the cooling trend in global temperatures observed during the 1940s to the 1970s was presented as a major flaw in climate modelling. In fact, the break in the warming trend is well known to have been caused largely by the cooling influence of sulphate aerosols temporarily dominating the greenhouse effect. Modern climate models include aerosols, and accurately track the cooling period, as well as steadily rising temperatures during the rest of the 20th century and up to the present time. These standard results, which must have been known to the programme makers and their interviewees, were not mentioned in the programme. So, as RealClimate scientists summarized in their comment on this deliberate misinformation, 'they are lying to us by omission'. Even worse, as the *New Scientist* has pointed out, the programme contained 'fabricated climate graphs, dozens of false statements and frequently misleading content'. The British broadcasting regulator, Ofcom, upheld some of the numerous complaints about the programme, but claimed 'that the programme was not in breach of any rules relating to accuracy'. Only news programmes have to be presented with 'due accuracy'.[20] This is a depressing claim by a public service regulator.

Among contrarian scientists and former scientists, the lonely figure with a distinguished research record is Richard Lindzen, atmospheric physicist at the Massachusetts Institute of Technology (MIT). Lindzen participated in the Channel 4 misrepresentations and also contributed to a *Newsweek* issue on

'Learning to live with global warming' (16 April 2007). While not denying the current warming, 'Lindzen claims that because we don't know what the ideal temperature of the planet should be, we shouldn't be concerned about global warming', as *RealClimate* summarizes. Instead of offering serious discussion of this extraordinary claim, which contradicts every scientific evaluation of the risks of future warming, Lindzen's contribution is just 'a series of strawman arguments, red-herrings and out and out errors'.[21]

While journalists who participate in the denial campaign may be ill-informed or obtuse, and most are certainly scientifically illiterate, the qualified individuals who are deliberately confusing and misleading public opinion share a grave moral responsibility for obstructing global justice and life-saving policies. Even well-informed and honest politicians have to contend with voters and colleagues whose understanding of the issues lags far behind the current state of science, in part because of the efforts of the deniers and contrarians. An important motivation for denial seems to be 'market fundamentalism', a strong (and irrational) ideological belief that government intervention in the economy is generally unnecessary or harmful. Since climate change is the ultimate market failure, and one that even further rising oil prices will take too long to 'correct', major policy initiatives are urgently required, and this is anathema to the fundamentalists.

As environmental writer Mark Lynas has emphasized, defamatory personal attacks on climate scientists and environmentalists by 'sceptics' have encouraged timidity in media reporting on climate issues, and reluctance by some scientists to be outspoken on questions of policy. An example is the cancellation by the BBC of a planned 'Planet Relief' – a day of climate-change related programming – after attacks by sceptics including those responsible for the Channel 4 'Swindle' discussed above. Attempting to be 'neutral' or 'impartial' on climate-related risks to the lives of hundreds of millions of (mainly poor) people – as suggested by BBC *Newsnight* editor Peter Barron's ridiculous remark that 'it's absolutely not the BBC's job to save the planet' – 'surely sets a new low for political cowardice in the media'.[22]

On the other hand, constant criticism and scepticism, at a level far beyond that of normal scientific debate at the frontiers of any field, even one with such momentous social and political ramifications, has forced climate scientists to take extraordinary care in the constant scrutiny of their own and each others' results. This should ultimately increase public confidence in their robustness, and help to generate the political support needed for far-reaching mitigation measures.

Conclusions

The most alarming current climate trend is the dramatically increasing loss of late summer Arctic sea ice and the resulting albedo effect of reduced reflectivity. This will accelerate warming in the whole permafrost region, as tundra and ocean without snow and ice cover absorb much more of the sun's incoming radiation. This, in turn, will boost carbon feedback as methane is released from thawing peat bogs, and could soon put global warming on an essentially irreversible path to overshoot the two-degree tipping point.[23] Many of the IPCC's predictions are now seriously outdated, though they are still regularly cited by policymakers in support of their ambitious sounding, but actually far too late targets, such as the 80 per cent reduction of emissions only by 2050. Unless rapid mitigation starts much sooner than in official targets, the feedback effects are likely to overwhelm later efforts and render subsequent stabilization of the climate enormously costly if not unattainable.

As we show in the following chapter, water shortages and soil erosion are already threatening food production in many areas. These problems will be exacerbated by climate change and growing populations, and represent the most serious medium-term threat to the poorest and most populous countries. Over a longer time horizon, sea-level rise could be much faster than current model predictions if loss of ice from Greenland (and perhaps also Antarctica) continues to accelerate and the ice cap begins to collapse. In subsequent chapters we show how climate policy has been largely constrained by fossil fuel and other industrial interests, as well as widespread lack of knowledge about the most cost-effective alternatives and the probable consequences of our current inaction.

3

Prospects for Agriculture

Introduction

It is widely recognized that global warming poses a serious threat to agriculture in the already hot and arid regions of many developing countries. These areas are expected to become hotter and drier, exacerbating existing strains on food production, while world population is likely to increase from currently nearly 7 billion to about 9 billion by the middle of the century. However, it is less widely realized just how serious are the problems already facing agriculture in parts of China and India, as well as in Africa and many other regions with the fastest-growing populations – problems that threaten world food supplies even without any further warming.

The success of the 'Green Revolution' in feeding a world population that has more than doubled over the last half century has diverted attention from the most critical resource required by the modern, high-yielding crop varieties, namely water. Irrigation is the world's largest consumer of fresh water and the global area of irrigated land has tripled in less than half a century. However, water supply for irrigation is now limited by competing demands from industry and domestic users, as well as progressive depletion of scarce, non-renewable water resources and declining rainfall in many already arid areas. Increasing populations in the poorest countries exacerbate all these problems, and securing water supplies is now a leading issue of economic development and security.

Ironically, the Green Revolution is also seen by many as the final rebuttal of the dire predictions made by early political economist Thomas Malthus, who argued in 1798 that population growth on limited land area would ultimately be halted by starvation. But the still rapidly growing populations of the developing countries now face multiple threats from depletion and pollution of water resources, rising temperatures that reduce yields in already hot areas, and progressive soil erosion and desertification under modern industrial agriculture and overgrazing. In addition to these threats, climate models generally predict an increasing probability of declining rainfall and major droughts in many arid regions in the future, as well as more frequent flooding in other areas.

While modern high-yielding crop varieties are close to physiological limits on further gains even under favourable conditions, their high water and chemical input requirements have prevented adoption in the poorest countries. But agricultural land is also being lost at an unprecedented rate in many regions, due to both urban expansion and road building in densely populated and fertile parts, and most ominously to advancing deserts and erosion of peripheral areas. Grain output per head of the growing world population has been declining, while stocks are shrinking. Many of the newly cultivated areas – especially former tropical forest where the topsoil is very thin and arid grasslands – are at the greatest risk from erosion. The most recent threat to food production comes from the boom in bio-ethanol in the US, already consuming a quarter of the corn (maize) crop, and from bio-diesel in the EU – after the farm lobbies' success in capturing huge government subsidies for products yielding little or no net reduction in carbon emissions.

Economic growth in many developing countries (outside sub-Saharan Africa) is putting additional strain on food supplies because demand for meat and dairy products has been growing nearly as fast as real incomes. These animal products require several times the total land area to produce the same calories of nutrition as directly consumed plant products such as grains or legumes. Intensive livestock rearing in advanced economies is particularly extravagant in its use of concentrated feed from prime cropland, as well as a serious source of water pollution, primarily from manure. Demand for animal products is boosted by prices that do not include the environmental costs of production, as well as government subsidies for large farmers in particular and industrial agriculture in general in many countries. The result of these trends, and an even more rapid rise in fossil fuel prices, was that grain prices doubled or more between 2006 and 2008. This dramatic increase imposed severe hardship on the poorest populations everywhere, but was followed by an equally rapid decline of commodity prices with the global recession that started in late 2008, though many food products have not fallen back to previous lows. As economies recover, the trend of rising fossil fuel prices will doubtless resume and continue to raise the costs of high-input industrial agriculture. This trend will increase the immediate relative advantage of conservation agriculture as an alternative to the destructive and unsustainable methods that now threaten food security.

A more sustainable, essentially organic agriculture based on no-till, conservation methods and cover crops instead of ploughing and chemical-intensive monoculture could become a major carbon sink as well as lowering cost and increasing resistance to drought and erosion. As we discuss below, these methods have been enormously successful wherever tried. Not surprisingly, however, large-scale transition faces serious political obstacles from many powerful interests that profit from the present system. Similarly, the introduction of realistic pricing for water is essential to halt the rapid depletion of aquifers and other reserves. Improved technology, including subsurface drip and sprinkler irrigation, has already been shown to dramatically reduce water consumption for a wide variety of food crops and fibres, while increasing yields and quality. All these relatively simple technologies save energy as well as securing future food supply, and thus offer an important contribution to climate change mitigation at little or no net current cost if political barriers can be overcome. The long-term, rising trend of oil (and water) prices means that organic agriculture will become more profitable than high-input, industrial farming, in addition to all other environmental benefits.[1]

Population Growth and the Malthusian Prediction

World population has nearly trebled since 1950, from about 2.5 billion to approaching 7 billion. Grain yields per hectare have tripled or more in many countries, compensating for loss of grain-growing land to competing crops, cities, roads and erosion, as well as the rapid expansion in demand for animal products that require much more land per calorie. The 'Green Revolution' that multiplied yields so dramatically is widely regarded as one of the scientific triumphs of the 20th century. Unbounded faith in further scientific progress sustains the popular belief that agricultural productivity will continue to grow faster than population and feed the extra 2 billion people expected by 2050 with a rising share of animal products, in spite of water shortages, shrinking cropland and increasing temperatures.

Claims that exponential population growth would ultimately outstrip limited land and food production began with Thomas Malthus, whose pessimistic predictions of famine and starvation gave the 'dismal science' of economics its name. But crop failure and famine have hitherto always been local problems, with the worst consequences often caused by government action or inaction, in spite of adequate global food reserves. Now, however, continued population growth combined with warming, unsustainable 'water mining', erosion and droughts in arid areas is adding to existing major strains on the world agricultural system, so the Malthusian warning seems more relevant than ever before.

While population growth was a major concern among ecologists before the Green Revolution, climate change has now taken centre stage, and *declining* population has even become a prime concern in the EU. Female education and job opportunities are key factors in reducing birth rates in developing countries, but also the usual consequences of economic and democratic political progress, so that development itself is often seen as the solution of the population problem. With income per head growing much faster than population in Brazil, India and China in particular (the so-called 'BIC' developing countries), the environmental impact of economic growth in general has become the focus of attention.

However, it is important to realize that growing populations in the poorest countries – and poorest classes – are putting severe strain on some of the most vulnerable environments as competition for resources increases, with about 80 million extra mouths to feed every year. In particular, deforestation and overgrazing for fuel and subsistence by poor rural populations are major causes of soil erosion and desertification all over the developing world. The poorest populations suffer from almost universal female illiteracy and high infant mortality and have multiple 'incentives' for large families. These include the insurance motive to provide for old age, the need for family labour in subsistence agriculture, lack of access to contraception, and the lack of education, cultural status and job-market opportunities for women.

Rising temperatures and more frequent droughts in much of the developing world will interact with growing populations to exacerbate all the above problems and reduce overall food supply. At the same time, growing demand for meat by the urban middle classes increases the pressure for overgrazing of marginal pasture lands, which encourages wind and water erosion, soil loss, and often irreversible degradation and desertification. As we discuss further in Chapter 4, the overall environmental impact of development, I, is often symbolized as the product of population, P, affluence, A, and technology, T, or $I = P \times A \times T$, where 'green' technology can serve to mitigate the effects of the other factors. Older, polluting technologies such as road transport or coal-burning power stations, on the other hand, further increase emissions. Underemployed and surplus rural populations everywhere migrate to the cities in search of work, but frequently only swell slum populations with little hope of betterment and dire social consequences. A recent report by the UN Population Fund predicts a near doubling of the developing countries' urban population by 2030, most of them under 18 and living in poverty and slums. UN-Habitat predicts that the urban slum population of the less developed countries (LDCs) will also nearly double, from 1 billion to 2 billion, in this period.[2]

China's authoritarian, 'one-child' population policy is well known and has dramatically reduced the country's fertility rate – the average number of children per woman – though not in the poorest, rural areas. Less well known is the more democratic example of Thailand, where a public campaign for birth control has also reduced the fertility rate below the critical level of two children per woman. Even more surprising, Iran is the only Islamic state to institute a comprehensive family planning policy, one that has reduced one of the world's highest birth rates, of seven children per family, to less than three. These examples show that major policy initiatives are both feasible and effective in very different environments, as well as necessary for really rapid reduction of population growth.[3]

The Green Revolution

The population explosion of the second half of the 20th century was made possible by a threefold expansion of world grain output, which in turn required a similar extension of irrigated area and a tenfold increase in the use of chemical fertilizers. However, the essence of the Green Revolution was selective breeding of short straw or 'dwarf' varieties, which essentially transferred the savings from shorter stalks into more grain, at the price of much higher demand for water and nutrients. Since modern crops have come close to the physiological limits to useful output, further productivity gains are likely to be much slower, and depend on measures such as multiple cropping where feasible. The increasing concentration of CO_2 in the atmosphere encourages photosynthesis, so plant yields could increase slightly if other conditions remained unchanged. However, nutrient quality declines substantially in tests, and transpiration is also reduced, which results in less cooling from the natural evaporation of water, and hence yields significant warming. This effect adds to GHG-induced warming, which substantially reduces yields in the already hot areas, which are also most threatened by water shortages.[4]

Intensive chemical use in industrial agriculture has also devastated natural predator populations, bred increasingly resistant strains of pests and weeds, and reduced the genetic diversity and natural resistance of the main commercial crop varieties. Thus a few modern high-yielding crops and varieties are grown worldwide, often in monoculture, and are particularly vulnerable to newly evolved epidemics, such as the new stem rust fungus, Ug99, to which virtually no modern wheat varieties were resistant. This pathogen is already spreading from its origins in Uganda, and has the potential to devastate much of the world's wheat harvest unless recently discovered resistant strains can be bred and cultivated in time.[5] After the initial successes of the Green Revolution, agricultural research was neglected worldwide in the belief that food shortages were a thing of the past, but now scientists are trying to make up for lost time and breed more robust varieties that can also tolerate drought and higher temperatures.

Another major potential threat to world food supplies has only recently been recognized. About a third of our total food calories (including most fruit and vegetables) come from crops that require pollination, but many of the natural pollinating insect populations have been decimated by industrial farming practices, including habitat destruction and toxic chemicals. Increasingly, European honeybees are relied upon for pollination in many different countries. In North America, hives are transported over long distances to follow the pollination seasons and make up for the declining population, as bees abandon their hives for no apparent reason and disappear, until the colony literally collapses. Rising death rates among bees around the world and the spread of 'colony collapse disorder' may have various causes, including parasites. Governments have done little to recognize the potential threat to food production and fund research.[6]

While world grain output per head of population has been declining for 20 years, surpluses in the most developed countries have been maintained with the help of about 300 billion US dollars in annual subsidies, or six times the world's aid budget. As Nobel Prize-winning economist Joseph Stiglitz explains:

When farming becomes more lucrative because of the subsidies,
the demand for land is increased, driving up the price. With the

price of land so high, farming has to become capital-intensive. It has to make heavy use of fertilizers and herbicides, which are as bad for the environment as the increased output is for farmers in the developing world.[7]

Most of the agricultural subsidies go to the richest farmers in the wealthy countries, while heavily subsidized exports to poor countries depress their own agricultural prices, undercut local producers, and increase poverty and displacement of the poorest rural populations. At the same time, EU and US rules prevent developing countries from exporting many of their agricultural products to the richest nations, thus further damaging the world's poorest farmers. This group is also the most vulnerable to the effects of current erosion, future warming, declining rainfall and worsening water shortages. Reform of trade and subsidy policies on its own will not be sufficient. Radical changes in agricultural practices, discussed below, are needed to reduce these threats and provide more food security. Education in the new methods, knowledge and technology transfer, and aid for the transition are all essential, but still far removed from an agenda that remains dominated by agribusiness multinationals and rich-country farming lobbies.[8]

Even in the developed countries, industrial agriculture is also generating progressive soil erosion and serious rural water pollution problems from fertilizer runoff and intensive livestock rearing. Vanishing wildlife habitats and the chemical 'treadmill' of increasing and more powerful toxic pesticide applications to overcome evolving pest and weed resistance are driving numerous species towards extinction. The publicity surrounding repeated scandals, such as 'mad cow' (BSE) and foot and mouth diseases, has raised concerns about appalling animal health and welfare in concentrated animal feeding operations (CAFOs), or very large-scale, intensive animal rearing under grossly overcrowded conditions – a basic component of industrial agriculture. These also result in serious health hazards for workers, and for consumers.

A major role in these developments has been the relentless pressure on farmers to reduce short-term costs from the market power of the ubiquitous large retail chains and agribusiness multinationals, while their combined political lobbying power has helped to block adequate environmental, health and safety regulation. This environment also requires large-scale, prophylactic use of antibiotics to avoid epidemics, as well as for their function as growth promoters to raise measured 'productivity' without regard for the external environmental costs. While they are restricted in the EU, illegal antibiotic use is widespread, and the US, with no restrictions, uses eight times the amount of antibiotics in animal feed as in human medicine. This misuse has helped to evolve increasing antibiotic resistance in many human pathogens and an epidemic of often fatal hospital infections, such as the recent episodes attributed to the MRSA (methicillin-resistant *Staphylococcus aureus*) hospital bacterium. The threat of additional major disease epidemics grows as industrial farming and intensive animal rearing spread in developing countries.

Following the swine flu pandemic, the potentially more lethal avian or bird flu virus H5N51 is expected, sooner or later, to mutate into a form that is contagious among human as well as bird populations and cause a much more serious global pandemic.[9]

The extravagance of an animal-based diet is illustrated by the following comparison. Average annual consumption of grain in India is around 200 kilograms per person, largely consumed directly. In the US, by contrast, 800 kilograms are consumed, mostly indirectly in the form of animal products. World demand for meat is increasing twice as fast as population growth, as the middle classes of developing countries move up the food chain with their rising incomes.[10] Italy, with 400 kilograms of grain consumption, occupies the healthy middle range, with a longer life expectancy than the US, better general health and much lower expenditure on healthcare. Excessive consumption of animal products in the rich countries is responsible for many health problems and 'diseases of civilization'. The global livestock population explosion is a major source of the powerful GHG methane, contributing almost 20 per cent of total anthropogenic GHG emissions. Most of the global fisheries, which have been a major source of protein comparable to livestock, are now close to collapse after decades of over-fishing and continuing lack of political agreement to protect the remaining stocks.

An epidemic of obesity and malnourishment with processed food (particularly among the relatively deprived) in the rich countries now matches the extent of hunger in the world's poorest populations, and is rivalling smoking as the leading 'disease of civilization'. Two-thirds of Americans are overweight (or obese), with other developed countries catching up, and worldwide more than 1 billion overweight people suffer increasing risk of type-2 diabetes and cardiovascular problems, while nearly 900 million are chronically hungry. Lack of exercise and intensive promotion (much of it targeting children) of unhealthy, highly sweetened, processed food and soft drinks by major retail chains and food multinationals with extensive market power have both contributed to this rapidly growing problem for current and future healthcare.[11]

The prices of animal products from industrial agriculture do not in any way reflect the huge environmental impact of their production. These include overgrazing and erosion of arid grasslands (three-quarters of which are already degraded to some degree), tropical deforestation to obtain more arable land for growing animal feed crops, and massive water pollution surrounding industrial livestock rearing. Just as lack of realistic water pricing fosters enormous waste, depleting aquifers and reducing groundwater levels in both developing and developed countries, so the failure to tax and price animal products in accordance with their full social costs helps to generate unsustainable consumption (in rich economies) and demand growth from the emerging middle classes (in the LDCs).

There are also two strong ethical arguments against intensive livestock production that provide additional support for much stronger regulation, and even prohibition in the long run. The first is the large-scale cruelty to animals involved, which philosopher Peter Singer has emphasized in his case for animal rights. The second is the destruction of biodiversity and damage to future climate caused by tropical deforestation in particular, which is largely driven by the soaring demand for cheap animal products from industrial agriculture.[12] It is sometimes claimed that intensive, industrial livestock production is less environmentally damaging than extensive overgrazing of vulnerable grasslands. This misses the point that neither method is sustainable, and the only alternative which is feasible in the long run is to produce smaller quantities of higher-quality animal products in environmentally friendly, mixed farming at realistic (higher) prices. As Rajendra Pachauri, Chair of the Nobel Prize winning UN Intergovernmental Panel on Climate Change (IPCC) urged in a recent lecture, eating less meat is one of the easiest ways to reduce emissions and protect the environment. In addition, as many studies have shown, there would be considerable health benefits for most consumers in rich countries from eating less industrially produced animal products, and major animal health and welfare benefits from a return to sustainable, mixed farming.[13]

Erosion, Desertification and Warming

Soil erosion and desertification are among the most significant threats to maintaining or increasing world food production, although they are usually invisible and difficult to measure. The impact of soil erosion – a precursor to desertification – has hitherto been largely neglected, though both are exacerbated by global warming, declining rainfall and water shortages in the most vulnerable areas. As soils lose organic matter and degrade, they become more susceptible to erosion and less productive, thus reducing the availability of arable land for food production. These problems, exacerbated by declining yields as temperatures rise and dwindling water reserves for irrigation, could generate catastrophic results in the medium-term future – resulting in the collapse of agricultural production in the most populous developing countries.

Soil erosion or the loss of the most fertile layer of topsoil only becomes spectacularly visible in dust storms, such as those that ever more frequently envelop Beijing and have been detected on the west coast of the US and in Southern Australia. Most of the time, however, as geologist David Montgomery explains in his pioneering book *Dirt*, erosion is an insidious and invisible process, resulting directly from modern agricultural methods, that leads to loss of topsoil, tens or even hundreds of times faster than natural rates of soil formation in problem areas.[14]

Several factors interact to cause the damage. The traditional method of cultivation by ploughing first buries organic residue and then leaves the surface exposed without crop cover for long periods and between rows (particularly under common monoculture). Heavy machines used in large-scale, industrial agriculture compress or 'compact' the soil even at depth, preventing water absorption and penetration by plant roots. Surface water then runs off and is lost, carrying away valuable topsoil. Reliance on chemical fertilizers depletes the organic or humus content of the soil, which then accelerates moisture loss, and allows the surface to be blown away in hot and dry conditions or washed away by heavy rainfall, particularly on hill slopes. Nitrate fertilizer pollution, pesticide residue and animal waste from intensive production are devastating local water supplies under modern farming around the world.

The end result of this progressive degradation, when all the topsoil has been lost, is barren subsoil or rock that will not support vegetation – the largely irreversible process known as desertification. Worldwide, the degradation of arable soil is reducing productivity, changing local and global weather patterns, and increasing temperature extremes – while threatening the world's food supply. The pace of desertification will only intensify with rising global temperatures and increasing populations in the most vulnerable areas – without a concerted international effort to promote the large-scale adoption of conservation methods. Around the world, there are already numerous environmental disasters resulting from unsustainable water and land use – disasters which are becoming increasingly serious with more frequent droughts and erratic temperatures.

Few visible alterations to the Earth's surface reflect the consequences of unsustainable natural resource use as dramatically as the now infamous desiccation of the Aral Sea in Central Asia. Due to inefficient irrigation and mismanagement of irrigation water for cotton production, water diverted from the sea's main feeder rivers resulted in the loss of over two-thirds of its volume in less than a generation. The methods of irrigation which drained the sea continue to compromise food security and ultimately sustainability as industry, agriculture and human beings compete for limited water resources. The demise of the Aral Sea has impacted on population health across Central Asia, as well as economic welfare. The irrigation infrastructure is dilapidated and losses in transport have resulted in severe water logging, salination and soil erosion – precursors to desertification. Summers in the already arid climate are hotter and winters colder with the loss of the sea, and desertification throughout the basin is now threatening productivity of remaining arable land. The Aral Sea disaster is considered to be one of the great environmental catastrophes of the 20th century. As the global climate continues to change, already fragile ecosystems around the world, with their growing animal and human populations, will similarly become ever more vulnerable to ecological collapse.[15]

Another cause of erosion and desertification is overgrazing of arid grassland, driven by rapidly growing demand for animal products. When too much of the surface vegetation has been damaged or removed, the soil in between can be blown away until remaining roots have no support left. In the most fertile regions, a thick layer of topsoil means that erosion can continue for decades with little effect on crop yields when high or rising use of chemical fertilizers is maintained. But much of the world's agricultural land has only a thin cover of topsoil; nearly a quarter of the area has already been degraded to some extent by erosion and is therefore particularly vulnerable to drought and overgrazing.

Nearly one per cent of the world's agricultural land may be lost or severely degraded annually due to erosion and human activity, though precise estimation is difficult. At the same time, the total arable area has been increasing, largely as a result of deforestation, but also from the cultivation of vulnerable steppes and grassland.

While this expansion has been responsible for much of the rise in global food production in recent years, yields in vulnerable areas may start to decline under the influence of rising temperatures and water shortages, reversing the trend. Furthermore, most of the newly cultivated lands are highly vulnerable to erosion and loss of productivity under industrial agriculture. There is still a large global land area (comparable to the existing arable area) that is considered potentially suitable for cultivation, which is one of the reasons for continued optimism by the United Nations Food and Agriculture Organization on future world food supply. However, while deforestation already contributes about 20 per cent of anthropogenic carbon emissions, extension of industrial agriculture to marginal areas and wasteland will only accelerate carbon loss and soil erosion.

In contrast to optimistic official predictions, a series of interacting factors will combine to threaten future food supply unless major changes in agriculture are implemented. First, rising temperatures and less rainfall in the already most threatened, arid areas will accelerate erosion and desertification. At the same time, hotter growing seasons in these regions will reduce grain yields by at least 10 per cent for each extra degree Celsius above 30 degrees during the growing season, unless much more resistant varieties can be developed in time, while world population will have increased by about 2 billion people by mid century if present trends continue. These effects will overwhelm the relatively small benefits of longer growing seasons and more atmospheric CO_2 in northern regions.[16]

Equally serious, much of the irrigation water that is a necessary input for the high-yielding varieties of the Green Revolution comes from rapidly depleting aquifers and groundwater, which are at best only slowly replenished, at much slower rates than current use. In the Great Plains of North America, practically all water for irrigation must be pumped from the Ogallala aquifer, a rapidly declining fossil freshwater resource. Additional demands from industry and development are also lowering water tables at alarming rates in parts of India, northern China and elsewhere, encouraged by lavish subsidies and political pressure for cheap water. Around the world, excessive water use has led to shrinking lakes, such as Lake Chad in Africa or the Aral Sea in Central Asia, and disappearing rivers, such as the Colorado in the US, the Yellow River in China and many others in developing countries.

Finally, the rapid growth of tropospheric ozone pollution produced by sunlight interacting with vehicle emissions is predicted to have increasingly damaging effects on crop yields (as well as human health) in the more prosperous developing countries, where car ownership and traffic are growing faster than GDP. Densely populated and rapidly urbanizing China is particularly vulnerable to this form of pollution, in addition to all the other problems facing its agriculture that are discussed later.

In summary, we are living in a 'food bubble economy',[17] maintaining production by using up the natural capital of topsoil and groundwater, or 'mining soil and water', as well as the fossil fuels that provide the massive energy and chemical inputs which power the Green Revolution but simultaneously degrade the agricultural environment.

Most economists and agriculturalists simply ignore these trends and believe that expanding cultivation and biotechnology will continue to increase yields over the next half century in a continuation of the Green Revolution progressing fast enough to feed a growing population in spite of accelerating erosion, declining water supplies and rising temperatures. However, high-yielding – and high-input – plants have already reached essential physiological limits to useful yields, though more resistant and hardier varieties will undoubtedly be developed. Genetic biotechnology has not provided any substantial yield gains, and concentrates on more feasible objectives such as resistance to herbicides and environmental factors (though also with limited success). Award-winning food policy writer Geoff Tansey shows how recent research and regulation has been dominated by multinational corporations and a World Trade Organization (WTO) that has been 'captured' by these and allied political interests. Policy is largely designed to secure monopoly profits for agribusiness, through patented seeds and other intellectual 'property rights', and with little regard for the welfare of farmers and consumers.[18]

The 'official' view of the rich countries and their agencies mirrors that of their multinationals' corporate lobby – developing countries should raise productivity by purchasing their patented seeds and agrochemicals. However, water shortage, soil erosion and climate are already severe constraints in many hot regions, problems that will worsen under climate change and be exacerbated by introduction of large-scale industrial agriculture. The high-input technology is in any case unaffordable for the poorest farmers, and will become even less viable as fuel prices return to their long-term rising trend. Instead, as we show below, conservation agriculture is the only feasible alternative for sustainable productivity gains and resilience to climate change.

In addition to world population increasing by around 80 million people a year, massive government subsidies for ethanol (biofuel) production from maize in the US, and biodiesel in the EU and elsewhere, are diverting agricultural land from food production and putting more pressure on prices.[19] China has become a major grain importer, as poor yields under worsening water shortages in the north and west have reduced domestic harvests and reserves. With world grain and other food prices having reached record levels in 2008, global recession has brought falling prices, but there are many reasons for expecting the upward trend to continue when the economy recovers, as explained in a recent Chatham House report.[20] There is ongoing strong pressure on LDCs such as Brazil to continue expanding cropland by destroying tropical rainforest or ploughing up the *Cerrado* – arid savannah with extraordinarily high biodiversity. Such newly cultivated land is exceptionally vulnerable to drought and erosion, often becoming infertile or desert in a few years, as experience from Central Asia to the Amazon has demonstrated.

The Example of China

China's phenomenal economic growth in recent decades is also rapidly expanding the demand for meat and grain products to feed the growing animal and human population, particularly the new middle classes who have profited most from growth. Per capita meat and milk consumption have doubled since the early 1980s, putting additional strain on agricultural resources as industrial agriculture begins to spread. In a generation, 15 per cent of the population have become overweight. Northern China supplies most of the country's grain, but is already running out of water. The Yellow River dries up almost completely in summers that are noticeably hotter and drier than 20 years ago. Most surface water is severely polluted, and groundwater tables have been falling by two to three metres annually under the combined demands of industry, households and the irrigation that is necessary to maintain crop yields. Much of the water used by agriculture comes from aquifers that are being exhausted far faster than natural replenishment rates. Water use by both agriculture and industry is extraordinarily inefficient, requiring much more water per unit of output than in advanced economies. Grain output and reserves have been falling in recent years, and China has become a major importer, adding to pressure on world market prices.[21]

Climate models generally predict that droughts are likely to become more frequent and more severe in arid areas such as northern China. Rising temperatures and increasing ozone concentrations will have similarly drastic negative effects on crop yields, while the Gobi Desert advances inexorably towards the capital city of Beijing. As the many strains on food supply outlined here continue to accumulate, and before any meaningful reforms are enacted, the potential impact of an extended drought in the region becomes ever more threatening. China's huge currency reserves would allow even some large-scale crop failures to be replaced by imports from the rest of the world. This would of course drive market prices for grain and food to unprecedented heights, unaffordable for the poorest people everywhere. As a result, China could effectively 'export' a domestic famine resulting from global warming to the most impoverished countries and populations in the rest of the world. The vulnerability of other crucial food growing areas in India and North America, as well as much of Africa, to water shortage, warming and drought only enhances the potential severity and plausibility of some future agricultural collapse.[22]

Continued global warming under business as usual, while relying on industrial agriculture, ever more expensive fertilizers and miraculous new genetically modified varieties in a second green revolution, will steadily raise the probability of a catastrophic food supply failure.

Food Security and Global Warming

As the trends of soil and water depletion demonstrate, to continue current 'worst practice' in agriculture would be a recipe for eventual disaster even without any further warming. Perhaps surprisingly, relatively simple and well-tried techniques can improve prospects for food security and simultaneously reduce future warming. The most obvious step to reduce depletion of water reserves is for governments in both developed and developing countries to stop subsidizing wasteful water use and introduce realistic pricing of this valuable resource. The alternative to wasteful irrigation is modern microtechnologies, including subsurface drip and sprinklers, which require some extra initial investment, but then use much less water and have proved to be extremely effective in arid areas such as Israel and the Southern High Plains of Texas. Switching subsidies from excessive consumption of water to this water-saving technology would be a major reform that could avoid penalizing the poorest farmers, as well as protecting future supplies.

An important measure to limit soil erosion has actually been more widely adopted in North and South America than elsewhere. Instead of ploughing, conservation low-till (or no-till) methods leave crop residue on the surface (without ploughing and with little or no cultivation) to form a mulch or organic cover that retains moisture and protects the soil from erosion. Additionally, a leguminous cover crop such as clover can be grown after the main harvest to fix atmospheric nitrogen and replace expensive and polluting artificial nitrogen fertilizer. Seed is sown in narrow slits cut through residue and surface soil. A common disadvantage of such minimum tillage farming is the increased use of herbicides to control weeds, but this can be reduced in the long run by crop rotation, biological pest control or rolling the cover crop as described below. A major benefit is that resistance to drought and wind and water erosion is dramatically improved, while the cost of energy-intensive ploughing and chemical inputs is avoided. In the poorest developing countries, simple hand tools can replace specialized seed planting equipment used elsewhere, so lack of knowledge among traditional farming populations remains the chief barrier to widespread adoption.

In addition to erosion, the most subtle damage from the combination of monoculture cropping, ploughing and intensive chemical use is the destruction of soil micro-organisms and organic matter. Much of the loss is the direct result of erosion, but fungi called mycorrhiza, which are vital for plant absorption of micronutrients and trace elements, are also damaged by cultivation and many chemicals in industrial agriculture. This is revealed in the striking decline of key nutritional elements in industrially farmed produce over recent decades.[23] The progressive decline of soil organic matter means that farmland has now become a significant carbon emitter, while losing topsoil through erosion. The second environmental gain from conservation tillage is the reversal of carbon loss, as organic matter accumulates in the surface layer again and the carbon content increases. Mycorrhizal fungi seem to slow down the decay of organic matter, and thus facilitate the accumulation of carbon in the soil.

Though carbon accumulation (or depletion) in soil is a slow process, Montgomery estimates that a third of the atmospheric carbon dioxide build-up since the beginning of industrialization has resulted from degradation of organic matter in soil. Furthermore, worldwide adoption of conservation tillage wherever possible could reverse the emission of carbon from soil under industrial agriculture and sequester a significant portion of global anthropogenic carbon emissions for many decades, while rebuilding soil quality and erosion resistance.[24] Since industrialized agriculture, food manufacture and retailing account for about 20 per cent of carbon emissions in advanced economies, energy saving in this sector, in addition to carbon capture in soil, could substantially reduce emissions of carbon. Globally, soils contain around twice as much carbon as the atmosphere or terrestrial vegetation, and according to the IPCC, agricultural land use contributes about 12 per cent of global carbon emissions. Halting (mainly tropical) deforestation would reduce emissions by about 20 per cent, so agriculture and forestry together have the potential to make a major contribution to mitigation for the next few decades, as well as reducing input costs, while the more expensive switch to clean energy production is completed.

Breeding new crop varieties that are resistant to disease and more tolerant of drought and heat is clearly an important component of future food security. Unfortunately it is one that has been seriously neglected for many years, as agricultural research funding plummeted after the initial successes of the Green Revolution. In addition to the threat to modern wheat from the new stem rust Ug99, the 'late blight' fungus-like infection that decimated potato crops in Ireland and elsewhere in Europe in the mid 19th century has evolved into a potentially equally serious problem for a crop that could make a much greater contribution to global food security than hitherto.

In rich economies, the humble potato has long been regarded as an inferior product, the demand for which declines as real incomes grow. However, potatoes have many advantages over staple grains. They yield 'up to four times as much complex carbohydrate per hectare as grain, better quality protein and several vitamins ... plus many of the trace elements poor people, and grain, lack'. Furthermore, 'potatoes are ... faster growing, need less land and water, and can thrive in worse growing conditions than any other major crop'.[25] It is thus not surprising that potato production is increasing faster than any other crop in the developing countries.

However, the risk from late blight has also grown, as the spores have evolved to reproduce sexually, and can thereby develop resistance to fungicides more rapidly than before. The benefits from a blight-resistant variety would thus be enormous, and various kinds of genetic modification hold promise of speeding up the otherwise slow process of cross-breeding and testing. In particular, Anton Haverkort of Wageningen University in the Netherlands is developing 'cisgenic' varieties, containing extra genes only from other potatoes, which may be more acceptable to Europe's GM-critical politicians and consumers than commonly used antibiotic marker genes.[26] Success would not only reduce the risk of famine in poor countries, but could also generate substantial climate and health gains for the developed world. As grain and grain-fed animal products become increasingly expensive, while the environmental and health costs of the latter become more apparent, cheaper potatoes would become attractive substitutes.

It is astonishing how little attention has been paid to the potential climate benefits of conservation tillage and organic farming, particularly when the long-term threat of erosion can also be limited, and farmers profit from fuel savings immediately. Combining conservation tillage with organic farming as described below yields additional benefits to soil and food quality and substantial savings from eliminating chemical inputs. Education in the new methods is, however, essential, and has been seriously neglected under the influence of agribusiness lobbies – an obvious policy failure that would be extraordinarily cost-effective to amend.

Organic Farming

There remains an essential tension between the objectives of conservation tillage and the continued use of herbicides and chemical fertilizers. Weeds and other pests become resistant, so higher doses or more toxic chemicals have to be used. Chemical fertilizers and herbicides do not augment soil organic matter, and by damaging microflora and microfauna may inhibit the formation of stable soil structure and humus content, as well as the uptake of micronutrients. Health hazards to farm workers, consumers and the aquatic environment are well documented, though still strenuously denied by the agrichemical lobby and its academic allies. In addition, the 'cocktail effect' of many thousands of chemicals, including agrichemicals, to which we are constantly exposed, has been little studied. The industry has strenuously opposed and watered-down new EU legislation on the Registration, Evaluation, Authorization and Restriction of Chemical Substances (REACH), though the risks of most individual chemicals in the environment have not been properly assessed.

Biological pest control, crop rotation, mechanical weed control and cover crops all offer alternatives to farmers with requisite skills. These innovations can only become more attractive with rising oil and derivative chemical prices expected when the world economy recovers from recession, though agribusiness has so far managed to steer research funding, farming education and policy away from such 'threats'.[27]

Organic farming, which avoids most manufactured chemicals, has a long tradition of emphasizing the health of soil, crops and animals, rather than maximizing profits at the cost of long-term health and soil fertility. Recurrent food scares and scandals have generated rapidly growing demand and premium prices for organic certification. However, there are costs of transition from conventional to organic status, as yields may decline substantially until soil fertility and biodiversity have been restored, which may take several years after a history of industrial agriculture. New skills and more labour are generally required, but chemical (and energy) inputs per unit of output are much lower. This trade-off will become still more favourable for transition when fossil fuel prices resume their upward trend again.

Smaller farmers in particular have been increasingly squeezed by the growing monopsony market power of the giant retail supermarket chains, which prefer to deal with a few large suppliers, and often suffer severe capital shortages and liquidity constraints, though generally producing higher yields.[28] Without government support for the transition, both financial and educational, they may not be able to make changes that would be both privately profitable in the long run and environmentally beneficial. Due to generous government support for transition, about ten per cent of Austria's agricultural area is organic, and several other EU countries have around seven per cent. The UK, which provides minimal assistance for transition, has converted less than half this area, so much of the rapidly growing demand for organic products has to be met by imports with high energy cost or 'carbon footprints' from transport, usually by air freight.

Ploughing for weed control is still widespread in organic farming. However, with extensive use of cover crops and rotation, better soil structure and higher humus content, organic ploughed land absorbs more water and is thus less susceptible to wind and water erosion than under conventional farming. The combination of reduced ploughing or low-till methods with organic cultivation is an important new advance in agricultural technology – described as the long-outstanding 'holy grail' of organic farming. This combination has been pioneered by the Rodale Institute in Pennsylvania in the US and further reduces energy inputs, to less than a third of the requirement under conventional ploughing and chemical use, while also raising some crop yields above those in both conventional and plough-till organic cultivation. The successful system is simple and economical – an appropriate cover crop, such as a legume, to suppress weeds and fix nitrogen in the soil, is flattened by a roller (which breaks the stems and also kills most weeds), followed by the seed drill for planting (all in one pass), with no further cultivation before harvest.[29] In developing countries and in some developed agricultural areas, complementary agroforestry combines the planting of trees or bushes in close proximity with conventional crops to yield additional, related benefits, including windbreaks and carbon sequestration.

Long-standing research with comparative trials of different methods at the Rodale Institute and elsewhere have established that well-managed, 'regenerative organic farming' can match conventional yields in some crops and conditions and be competitive even without premium market prices for certified organic products. This advantage can only increase as energy and chemical prices rise. Yields under drought conditions have been much greater, due to the superior water retention ability of enhanced soil organic matter. Most importantly for climate policy, organic no-till methods in these trials could sequester twice as much carbon in soil as standard no-till (as well as avoiding the substantial carbon emissions from conventional agriculture). Extrapolated to worldwide adoption, these results suggest a potential for carbon capture and storage in the soil up to nearly 40 per cent of total anthropogenic carbon emissions. This and much other evidence on the environmental benefits and commercial viability of organic farming was recently reviewed at the United Nations Food and Agriculture Organization Conference on Organic Agriculture and Food Security in May 2007.[30]

Though only beginning to attract interest in developing countries, there is growing evidence that organic and low-till agriculture offers particular promise for both higher yields and more sustainable rural development. By substituting relatively cheap local labour and other resources for expensive imported chemicals and machinery, in regions where resistance to drought and erosion is even more important than in temperate zones, these methods can reduce irrigation water demands, contribute to food security and help to reverse the flight of displaced rural poor. However, an essential precondition for any improvement remains the halting of heavily subsidized food exports from rich countries that undercut local suppliers.

When prices for energy and oil-based chemical inputs recover, organic and conservation methods will offer cost savings in spite of being more labour-intensive (as well as agricultural sustainability in the long run) and premium prices for higher-quality produce where markets are developed. However, farmers need education in the new methods and availability of improved seeds that can be harvested and resown without dependence on multinational monopoly suppliers of hybrid varieties that have been specifically developed to maximize agribusiness profits. It may also turn out to be possible to develop genetically modified varieties that *complement* organic farming methods (thus avoiding herbicide use), if research efforts are appropriately targeted and no longer dominated by agribusiness.[31]

Cuba remains a pioneering example of nationwide conversion from high-input agriculture to near-organic farming that has been largely ignored by the rest of the world. This transition was essentially enforced by the collapse of the Soviet Union (Cuba's main aid and trade partner), the continuing US embargo and the resulting food crisis, as fertilizer and energy imports were drastically curtailed. Large industrial state farms were divided into small cooperatives using local resources, and farmers' markets have flourished. Calories consumed fell by about a third, diets changed, physical activity increased, and the result was an average weight loss of eight kilos per person. Most interestingly for Western observers, major declines in cardiovascular, diabetes and stroke mortality led to a 20 per cent drop in the total mortality rate. Many shortages persist, not least because Cuba remains the second poorest county in the Americas, due to inefficient central planning and political repression, as well as the continuing US trade embargo. But education levels are very high, infant mortality is lower than in the US, and the food crisis has been largely overcome with a remarkable system of low-input, sustainable rural and urban agriculture. Any political liberalization and decentralization of the economy, following the long rule of Fidel Castro, might help to generate much more interest in this example among other developing countries.[32]

Biofuels

While dependence on imported oil and gas can be reduced by domestic production of biofuels in the EU and US, the most popular and heavily subsidized ethanol may actually have a negative total energy and carbon balance. In a tropical climate such as Brazil's, ethanol production from sugar cane is more efficient, provided that tropical forest or savannah is not destroyed to provide land for cane plantation, or for food crops that have been displaced by cane. Cultivation of such 'virgin' land generates long-lasting carbon emissions, which are likely to more than offset the fossil fuel savings. Similarly, biodiesel production for renewable fuel targets in the EU encourages tropical deforestation for palm oil plantation in Malaysia. Diversion of agricultural land to biofuel production also reduces food output and was an important contributor to rapidly rising food prices before the financial crash of 2008.

A much more promising approach than bioethanol or biodiesel is the production of biogas. Instead of competing with food production, any kind of biowaste or biomass can be turned into biogas by anaerobic fermentation in 'biodigesters', leaving a residue which provides a valuable organic fertilizer. Biogas production is expanding rapidly in the EU, and offers many advantages even over prospective 'second generation' bioethanol from cellulose, which involves the development of complex technology and is still far from commercial production. There is great potential for sustainable growth, without chemical inputs, of high-yielding, hardy perennial grasses on marginal land or wasteland (in other words land that is unproductive or unsuitable for food production), which can be harvested as feedstock for biogas production.

Biowaste can be heated without oxygen (pyrolysis) to produce biofuel in gas and liquid form and leave a charcoal residue called biochar, which may have beneficial effects on soil biota and fertility. The *terra preta* or dark earth regions of the Amazon, which contain ancient biochar, are much deeper and more productive than the shallow and fragile topsoil beneath most of the tropical rainforest; however, there has been little testing of new biochar in other soils. The hope expressed by some scientists and environmentalists, that large-scale use of biochar could sequester a substantial part of global carbon emissions in varied soils and climates, is thus based on untested assumptions. Other potential problems have also been neglected. To reverse the depletion of soil organic matter under industrial agriculture and erosion, most biowaste should be composted and returned to the land, a process that will also sequester carbon, but which cannot be substituted by biochar. Extensive production of biomass in industrial monocultures is likely to have serious environmental consequences and lead to further degradation of marginal land, loss of biodiversity and displacement of indigenous, subsistence populations.[33]

The alternative, and perhaps more benign, process of hydrothermal carbonization can 'pressure cook' wet biowaste in the presence of a catalyst to produce a humus-like residue containing all the original carbon and suitable for use as an organic fertilizer (or biofuel) and wastewater. This 'exothermic' reaction requires no prior drying or external energy source, but has not yet been tested on a large scale.

By contrast, the direct burning of wood and biowaste for domestic cooking in developing countries wastes most of the energy, and is a major source of indoor pollution that is responsible for millions of premature deaths a year (probably more than from outdoor, urban air pollution). It also drives deforestation and destroys much of the organic waste that could be used instead to maintain soil fertility, enhance erosion resistance, and reduce dependence on imported chemical fertilizers and depleting groundwater for irrigation. Cheap solar cookers are available to replace biowaste burning, and their wide dissemination with Western aid, together with the necessary education in no-till and organic agriculture, would be key steps to initiating more sustainable development under the threat of further warming, declining water supplies and more frequent droughts. We discuss the costs and benefits of these approaches in more detail in Chapter 9.

Forms of agroforestry, mentioned above, do have the potential to sequester a substantial portion of the world's carbon emissions, with major additional benefits. Fast-growing trees planted around the perimeters of fields provide shelter and biohabitats, as well as long-term biofuel harvest and protection against erosion. Worldwide, hundreds of millions of hectares of deforested or marginal land could be planted with sustainable, mixed forest (rather than industrial monocultures, with all their damaging environmental effects). As well as the long-term timber harvest, tropical forest can sequester carbon at a rate of many tonnes per hectare every year, over a growing lifetime of decades. Together with conservation agriculture, stopping deforestation and developing a major global reforestation programme of this kind could sequester most emitted carbon (while the rest could be removed by energy saving), until the transition to renewable energy is completed.

Conclusions

In spite of official complacency, the 'food bubble' generated by industrial agriculture and soil and water 'mining' is unsustainable. Deforestation to expand the cultivated area is a major driver of global warming, which in turn will exacerbate existing problems of declining water resources and progressive erosion, though the precise path of change cannot be predicted exactly. Even the best conservation methods will not protect all areas against the worst extremes of future weather if global warming progresses unabated, but they do offer more robustly sustainable food supply, with ever more impressive cost savings compared to high-input agriculture as oil prices rise again after the recession. In addition to securing future food supply, reducing emissions and sequestering atmospheric carbon with conservation and no-till agriculture could provide a major contribution to mitigation efforts. This could be matched by agroforestry and large-scale afforestation or reforestation to stabilize total atmospheric carbon during the switch to renewable energy. Essential complementary measures are realistic pricing of water (and pollution) to protect declining reserves and taxation of animal products to reduce the devastating environmental impact of unsustainable intensive rearing. The main obstacles remain lack of public education and government capture by agribusiness lobbies.

4

Economic Growth, Wellbeing and Sustainability

Economic Growth: Falling Behind or Moving Forward

Comparing life in a village in Roman England with medieval life 1000 years later, no major changes would be noticeable. The villagers would cultivate small plots of land and keep some livestock close to their homes, have a life expectancy of less than 35 years, and live in hovels, cold in winter and dark at night. Living standards, real income and consumption were more-or-less stagnant. We often forget that economic growth as we know it is a phenomenon of the last 250 years, propelled by the Industrial Revolution in Western Europe and a continuous stream of technological advancements.[1] This unprecedented and almost uninterrupted rise in real income or GDP per capita since the mid 18th century was soon perceived to be an end rather than the means to something else, and economic growth became a synonym for progress in general.

The disparity in historical growth performance across the globe is apparent from the current world income distribution. The richest 20 per cent of the global population in the developed economies consume about 85 per cent of global output. The rest live in less developed countries (LDCs) and about 3 billion of them, or nearly half of the world's population, still subsist on less than two dollars per day (or the equivalent in terms of subsistence production). A few hours' flight from New York or London is enough to reach villages in developing countries where life has hardly changed for centuries. Political economists as early as Adam Smith, with his theory of the division of labour, sought explanations for the divergence in growth patterns between the fortunate rich and the ill-fated poor nations. Many Nobel Prizes have been awarded for work on economic growth. It seems that investment in physical capital and infrastructure, human capital or education, restraining population growth, openness to trade, technological progress, and good institutions or social capital all contribute to increased rates of economic growth. Some middle-income countries have been able to catch up with the front-runners (a phenomenon called convergence), although many of the poorest economies have stagnated or even contracted.[2]

There is certainly a wide range of interlinked factors that affect economic growth and performance (including climate). While most developing nations experienced modest but positive economic growth over the last three decades, the economies of most sub-Saharan countries contracted. This pattern contrasts with the experience of a few successful growth 'miracles', such as Thailand, Malaysia, Taiwan, South Korea and India (and mainland China more recently). The rapid industrialization of the most populous country, China, in particular (with its dependence on dirty coal) has drastically increased consumption of non-renewable resources and carbon emissions, with China now rivalling the US as the world's worst polluter.

As we discuss in detail in Chapter 5, LDCs are most vulnerable to climate change and environmental degradation in general. They lack basic infrastructure and resources to protect themselves from droughts, floods and disease, and more frequent extreme weather conditions will fall disproportionately on the poor living in their territories. Countries located in tropical and semi-tropical regions with extensive coastlines will be particularly hit, as it is already the case for the 43 low-lying small coastal countries belonging to the Alliance of Small Island States (AOSIS).[3] Certainly, poverty also contributes to environmental stress, as the destitute often destroy their immediate environment to survive. At the micro level farmers overgraze pasture and destroy forest with 'slash-and-burn' agriculture, while businesses discharge their waste into local waterways and the atmosphere without penalty. At the macro level, governments fail to enforce even minimal environmental standards and penalties or taxes on polluters, while neglecting green technologies such as solar and wind power that would offer major economic as well as environmental benefits. At the same time, international corporate interests lobby intensively for high-input, labour-saving Western technology in both industry and agriculture, with consequent damage to the environment and traditional employment.

In the poorest countries, environmental degradation and resource depletion get worse as economic development accelerates. However, higher incomes, which encourage growing demand for a cleaner environment, a structural change towards services and the imposition of environmental regulation, often reverse the pattern. This relationship (often called the Environmental Kuznets Curve) holds for several air pollutants, such as sulphur dioxide and nitrogen oxides, which result in local acid rain and respiratory problems, but not for carbon dioxide, the primary greenhouse gas.[4] As we discuss in Chapter 7, to address such global public 'bads' as global warming, what is needed is coordinated collective action among nations that restrains free-riding problems in environmental policymaking, rather than sole reliance on technology and markets where polluters do not pay.

A Sustainable Development Path (from Malthus to Kyoto)

After centuries of economic growth, at least in the developed world, and popular faith that the rest will eventually catch up, it is easy to forget that there may be limits to how much longer our planet can support ever-increasing consumption. In this context, 'sustainability' has become one of the most popular terms in environmental discourse over the last three decades, reflecting both concerns over the health of our environment and about (so-far) robust economic growth.[5] The term 'sustainable' has become widely used as a substitute for 'environmentally friendly' to characterize any kind of economic and social activity that inflicts minimal harm on the environment (one often reads about sustainable architecture, sustainable agriculture, sustainable cities, sustainable tourism and business sustainability, among others).

Ultimately, sustainable development addresses concerns about the feasibility of continuous economic development on a planet of limited resources and fragile ecosystems. The Industrial Revolution and the Enlightenment in the 18th and 19th centuries were based on unquestioning faith in the ability of science and technology to harness nature and support ever-increasing material welfare. Though Britain had been largely deforested by the end of the 18th century for the production of charcoal as fuel, coal subsequently provided the foundation for industrial expansion and the belief that nature supported, rather than constrained, continuous economic progress. Thomas Malthus, with his *Essay on Population* in 1798, was one of the first intellectuals to criticize the cornucopian optimism of the time and stress that an ever-expanding population was unsustainable with limited land and food production.[6] IPCC reports and environmentalists now echo Malthusian pessimism by emphasizing that growing population and consumption both directly impact on the entire planetary environment.

In the 19th century, John Stuart Mill had already related wellbeing (or utility in the terminology of economics, as we discuss later in Chapter 6) to the pleasure derived from a healthy natural environment. But only in the second half of the 20th century did critical thinkers begin to realize that our lifestyle and consumption patterns were not viable in the long term due to environmental constraints, and the environmental movement hence gained momentum. Prophetic writings such as 'The economics of the coming spaceship Earth' by Kenneth Boulding in 1966 and Rachel Carson's *Silent Spring* in 1962 were long derided or ignored. Now they seem more relevant than ever before as climate catastrophe and mass extinction become the likely predictions of the most sophisticated scientific models with continued growth of GHG emissions or 'business as usual'.[7]

In 1983 the World Commission on the Environment and Development was set up by the United Nations to address growing concerns 'about the accelerating deterioration of the human environment and natural resources and the consequences of that deterioration for economic and social development'. In its 1987 report *Our Common Future* (also known as the Brundtland Report after its Chair) the notion of 'sustainable development' emerged.[8] From its almost 400 pages, the definition of 'sustainable development' as 'development which meets the needs of the present without compromising the ability of future generations to meet their own needs' stood out. While this stresses the need for intergenerational equity in terms of welfare, the Brundtland Report also emphasizes the importance of equity within generations: 'in particular the essential needs of the world's poor, to which overriding priority should be given'.

What the Brundtland Report tried to achieve was coordinated global action on environmental problems combined with economic development. It accepted that there are environmental limits to growth but also that poverty and environmental degradation are interlinked and need to be addressed jointly: environmental degradation affects mostly the poor and it is the poor who cannot afford to deal with it in the first place. The report claimed that growth was also essential in the rich countries, which are expected to provide aid more generously for the poor without compromising environmental protection and the welfare of future generations.

What followed the Brundtland Report was the UN Conference on Environment and Development in Rio in 1992, with an unprecedented representation of countries and heads of state (172 countries, 110 heads of state). The sustainable development rhetoric was already becoming popular and many countries participated without fear of having to make uncomfortable concessions. The Framework Convention on Climate Change, as part of the summit, acknowledged for the first time (at a political forum) that carbon dioxide emissions were contributing to global warming and that the industrialized countries had to take action (initially to stabilize emissions at 1990 levels by 2000).[9] The convention included preparations for a binding agreement to tackle the issue, and in 1997 the Kyoto Protocol on climate change was finalized. Based on the same rhetoric of sustainable development as in the Brundtland Report, it was agreed that global GHG emissions should be reduced by only 5.2 per cent compared to 1990 levels by 2008–2012 and that this relatively small burden would fall on the industrialized nations (Annex I countries). Poorer nations would thus be unconstrained in their development, and richer nations could maintain economic growth. Modest as this goal was, the first step had been taken to acknowledge the threat of global warming for the welfare of future generations, although this welfare was still perceived purely in terms of material consumption.

IPAT: Impacts, Population, Affluence and Technology

The scale of our current environmental impact is unprecedented in the history of humanity. As we discussed in Chapter 2, the concentration of CO_2 in the atmosphere has been continuously increasing from its pre-industrial level of 280ppm to around 390ppm today, and we have already experienced global warming of approximately 0.8 degrees since the early 19th century. Even worse, our environmental impact has intensified in recent years, and, as earlier chapters have shown, unless serious mitigation efforts are quickly implemented, a doubling of pre-industrial atmospheric carbon – and probable agricultural catastrophe – will take place in a few decades. Global warming is, of course, only one of the many environmental challenges humanity faces as a result of expanding economic activity since the Industrial Revolution. Natural habitats have been continuously degraded by our over-harvesting and excessive pollution, resulting in widespread deforestation, species extinction and water scarcity. Global warming will simply reinforce the environmental challenges humanity has been facing for many decades as a result of expanding consumption and population pressure.

Economists often decompose such environmental impacts (I) into three parts: the level of human population (P), our affluence measured by income per capita (A) and the environmental friendliness of technology in use (T). The IPAT equation, a simplistic but rather intuitive relationship attributed to Paul Ehrlich and John Holdren in the 1970s, relates our global environmental impact to the product of human population, income per capita and technology ($I = P \times A \times T$).[10] In order to embark on a sustainable path and reduce GHG emissions and other human impacts on the environment, some contribution has to come from the right-hand side of the equation, namely stabilizing population, constraining material growth and/or adopting environmentally friendly technologies.

So how do our prospects for a sustainable future look so far? As every single dimension of global-level environmental health has deteriorated over the last few decades (from carbon emissions to water scarcity and deforestation), we are undoubtedly heading towards an environmental catastrophe. Without urgent and decisive policy measures targeting population levels, unsustainable consumerism and dirty technologies, there is no scope for optimism.

For global warming, the time bomb is ticking even faster. If we are serious in tackling climate change and avoiding the tipping point of a two-degree temperature rise, we need to adopt more aggressive strategies for carbon mitigation. Which of the right-hand parts of the IPAT equation, though, offers a glimpse of hope? As we will discuss in Chapter 5, there does not seem to be much hope from the population factor (at least in the short or medium term). Current trends predict that the global population will increase by at least 2 billion people by 2050 in an already overcrowded planet, with developing nations like China and India leading the way.[11] While fertility rates are declining over time, it is unlikely that the global population will stabilize before mid century.

The average output per person around the world is also rising fast. Even a modest annual growth rate in GDP per capita of three per cent (much below the recent double-digit growth performance of China), would result in a fourfold expansion of production by 2050. Attempts to constrain GDP growth would be highly unpopular, especially (but not only) in developing countries, where the environment has low priority. With global population and average income on the rise, there is little hope that carbon mitigation (or sustainability more broadly) will come from the *P* or *A* parts of the IPAT identity, at least in the immediate future, unless production and population adjust (by necessity) as a direct result of a global warming catastrophe. Much more hope in mitigating our environmental impact is linked to the technological parameter, *T*. Generous technology and knowledge transfers and investment in renewable and energy-saving technologies, which we analyse in detail in Chapter 9, will thus need to more than compensate for the environmental pressure from population and income growth for a global climate catastrophe to be averted.[12]

Material Growth, Welfare and Happiness

In both popular media and academic discussion, the 'welfare' of a country, or individual, is generally identified with their 'standard of living' – in other words real income or consumption. Economic growth that raises average real income (after allowing for inflation) is automatically assumed to increase average welfare in the common sense usage of making (some) people feel better off. As we discuss in Chapter 6, social welfare is traditionally regarded as a 'sum' of individual welfare, mainly dependent on the objective income measure. Of course, average income may increase simply because rich people are getting richer, while the poor remain poor or more people descend into poverty, as has been happening in many countries in recent years. These issues of income (or welfare) distribution are receiving increasing attention because of their obvious political significance, at least in democracies, but most governments (apart from the Nordic countries) have cut taxes or maintained privileges for the rich, thus directly increasing inequality in recent years.

Rather than simply assuming that individual wellbeing depends on income, social scientists for the last 30 years have been actually asking people to evaluate their own welfare, usually in terms of questions about 'satisfaction with life' or simply 'happiness', as indicators of 'subjective wellbeing' (SWB), and relating their answers to objective data on the person's income, family situation, health, work and many other factors. While economists were initially sceptical about subjective opinions on such emotional issues as happiness, the responses to repeated surveys of this kind have displayed remarkable consistency across countries and over time, so that the key results are now well established. It is all the more astonishing that the majority of economists and policymakers continue to ignore them.

In the advanced economies of Western Europe, Japan and North America, average SWB is fairly stable, though it has actually declined in several countries over the last decades of substantial economic growth. Of course, this contradicts the almost universal belief that income growth always raises welfare and is known as the 'Easterlin Paradox'. However, as poor countries grow richer, more people often do feel happier as they gain access to basic necessities. In addition to this effect, it turns out that social trends, such as increasing 'tolerance', 'sense of freedom' or democracy in Eastern Europe, help to explain the observed upward trend in SBW in some poorer economies. There are surprising exceptions, however: in spite of very rapid economic growth, SWB in China and India has fallen over nearly two decades, which is a remarkable illustration of the social and environmental costs of excessive material growth. Recent studies also point to a substantial variation in SWB in Chinese cities, with citizens living in urban centres with high levels of atmospheric pollution and traffic congestion reporting significantly lower levels of welfare.[13]

Using survey data on individuals and their characteristics over time and across countries, David Blanchflower shows that education, as a proxy for relative income and status, has a strong effect on life satisfaction, while divorce and unemployment have major negative consequences. In contrast to much traditional thinking, unemployment is much worse for welfare than inflation. Per capita national income has no additional explanatory power in rich countries, but is important for life satisfaction in poor countries where basic necessities are not necessarily met.[14] Average life satisfaction in rich countries is generally higher than in poor countries, as expected.

How can these disparate results and in particular the Easterlin Paradox be explained? Once basic needs for food and shelter have been satisfied, further material wants are strongly influenced by social comparison. People look at the consumption patterns of reference groups such as neighbours or those with similar or higher incomes, and form aspirations or ambitions to match or exceed their consumption. A major cause of unhappiness turns out to be the gap between aspiration and achievement. As all or most incomes increase with economic growth, relative positions do not change much, but aspirations grow with the economy, so the income people say they need to get by with comfortably is generally higher than their current income, whatever its level, and the gap remains. This process is known as adaptation and is familiar to everyone from personal experience – yesterday's luxuries become today's 'necessities'.

On the other hand, a rise in *relative* income, say through promotion to a better-paid job, does bring real benefits in terms of status, consumption and comparison with reference groups. However, reference groups also change as people move to more attractive and more expensive neighbourhoods or compete with new rivals at a higher level of their organization. The aspiration gap may shrink but not disappear. People with the most materialist aspirations are generally the least happy, and competition for career advancement becomes a 'rat race' just to 'keep up with the Joneses', let alone overtake them. Individuals regularly overestimate the benefits of effort to earn higher income and status by forgetting that their aspirations will ratchet upwards with material 'progress'.[15] Even when the benefits of effort in terms of gains in relative income and status are correctly perceived, people will generally work more than is socially optimal, because each individual's advancement reduces the relative position of neighbours or rivals, thus imposing an external cost on society.

The simplistic, traditional model of isolated economic actors whose wellbeing depends only on their own consumption thus ignores rivalry and aspirations, and leads to the perverse policies that drive excessive growth, overwork in the rat race and environmental destruction. A more realistic, psychologically based view of human behaviour suggests that income taxation can raise true welfare by discouraging excessive effort and competition for relative income and status.[16] In contrast to material consumption, the enjoyment of family and personal relationships is not normally compared to others' enjoyment, and is not eroded to the same extent by adaptation and rising aspirations. More time with friends and family would essentially make most people happier, without imposing costs on neighbours.

An argument against major investment to mitigate GHG emissions and global warming is that economic growth would slow down and reduce welfare in the future. But as we have seen, the evidence is overwhelming that slower growth in the rich countries would not reduce happiness.

Some economists have claimed that economic growth is generally correlated with increasing SWB by confusing short-term cyclical fluctuations with long-term trends. Thus during cyclical downturns, as in 2008–2009, we can always observe declining growth rates of GDP, rising unemployment and insecurity, and hence falling average SWB. In recovery after recession, the opposite movement takes place. However, over two decades or more, Easterlin finds no significant relationship between economic growth and 'improvement in life satisfaction' in 16 advanced economies. More surprisingly, there is no relationship in developing countries either. Even rapidly growing Korea, Chile and China have not seen improved average life satisfaction over long periods.[17]

As already remarked, the biggest income effect on reported happiness in any one country is between those in (relative) poverty and those in the middle of the income distribution (or above). Even in wealthy countries, relative deprivation often means frequent unemployment, poor education and alcohol addiction. And in spite of economic growth, declining demand for unskilled work has been increasing the proportion of the population in poverty in a number of countries. The importance of relative income has recently been strikingly confirmed by studies showing a negative effect on happiness of an increase in neighbours' income of about the same magnitude as the positive effect of a similar rise in one's own income.[18]

For those who are above the relative poverty line in any country, it is important to remember that income is far from the most important determinant of happiness or wellbeing. Unemployment and divorce are major causes of unhappiness, while family, health, social relationships and job satisfaction, together with largely inherited personality traits, are the most important factors influencing happiness. In comparisons between advanced countries, a few indicators of community and trust in society can explain not only most of the differences in average reported happiness, but also much of the variation in the opposite extreme – rates of suicide. At the same time, recent studies point to a positive relationship between generosity and happiness (this confirms the 'hedonistic paradox', that a person who explicitly seeks happiness may be less likely to find it compared to an altruist who assists others.)[19]

One of the negative by-products (or 'externalities') of economic growth – in addition to environmental degradation – has been the erosion of community and trust or 'social capital' in industrial economies. This loss is manifested in the dramatic increase in family breakdown, youth suicide, clinical mental illness and crime in the last half century of unprecedented economic 'progress' and growth in real incomes, developments which are routinely ignored by most economists in their misplaced identification of more consumption with greater welfare.[20] While this fundamental error has dominated policymaking in the post-war era, it is notable that countries with the strongest commitment to deregulating markets in favour of unrestrained growth, such as America and Britain, have the highest shares of relative poverty, and much lower happiness scores than, for example, the Scandinavian countries.[21] These have maintained social capital and avoided poverty with highly progressive taxation to fund extensive welfare, education, training and redistribution, policies which – ironically – have been scathingly criticized by neo-liberal economists and market fundamentalists.

A new European survey, the most comprehensive of its kind, by Cambridge University and the New Economics Foundation, captures several different but related dimensions of personal and social wellbeing, and finds Britain far below the Scandinavian leaders in most of them. This study shows how detailed 'national accounts of wellbeing' could be based on such surveys, and provide a much more realistic and useful guide for policymakers than the crude and misleading GDP measure, which is still almost exclusively relied upon. The proposal is the latest in a growing number of calls for SWB to be included in national and international decision-making.[22]

The Ecological Footprint

A very simple indicator of the unsustainability of current consumption levels is the crude but suggestive 'ecological footprint'.[23] The main idea is that there are only about 1.8 'global hectares' (gha) of ecologically productive surface area per inhabitant of the Earth.[24] Humanity's demand on the biosphere (in terms of productive surface) constitutes our global ecological footprint, and is about 2.2gha. This includes the area required to absorb all waste, including GHG emissions, in natural sinks. Thus our global ecological footprint already exceeds the total sustainable capacity of the biosphere, which constitutes our 'ecological deficit'. Clearly this deficit cannot be sustained indefinitely, and the growing pressure we impose on ecosystems will sooner or later translate into food shortages, biodiversity loss and accelerated climate change.

Perhaps not surprisingly, the average ecological footprint per inhabitant of the US is among the highest, at 9.5 global hectares, twice the EU level and about five times the average available area of 1.8gha per person. Such large differences in environmental impacts are also typical across households in developed economies, with the carbon footprints of richer households often exceeding those of poorer families by a factor of 10.[25] This of course depends on current technology and consumption habits, and could be reduced by greener technology and consumption. However, if developing countries' material living standards and greenhouse gas emissions per head were to approach the European or US average over time, without a radical switch to renewable energy and cleaner technologies, the ecological deficit implied by our global footprint would expand dramatically. Carbon sinks will deteriorate, and as temperature rises and ecosystems collapse, humanity will be forced by necessity to drastically reduce its ecological footprint.

The Illusionary Comfort of Sustainability (Strong vs. Weak Sustainability)

In order to produce the unprecedented levels of consumption currently enjoyed by wealthy countries, we need to complement our human labour with large amounts of other factors of production. Economists classify these productive inputs into four categories: physical, human, natural and social capital. Physical capital consists of the stock of machinery, buildings and infrastructure that is used in any productive activity. Human capital consists of those skills, abilities and knowledge embodied in labour. But all kinds of capital (except non-renewable resources) can increase as a result of investment (which is the alternative to current consumption), provided the investment is more than the amount of capital that has been 'used up' or become obsolete in the period of production.

Natural 'capital' is more difficult to define precisely, but we can think of it as all those environmental services and resources or 'raw materials' provided by nature. These include (potable) water, breathable air, fisheries, forests, land, non-renewable resources (such as fossil fuels), and the overall services that nature provides for recreation (amenity value), waste assimilation and life-support. Social capital is much more abstract, and depends on the institutional framework within which economic activities take place (such as the extent of property rights and the role of bureaucracy and corruption). Just as importantly, social capital includes the whole network of informal personal relationships – such as trust in neighbours, friends and authorities – on which both everyday life and all economic transactions ultimately depend, and which are so important for life satisfaction or happiness.

Natural capital depreciates through exhaustion of fossil fuels, aquifers and other non-renewables, as well as the destruction of fertile soil or forests. Pollution of air and water threaten future health and agriculture. Neoclassical economists assert that this does not necessarily imply the end of a sustainable world, as long as there is sufficient investment in other kinds of capital. If the 'total stock' of capital in some appropriate sense is maintained (whatever its composition), then sufficient substitutability between man-made (physical, human and social) and natural capital should enable future generations to enjoy at least the same level of welfare as today. The assumption of a non-declining stock of 'total capital' in the economy is known as 'weak sustainability'. While there are obviously always *some* possibilities for substitution between different kinds of capital, relying on weak sustainability as an excuse for large-scale destruction of natural capital requires a high level of corruption or a naïve faith in future technology that owes more to science fiction than to any relevant discipline.

Ecological economists, environmentalists and ecologists believe that natural and man-made capital are often complements rather than substitutes. The natural environment has intrinsic value, in addition to its direct effects on human welfare. True or 'strong' sustainability emphasizes conservation of natural capital and stabilizing population, rather than maintaining the material productivity and consumption growth that is actually eroding natural and social capital in the advanced economies. The combination of a growing world population and consumption with unavoidable further warming does mean that numerous species risk extinction by mid century and that many human lives will be lost. Strong sustainability remains an ideal rather than a precise guide for policy, and is thus often rejected as irrelevant, but without wide acceptance of this ideal instead of continuing current growth patterns, our chances of averting climate catastrophe and agricultural collapse will be slim.

Genuine Savings and Investment

A famous weak-sustainability rule of thumb, known as the Hartwick rule, suggests that all revenues from exhaustible resources (after deducting extraction costs) need to be saved and invested in other forms of capital (human, physical or natural).[26] This of course only applies to those kinds of resources for which markets and realistic prices exist. To verify weak sustainability more generally, economists compare total investment in new capital with the estimated monetary value of all the kinds of capital used up or worn out (depreciated). This difference between new investment and all capital 'consumed' or lost in a particular year is called 'genuine' savings or investment, which obviously have to be positive for weak sustainability to hold. The new capital added to the economy can also be in the form of natural capital, such as investment in abatement, planting trees or searching for new resource deposits. Whatever the limitations of the concept, it can provide a useful early warning signal: negative genuine savings strongly suggest that the economy is on an unsustainable development path of imminent environmental collapse and deteriorating welfare. Recent studies reveal that this is the dismal reality for many parts of the world, ranging from Scotland to Namibia.[27]

The genuine savings measure is far from ideal. It assumes that man-made capital can always replace degraded natural resources to sustain human living standards and happiness. It ignores the fact that natural resources may be useful in the future in ways unknown to current consumers, and with no available substitute (loss of plant species, for instance, may hinder future medical progress). Furthermore, in order to measure substitution and genuine investment, we need to attach monetary values to natural resources and their services, which are often not traded in real markets. As we discuss in Chapters 6 and 9, such estimated values (or 'shadow prices') may underestimate the true, long-term benefits of natural wealth, in particular to future generations, who are not represented in current decision-making. Last, a country may also preserve its own resource base by importing, say, tropical timber, minerals or goods manufactured with intensive energy use and pollution from other nations with lax environmental regulations (and thus contribute to negative genuine savings abroad). A third or more of China's emissions are thus caused by manufacturing for export to rich countries.

GDP (Grossly Distorting Perception)[28]

Even the most casual attention to media reporting on economic policy confirms a near obsession with one measure of economic performance – gross domestic product (GDP) and its growth from year to year. GDP is simply the market value of all final traded goods and services, or the sum of consumption and investment. As noted above, average consumption (and GDP) per capita at a point in time has little relationship with subjective wellbeing in comparisons among the richer countries, and growth of life satisfaction is unrelated to economic growth in this group, as well as among many developing countries. Not only has this fundamental flaw in our key economic indicator been basically known (though largely ignored) for 30 years, but the most obvious and well-known economic inconsistencies in the concept of GDP are also neglected. Thus non-market activities, such as housework or childcare in the family, and the value of additional leisure when working time is reduced, are omitted when GDP growth rates or levels are compared.

As emphasized already, capital of any kind depreciates in various ways, and to maintain a given capital stock, there must be sufficient investment every year to replace the annual loss or depreciation. Business accounts report a surplus only after subtracting an allowance for the depreciation of their physical capital (as well as other costs of current output) from total revenue. Net national product (NNP) is defined by subtracting depreciation of man-made capital from GDP, but this measure is seldom used, because accounting and tax conventions affect the value of depreciation, so NNP is considered to be unreliable and subject to arbitrary errors. Astonishingly, however, neither business nor national accounts even attempt to allow for the natural resources that have been used up or destroyed. One reason is that it is usually very difficult to put a monetary value on damage to the environment caused by GHG emissions and our unsustainable consumerism. Many natural resources are sold on world markets, so it would actually be easy to incorporate their depletion into accounting rules, but even such reforms are strongly resisted by business lobbies. Nobel Prize-winning economist Joseph Stiglitz describes one such episode from his term as Chair of former US President Bill Clinton's Council of Economic Advisors, when he campaigned for improved national accounts.[29]

Greening the GDP

There have in fact been various attempts to provide more comprehensive or greener versions of GDP, adjusting for negative environmental (and other) externalities of economic growth. In the 1990s the United Nations Statistical Division created the System of Integrated Environmental and Economic Accounting (SEEA) to provide some guidelines on how to construct an environment-adjusted measure of GDP. The new measure subtracts from GDP all capital depreciation (both in physical and natural capital through resource depletion), as well as estimated costs of environmental degradation. However, this attempt to create a measure of sustainable income has not been widely used, although it improves on the UN's earlier and frequently cited Human Development Index (HDI), which, as we discuss in Chapter 6, only adds education and life expectancy and ignores sustainability.

The much broader-based Index of Sustainable Economic Welfare (ISEW) has been constructed for several countries by Friends of the Earth and the New Economics Foundation and has been declining or remained stationary in recent decades. The similar Genuine Progress Indicator (GPI), originally developed by Daly and Cobb and continuously updated and extended for the US economy (but also at a smaller-scale for US regions and cities),[30] has also attracted attention in recent years. After rising until 1970, the US ISEW has been falling since, currently reaching a lower level than in 1950. These indices are constructed using GDP data after adjusting for non-market output, income inequality, and depreciation of both man-made and natural capital, as well as externalities and clean-up costs. They thus subtract from GDP the estimated monetary value of a broad range of externalities which are generated by our unsustainable consumption patterns.

The GPI includes estimates of damage caused by GHG emissions, and it is striking that these amounted to more than a trillion US dollars in 2004. Alarmingly, this is the second highest cost included in the GPI index, after depreciation of non-renewable resources, and the fastest rising cost over the last few decades. There are similar estimates for other countries. While no substitute for direct survey evidence on happiness, and subject to unavoidable uncertainty in attempting to quantify environmental damage, the GPI index includes important aspects of sustainability and welfare that are totally ignored in the conventional GDP measure of market activity.

Rather than trying to modify GDP to obtain a meaningful index of welfare, an interesting new approach by the New Economics Foundation measures the ecological efficiency with which nations attain subjective wellbeing or happiness, the Happy Planet Index (HPI). This is defined as the product of life satisfaction with life expectancy (happy life years) divided by the ecological footprint, or 'the average years of happy life produced by a society ... per unit of planetary resources consumed'.[31]

As examples of how the HPI works, resource-rich Sweden has a large ecological footprint to attain a high level of happiness, and thus scores lower than countries such as Austria or Iceland that achieve similar 'happy life years' with much smaller footprints or lower resource use. The UK, with relatively low life satisfaction and a moderate footprint among advanced economies (though still three times the available 1.8gha per person), has a HPI just above Sweden, though far below the leaders. Some relatively poor countries such as Cuba and Costa Rica manage to achieve surprisingly high levels of life expectancy and satisfaction with very modest resource use, thus coming close to the top of the HPI ranking, indicating much greater ecological efficiency than even the best-performing advanced economies. There are surely interesting lessons for development and sustainability to be drawn from further study of this promising new approach.

Ecologists vs. Economists

Ecologists are concerned with the integrity and stability of whole ecosystems, and thus have a keen interest in the adverse impacts of human actions on their functioning. For this reason, they interpret sustainability quite differently from most economists. Their central concern is the survival of the entire biosphere, not just a given level of human prosperity or the wasteful consumption of the richest nations. Of course, as we have argued at length, there is abundant evidence that the current pattern of Western material consumption is already unsustainable, let alone its imitation by the LDCs as the world warms up. Reflecting on ecology raises profound questions about the valuation of non-human life, which, as we discuss in Chapter 6, receives much more attention in the ethics of Eastern religions, especially Buddhism. However, more pragmatic and widely shared concerns about the survival of our own children, as well as those in the most threatened, poorest parts of the world, are in themselves quite sufficient to justify urgent and drastic action to reduce the environmental cost of conventional economic growth.

Ecologists and environmentalists tend to be sceptical about substitution possibilities and the scope for new technologies to replace natural resources that are often irreversibly destroyed by traditional economic growth. This is particularly relevant for what is often defined as 'critical natural capital', which provides our life-support ecological services, but the 'criticality' of natural capital and the inherent value attached to it are closely linked to social perceptions, rather than any strict biophysical limits and threshold effects determined by natural scientists. From this position, the basic ideas of strong sustainability form the only meaningful and morally acceptable guide to future development. Clearly, past economic growth has diverged very far from this ideal, and global warming already threatens numerous ecosystems (with much tropical rainforest and biodiversity likely to be destroyed by temperature increase and drought by mid century).

The ultimate threat from water shortage, soil erosion and further warming is not just to ecosystems, but to the lives of perhaps billions of the world's poorest people in hot and arid regions, who face the risk of large-scale famine if present trends continue. Sustainability indicators for the wealthy northern countries alone, which may even benefit from climate change, are both ethically and strategically bankrupt in a nuclear-armed world order and a global economy that is threatened with partial collapse.

Ecological economists try to combine insights from various disciplines and arrive at a more inclusive and holistic evaluation of costs and benefits of policies than the narrow monetary estimates usually used by economists and governments. These in turn are often dominated by industry lobbies that influence public opinion and actively promote deception and distortion of scientific evidence to conceal environmental and health costs. This is particularly easy to do when the costs are difficult to quantify, and affect poorer countries or future generations. Decades of false claims by the tobacco industry and more recently by the fossil fuel lobby[32] are facilitated by an environment where media and politics are generally subservient to business interests, with public legitimacy based on the false ideology that economic growth makes everyone happier.

Conclusions

Economic development has been at the expense of our global environmental health. A truly sustainable future, on the other hand, requires economic development that does not compromise the health of ecosystems, climate stability or the wellbeing of the future poor. But how do economists perceive such a 'sustainable future'? As highlighted above, sustainability is often an ambiguous concept, with some emphasizing the role of continuous material growth and others putting more emphasis on environmental protection. Whatever the definition, unmitigated climate change is certainly inconsistent with sustainable development. Generous investment in renewable technologies and knowledge transfers will be necessary to decouple economic growth from GHG emissions and environmental degradation more generally, particularly as China and India's current economic ascent imposes enormous environmental harm. National accounts, which are used to calculate our most common estimate of welfare – GDP – currently do not correct for the loss of environmental assets and pollution. Even when green accounting tries to incorporate such damages into a more comprehensive measure of wellbeing, monetary values cannot be accurately provided for all non-marketed environmental services, nor can material consumption and environmental quality ever be complete substitutes.

Even more importantly, there is increasing evidence that long-term growth rates of average income and life satisfaction are unrelated in many countries, both rich and poor. Our unsustainable consumerism not only fails to raise average wellbeing, but also comes at the expense of social and environmental capital. This suggests that sacrificing consumption in richer countries for investment in public goods and aid transfers is likely to achieve a convergence in happiness globally, though at no cost for those already rich. Rivalry and aspirations for higher relative income result in continuous competition, excessive growth, and an ever-expanding list of consumer needs and habits. While our ecological footprint suggests we already live beyond our means, we mistakenly prioritize relative consumption over more fundamental determinants of happiness, namely social relationships and environmental quality.

5

Development in a Changing Climate

Millennium Goals for Development and Environment

We live in a world of collapsing ecosystems and environments, from fisheries and rainforests to clean air and water, as well as persistent, extreme poverty in most developing countries, where climate change is only one of many serious challenges. The eight Millennium Development Goals (MDGs), agreed at the UN Millennium Summit in 2000 (by 189 countries), attempt to create a road map for improvement in the main problem areas. The plan reflects high aspirations in many development dimensions, but little progress can be expected without major policy changes, as Africa's disappointing performance, in particular, so far suggests.[1] Generous technology, aid and knowledge transfers need to be complemented with radical policy changes in environmental protection, gender equality, international trade and poverty alleviation.

The MDGs for 2015, in brief, are to eradicate extreme poverty, achieve universal primary education, promote gender equality, reduce child mortality, improve maternal health, combat diseases (such as HIV/AIDS, malaria and typhus), ensure environmental sustainability and develop a global partnership for development.[2] Under the environmental sustainability objective alone, there is a formidable list of more detailed targets, including halting biodiversity loss, improving access to safe drinking water and sanitation, reversing deforestation, and mitigating climate change.

It is obviously counterproductive to target global warming in isolation. Developing nations, and the poorest countries in particular, have special needs and characteristics that all merit urgent attention. Most of them are far behind schedule for achievement of all MDGs, and are still further handicapped by rapidly growing populations and, until recently, fast-rising food and energy prices. Developing nations generally, and most outside observers, see economic growth as one of the essential elements needed to achieve their MDGs. Economic growth will in principle allow governments and individuals to increase their spending on education, health, the environment and general infrastructure, though, as we discuss below, these 'public goods' are frequently neglected, with the richest classes capturing most of the benefits of growth for themselves. The crucial question here is whether growth will continue to come at the expense of even higher greenhouse gas emissions, more deforestation, environmental degradation and inequality. Is there a way to achieve all the development goals simultaneously?

This chapter focuses on the challenges faced by developing nations, especially those with large populations, suffering widespread and extreme poverty. In a world of 6.7 billion people, about a billion live on the estimated 'equivalent' of less than a dollar per day, though many are subsistence farmers who scarcely interact with the market economy. The majority of the poorest live in sub-Saharan Africa and South Asia, with East Asia achieving the greatest improvements in reducing poverty since the 1960s (mainly driven by China's growth performance). If one stretches the poverty limit to $2 a day, the results are even more discouraging. Most of the people so living are found in populous developing nations, such as Nigeria, Bangladesh, India, Indonesia and China, where the shares of total population under the $2 poverty line are an astounding 92, 84, 80, 52 and 35 per cent respectively. For most sub-Saharan nations, the share consistently exceeds 70 per cent of the total population. These are the Earth's 'bottom billions', a staggering 2.6 billion people, or 40 per cent of the global population, that live – and die prematurely – on only a tiny fraction of the richest countries' per capita GDP.[3] At the same time, aid from the leading developed economies of the OECD remains much smaller than their subsidies for the most polluting fossil fuels, or for their richest big farmers. The US continues to provide only 0.17 per cent of GDP as development aid, which is the smallest share in the OECD.

There are thus two reasons for a chapter on development under the growing threat of climate change. First, the poorest countries and the poorest segments of their societies will suffer the most from global warming. Low incomes prevent both governments and individuals from investing much in either adapting to or preventing climate change.[4] Many of the poorest countries contain some of the already most environmentally degraded regions, where the effects of climate change will be particularly devastating. Many farmers in these regions are vulnerable to the expected increased frequency of droughts, heatwaves and floods. Large-scale agricultural collapse due to warming and water shortages will almost certainly be the most important climate change impact on the world's poor if present trends continue much longer, leading to astronomical food prices, mass starvation and migration, as we discussed in Chapter 3. Food price inflation in 2007–2008 strained the budgets of those who spend most of their incomes on basic necessities, with accompanying food riots in many poor regions, and export bans by producers worried about their own food security. While worldwide economic recession and financial crises in late 2008 have generated sharp falls in food and energy prices, economic recovery will surely reignite the upward trends.

Apart from the fact that the less developed countries will be hardest hit by changes in climatic conditions, there is another major reason why they deserve our particular attention – developing nations are increasing their carbon emissions much more rapidly than the old industrial countries. China has recently surpassed the US as the largest contributor to global emissions, coupled with rapidly progressing domestic environmental degradation. This suggests that unilateral reductions of emissions by the Annex I industrialized nations under Kyoto may simply be counterbalanced by increases across developing countries. Unless there is some concerted global effort by all nations simultaneously, any efforts by developed nations to reduce their GHG emissions will have only limited effects.[5]

Time to Double – 70/x

There is a rule of thumb in mathematics that gives a practical sense of what a growth rate implies. We know for instance that China's economy has been growing by about 10 per cent annually for many years. We also know that India's population grew at an average annual rate of 1.5 per cent over the last decade. It is sometimes useful to translate such numbers into an alternative and more intuitive measure. Dividing the number 70 by the growth rate of any statistic, we obtain the number of years it takes for the variable to double.[6] Assuming that the above growth rates persist over time, it follows that China could double its output in 70/10 = 7 years. With emissions increasing nearly as rapidly, China could be producing half the world's output of GHGs in a decade or two without radical policy changes. Similarly, a sustained growth rate of 1.5 per cent implies that India could double its population size in 70/1.5 = 47 years.

The Dragon Is Rising

Though not one of the poorest countries, and in spite of its success in lifting many out of poverty, China still has a large, impoverished and vulnerable 'underclass' that has benefited little from growth hitherto. In addition, the sheer size of its economy and GHG emissions imply that this developing country already has major impacts on commodity markets and prices, and in the long run on global climate. China's GDP is currently estimated at approximately $7000 billion on a 'purchasing power parity' basis (in other words when taking into account that many commodities are cheaper in China than in the US and that the official exchange rate undervalues the Chinese currency).[7] This is approximately half the size of the US or EU economies. India's GDP is also rapidly expanding and is currently estimated at just over $3000 billion. While there is a strong relationship between economic activity and carbon emissions, China is currently using much 'dirtier' and more energy-intensive technologies than the US, which in turn is twice as energy-intensive as Europe. China's economy, despite being half the size of that of the US, is still responsible for about the same total amount of carbon emissions.

Luckily for the world, the double-digit growth rates of many large, developing economies and their emissions are unlikely to continue unabated. Air pollution in China, for example, is already so bad that half of Beijing's traffic and much industry had to be banished for the duration of the Olympic Games in August 2008. The ultimate health effects of even catastrophic air and water pollution may take decades to appear as mortality statistics, but pressures to provide environmental public goods, such as clean air and water, and restrain excessive polluting growth are now likely to grow, as basic consumption needs are met. These pressures will be reinforced as the most easily accessible coal resources become exhausted, fossil fuel prices begin to rise with the recovery of the global economy and costs of renewable energy decline due to spectacular technical progress.

There are, of course, still major pressures for material growth, not least from the rapidly growing (albeit still relatively small) middle classes of the big developing countries. Average Chinese income per person (in terms of purchasing power), after three decades of fast economic growth, is still only a small fraction (around 12 per cent) of its American equivalent. To illustrate how energy-intensive the Chinese economy has become, its per capita carbon emissions are now about a quarter of those of the US, yet China still has only one car per 70 inhabitants, while the US has nearly one car per person. Meat consumption has already reached two-fifths of the US level, adding major strains to agriculture already threatened by growing water shortages, as we discussed in Chapter 3.

Just before the 2008 global recession, China's carbon emissions were still growing by about eight per cent annually, nearly as fast as the economy, suggesting that the country is making only slow progress in becoming more energy efficient, though the government has set extensive industry targets for greater energy efficiency. The two new coal-fired power stations being completed per week are more efficient than the old ones (some of which have been closed), but with only a few, limited experimental projects for carbon capture and storage (CCS), total emissions could double in a decade without major policy changes. At the same time, no one is measuring the innumerable forms of local toxic air and water pollution or their growth, since most of their sources are illegal and unrecorded. Rampant corruption among local officials means that existing legislation for environmental protection is largely unenforced.

China's Clean Revolution is the unlikely title of an August 2008 report by the Climate Group, an international NGO, which argues that the Central Government has recognized at least some of the dangers resulting from current policies. China already has the world's largest renewable generating capacity and plans to expand this to 15 per cent of power generation by 2020. China is also a leading producer and exporter of all kinds of renewable technology, and already has 60 per cent of the world's solar water-heating capacity. However, with most of its energy still coming from dirty coal, this is an entirely inadequate response to the country's own looming public health crisis, let alone to the threat of climate change. China's central planners also have the world's most ambitious plan to develop nuclear power, though in the West, at least, this is the most expensive form of energy supply, requiring large-scale government subsidies and guarantees for the few units currently planned.[8] Just how long the Chinese central authorities can continue to inflict ever-worsening pollution on most of the population, as the price for material growth, remains to be seen.

The burgeoning middle classes who everywhere demand more cars and more meat are beginning to feel many of the environmental effects of these products in the form of congestion, pollution and, until recently, food price inflation. Higher incomes and flight to the suburbs, traditional routes for prosperous individuals to escape the environmental consequences of economic growth, can only temporarily protect them from the eventual global consequences of local and regional devastation inflicted by old-fashioned, dirty technology throughout the developing world. The continuous upsurge in fossil fuel prices between 2002 and 2008 (dictated by the traditional market forces of scarcity and surging demand for energy from emerging economies like China and India) provided a glimpse of hope for a long-overdue change to cleaner technology, at the same time as imminent, and potentially devastating, public health and environmental problems were becoming increasingly political issues. While the late 2008 global recession might undermine such a process of change by shifting attention away from longer-term environmental problems, tackling global warming and a global recession should not be seen as competing goals, particularly when investment in greener technologies and infrastructure can provide the solution to rising unemployment and falling production.

It comes as no surprise that China's astounding take-off dominates the international development debate. China has achieved remarkable economic progress, with fast rates of GDP growth, large inflows of foreign direct investment, huge trade surpluses and drastic reductions in domestic poverty. Today, less than 10 per cent of the population lives below the $1 per day poverty line, compared to 60 per cent in the late 1970s. Sustained economic growth has had enormous effects – not all of them positive – that have radically transformed the Chinese economy and society within a generation. The Chinese development model gradually reduced the state sector and intervention in favour of private entrepreneurship, gave control of land to farmers, and welcomed foreign direct investment. At the same time, higher average consumption and improved literacy rates played a key role in reducing infant mortality rates and raising life expectancy at birth.[9]

The Chinese development model has been widely praised for raising large numbers out of extreme poverty and improving living conditions for perhaps a majority of Chinese families, particularly in eastern provinces. While achievements on the poverty front are generally recognized, however, China's rapid industrial development has come at the expense of air and water pollution and soil degradation. Economic growth has also not benefited everyone equally, with rural areas, particularly in western China, lagging behind the booming urban centres of the east. Recent reports of violent protests in rural Hunan in Central China in 2007 revealed the plight of China's poor.[10] Recent research on measures of subjective wellbeing (SWB) also provides evidence of the costs of reckless economic growth and planning. Subjective happiness and life satisfaction for the average Chinese have deteriorated dramatically between 1990 and 2007, despite the large gains in average GDP per person reported by official statistics.[11] This development is all the more remarkable because most poor countries do seem to benefit from economic growth with increasing SWB, though India is another notable exception.

The world keeps a close eye on Chinese developments in the economic and political spheres. China has approximately a fifth of the world's population, and globalization has linked the rest of the world with the Chinese economy. But it is certainly not only a matter of size. The Chinese development model is widely perceived as one of the most successful examples of recent economic development. This largely ignores the fact that China will have to pay an enormous price for its breakneck pace of development in terms of environmental degradation and future health costs. Less developed nations may be tempted to try to replicate the economic policies and development model of a country whose economy expanded six times in the course of 20 years. The allure of the Chinese model may thus put other developing nations on track to repeat its policy mistakes of inequitable and environmentally destructive industrialization.

China has gradually become not only a major recipient of foreign direct investment from developed nations, but also a key investor herself in other developing economies. There is increasing evidence, however, that Chinese foreign investors are less likely to comply with already insufficient international standards and norms on environmental protection and labour rights when compared to American and European investors. This is likely to instigate a race to the bottom in environmental standards for many developing countries, where domestic firms choose trading partners according to criteria of profit and cost-effectiveness, and do not necessarily view environmental protection as an integral part of their corporate social responsibility.[12]

The Impacts of Climate Change on the Poor

The effects of global warming will be felt across the whole planet, but some regions will be hit harder than others. It is now widely acknowledged that the poorest nations and the poorest segments of their populations will bear the largest costs of climate change, interacting with already severe water shortages and pollution problems. Halting and reversing existing environmental degradation, as well as adapting to adverse new climatic conditions, is particularly difficult when resources are lacking and governments are corrupt and undemocratic. As usual, the poorest individuals in those 'bottom billion' countries are the worst equipped to cope with deteriorating environments and future complex climate change impacts.

In Chapter 3 we discussed in detail the devastating impact climate change is expected to have on agricultural productivity. Higher temperatures, increased frequency of droughts and floods, and growing water scarcity will all adversely affect agricultural production in vulnerable areas. In some regions in higher latitudes and temperate climates, increased temperatures may extend growing seasons and allow more multiple cropping, but any positive impacts will be dominated by the threat of major droughts in hot and arid parts of the planet. The majority of the Earth's bottom billions live in these areas and will experience the largest declines in agricultural productivity, and soaring food prices in consequence.

For most developing countries, with the exception of some mineral-rich nations, agriculture plays the dominant role in the economy. In many areas where agricultural productivity is expected to decline, the majority of the economically active population derives its livelihood from activities dependent on agriculture. In developed economies, by contrast, only a small fraction of the labour force is employed in the agricultural sector.[13] Even in fast industrializing and urbanizing China, more than 60 per cent of its vast population is still rural and largely dependent on agriculture. And the dramatic food price inflation that will follow any large-scale collapse of agriculture in major food-growing areas will of course also expose the urban poor to mass starvation wherever the resources or political will to implement aid and redistribution are lacking.

The list of climate change impacts on the poorest billions is of course much longer and discussed in detail throughout the book. Increasing populations will exacerbate all those problems in the poorest countries with the highest birth rates. Rising sea levels will disrupt agriculture and pollute groundwater in coastal areas and result in massive population migration. In hot environments, water scarcity, land degradation and food shortage may result in serious conflict over these ever-scarcer resources. Extreme weather events and intensified ocean acidification will have devastating effects on coral populations, the dependent marine life and human populations in nearby areas.

Much attention has been given to the impact of rising temperatures on health and the spread of infectious diseases. As temperatures rise more in northern latitudes, warmer winters will bring some benefits, but many pests will also be able to spread and survive the cold season. In contrast, even moderate warming will have serious health effects for many of the world's poorest billions living in tropical and semi-tropical regions. For example, the spread of malaria is limited by temperature. In warmer conditions, malaria-carrying mosquitoes will spread more easily to areas north and south of the tropics, as well as into higher elevations.[14] Dengue fever, an infectious disease related to yellow fever, is also on the rise in many tropical climates. New and essentially untreatable infections, such as avian flu, antibiotic-resistant tuberculosis or the black stem wheat rust fungus Ug99, threaten human, animal and plant populations with increasing frequency, even without help from climate change. The health impacts of old and new epidemics, as well as of global warming, are magnified by modern mobility and transport. But as usual, the worst impact will be on the world's poorest nations and populations, where most households have little capacity to relocate or protect themselves, and public medical care is rudimentary.

Development and Sustainability as Conflicting Goals

Climate change, unless concerted effort takes place soon, will in effect be a tragedy of the global commons. We need to learn to manage our global footprint not as single independent nations, but rather by coordinating our actions. This applies most particularly to our carbon emissions, as they accumulate in the atmosphere, irrespective of where they are emitted. Increased pollution by the large and fast-growing developing countries can offset mitigation efforts by other sovereign states.[15]

The problem with most developing nations is that the environment is not an overarching priority at this stage of their development process. Many of the largest developing economies have been growing at 7–12 per cent per annum, and at the moment are unwilling to sacrifice economic growth for the sake of a global environmental good, or even for their own local environment and public health. A common argument from developing nations is that they are not to blame for most of the increase of greenhouse gases in the atmosphere since pre-industrial times. Rich countries that built their previous successful economic development on natural resource exploitation are responsible for most of the existing stock of GHGs, and hence should contribute most to clean-up costs and mitigation efforts.

The argument is, of course, valid to a large extent, and this is exactly the reason developing nations face no binding targets for carbon emissions under the Kyoto Protocol. But is there any way we can take them on board in a concerted effort to constrain global emissions? It all boils down to the extent that the environment and economic development remain conflicting goals for the developing world. We need to implement a development strategy that combines carbon management and environmental protection with healthy economic growth to meet the concerns of the global South. Lower emissions and sustainable growth can be simultaneously attained with the right policies, market initiatives and interventions, as we explain in Chapters 7 and 8.

Thinking on an Empty Stomach

Climate change mitigation should not be an exclusively top–down approach, relying on government agencies and international donors to take all the action against carbon emissions. Local communities and individuals have an important role to play in curbing global emissions by adopting environmentally friendly modes of agriculture and transportation, minimizing energy consumption at home, and putting pressure on their elected representatives to take action on environmental issues. Nevertheless, environmental awareness tends to be a rather exclusive prerogative of the small urban elites in most developing countries. Limited access to education for the world's bottom billions necessarily inhibits environmental awareness for the global poor. Governments often lack necessary funds for public investment in education, and poor households have more urgent and immediate survival needs than environmental quality and its usually less obvious and deferred benefits, let alone the longer-term threats of further climate-enhanced degradation.

For these reasons, many of the world's poor are either unaware of climate change and its consequences or have a rather partial and often distorted perception of the problem. A recent study conducted in Nairobi, Kenya, examined local perceptions of climate change and concluded that global warming is generally not considered a significant problem, in contrast to corruption, unemployment, street crime, HIV/AIDS and poverty.[16] *Climatic Change*, a specialist journal on global warming issues, devoted a special issue in 2006 to the psychology of climate change, suggesting a strong link between perceptions of climate change risk within societies and decisions taken to prevent or adapt to global warming.[17] The complexity of the climate change problem, the large uncertainties involved and often a poor communication of relevant scientific evidence all work against a wider public awareness of climate change.

There is also widespread ignorance about the most basic scientific facts of climate change. Stratospheric ozone depletion is most commonly confused with global warming, along with a long list of irrelevant responses in opinion surveys on the causes of climate change, ranging from space exploration to acid rain. Even in highly developed nations, such as the US and UK, close to a quarter of survey respondents regard ozone depletion as the major cause of climate change.[18]

Aid and Technology Transfers

The rich countries currently provide about 0.3 per cent of their total national incomes as development aid – and this is nearly twice the share of the lowest ranking (and richest) donor, the US. Leading development economist Jeffrey Sachs estimates that about 2.4 per cent of GDP would be necessary to achieve all the Millennium Development Goals, and reduce carbon emissions to safe levels.[19] This is not very much more than current US military expenditure alone, or half its share of 'defence' in GDP, and is comparable to the amount spent on wasteful and perverse subsidies in the rich countries. For aid to be more effective than in the past, a larger flow would need much more careful monitoring to avoid diversion to corrupt governments and greedy multinationals. Sensible saving and redirection of public spending could thus essentially ensure a stable and sustainable future world. In the short term, the poorest countries would be the most direct beneficiaries, but from a longer-term perspective, the donor countries can only thus ensure their own future prosperity (and perhaps even survival) in a cooperating rather than collapsing international order.

Much of the apparent conflict between growth and the environment in the developing countries arises from their reliance on outdated technology, instead of using the well-tried and tested alternatives that are already available. These issues are discussed in detail in Chapter 9, but the point here is that these alternatives have largely been developed in the rich economies, with little effort to transfer or adapt the newer, cleaner technologies to the poor countries. There is thus a widespread misperception that environmental degradation today is the necessary price for economic growth and higher consumption in the future. There is also little awareness in developing countries of the health costs of current pollution, and of how realistic accounting for mortality and morbidity would reveal huge social returns to environmental clean-up.

Western consumers benefit from cheap imports as long as wages and environmental, health and safety standards remain low in the developing economies. In the long run, these consumers will also suffer from the consequences of climate change on agricultural productivity. However, the poor nations remain the most vulnerable, and part of any serious aid effort (reinforced by self-interest) should provide support for the clean technologies that are already competitive with – or cheaper than – dirty coal. These include combined heat and power from smaller, decentralized generating units in appropriate areas such as northern China, and modern wind power in suitable sites. The rapid growth of a large-scale alternative energy sector in China offers an ideal partner for implementing the mass production and further cost-reduction of these technologies, as well as the major new breakthroughs in solar energy coming from specialist companies. This is particularly appropriate at a time when bottlenecks in the production and supply of large wind generators have resulted from 30 per cent annual growth rates in demand, and caused costs to rise rapidly after years of steady decline. Alternative energy production is of course also affected by the recent rise in the cost of cement, steel and other primary resources, needed for the construction of wind turbines or energy transmission, which in turn has been largely generated by the extraordinary pace of conventional (and highly polluting) economic growth in large developing countries, headed by China.

It is widely recognized that one of the most cost-effective forms of aid is to provide appropriate incentives for developing countries to stop tropical deforestation and biomass burning. Preserving biodiversity and other ecological services for future biotechnology and ecotourism in particular, as well as for their wider climate benefits and existence values, offers huge returns to modest investments. However, the enforcement of both existing laws and new agreements under pervasive corruption and pressures for short-term exploitation is fraught with problems. A cheap solar cooker costing about $10 can easily provide an economic alternative to domestic biomass burning – a major source of indoor air pollution – and an inexpensive means to reduce carbon emissions in the poorest regions. The subsequent health benefits of removing indoor air pollution are much longer-term than the immediate effects of providing clean water and sanitation (the lack of which is the major cause of child mortality), however, and hence tend to be neglected in spite of their very low cost.

To prevent carbon emissions and local pollution from industrial activities in developing countries on a larger scale, more funds will be needed from richer nations. Technologies that either improve energy efficiency or rely on renewable resources need to be subsidized and transferred to developing markets, in cooperation with domestic policy initiatives, such as China's rapidly growing clean energy. In time, learning-by-doing will render the new technologies competitive without the support of external funding. In the meantime, the rich have to provide financial assistance (either directly or via the Clean Development Mechanism we discuss in Chapter 7) to achieve carbon reductions in the developing world. Currently, the World Bank claims to be a key player in financing clean energy transitions (with its Prototype Carbon Fund and more recent Climate Investment Funds), aiming at transferring technologies and know-how that reduce carbon emissions in developing economies. Although a step in the right direction, the World Bank unfortunately still remains a large underwriter of fossil fuel energy projects in many parts of the developing world, hence playing a counterproductive role in the dissemination and adoption of greener technologies.

Transportation

Worldwide, transport accounts for about 14 per cent of total carbon emissions, nearly as much as deforestation.[20] The share of the developing countries is rising rapidly, and, as with other technologies, they seem determined to imitate the most destructive aspects of earlier, Western urban development. Car and oil lobbies have helped to generally suppress the alternative model of urban planning based on public transport and cycling, which has been spectacularly successful in at least one developing city, Curitiba in Brazil. China promoted the use of bicycles as the main urban transport mode, and some 500 million bicycles provided unprecedented mobility by the 1980s. But the subsequent switch to priority for cars has exacerbated already appalling air pollution and traffic congestion, and displaced bicycles, which are often perceived by middle-class drivers as obstacles to 'progress'.

Growing political awareness of these problems, perhaps aided by the Beijing Olympics, has triggered the beginnings of an interesting U-turn in the shape of the E-bicycle. This has a rechargeable battery to power a light electric motor, providing an economical and clean powered transport option, the latest versions of which even use braking energy for recharging and still greater economy. Rapidly growing demand will be boosted by higher fuel prices, and 'hybrid' E-bikes could become a major export hit.

Curitiba has been a remarkable and rare example of green and integrated urban development in a developing country, of immense importance and relevance for the rest of the world. Surprisingly, though, only Columbia's capital city, Bogota, seems to have taken some steps in this direction.

Conspicuous failure to replicate the enormous welfare and environmental benefits of this model more widely is difficult to explain. The Curitiba story does seem to have features of a historical accident, owing much to a talented town planner, Jaime Lerner, who founded the Urban Planning Institute of Curitiba (IPPUC) and then became long-term mayor of this rapidly growing city in the 1970s and 1980s. He finally became Governor of the State of Parana, and recipient of innumerable international honours and awards.

The integrated, green development of Curitiba has accommodated above-average population growth for decades, with the population now reaching 1.6 million. There are several key elements for this successful experiment in the developing world. Much of the central area is pedestrianized, combining high-quality residential and commercial use. Main routes are served by frequent, cheap and fast buses in dedicated lanes, with convenient, covered stops for rapid access and exit. Cycling is encouraged by 200 kilometres of cycle tracks, and about one-fifth of the city area has been converted to green parkland. Though car ownership is relatively high, car use and air pollution are lower than in any other Brazilian city, while the share of public transport is much greater, accounting for 75 per cent of weekday commuting. No less than 70 per cent of garbage is recycled. The most remarkable statistics are reported by environmental writer Bill McKibben:

> In a recent survey, 60 per cent of New Yorkers wanted to leave their rich and cosmopolitan city; 99 per cent of Curitibans told pollsters that they were happy with their town; and 70 per cent of the residents of Sao Paulo said they thought life would be better in Curitiba.[21]

It is, of course, much more difficult to implement integrated green planning in the megacities that have become environmental disasters after decades of domination by the dirtiest technologies, for the sake of private profit and at the expense of public health. Curitiba had the huge advantage of starting on the right track as a relatively small city. However, the urgency of change grows with the costs of congestion and damage to health and welfare. The newest technologies of hybrid buses, electric light rail and E-bikes offer major further environmental benefits and cost savings as fuel prices rise, and the incentives for change are greatest in the poorest countries, which can least afford extravagant use of energy. But these innovations will be much more rapidly adopted under appropriate planning that provides dedicated road space for clean and public transport and extended pedestrian areas.

Deforestation

There is an urgent need to slow down and finally halt deforestation in tropical and semi-tropical countries. Forest clearance – particularly in Brazil, which has the largest forest cover globally – has reached unprecedented levels in recent years and accounts for perhaps a fifth of our carbon footprint. While difficult to measure precisely, probably around 15 million hectares annually suffer degradation and destruction, largely driven by slash-and-burn farming, global demand for timber and, increasingly, biofuel production that requires forest clearance for palm oil and sugar cane plantations, particularly in Indonesia and Brazil. Similarly, changing consumer habits in China and other fast-developing countries exert pressure to convert forest into farmland, for meat and soy production for their expanding middle-income populations. Perhaps half the original mature tropical forest has been lost in the past 50 years.[22]

Much of the destruction is already illegal, and facilitated by corrupt local officials. Interestingly, though, well-defined property rights protection and alternative economic incentives could decrease the current rate of deforestation in the Amazon and other tropical regions rather inexpensively with appropriate government commitment. In tropical regions, forest clearance creates grazing or cropland of low quality that is quickly exhausted and abandoned. Small economic incentives, either in the form of a 'payment for environmental service' scheme by developed countries or ecotourism charges, could easily create attractive, alternative and sustainable livelihoods for local communities.

The causal links between global warming and deforestation are certainly complex, and climate change is also expected to have direct impacts on forest cover. Reduced rainfall, increased frequency of droughts and higher temperatures will result in recurrent and extensive forest fires, like the 2007 summer fires in Greece that destroyed about 2000 square kilometres of forest in a few days (as well as numerous properties and human lives). Forest fires also release stored carbon back into the atmosphere, further enhancing the greenhouse effect. This is partially compensated for by a northward migration of forests, as colder northern latitudes gradually become more suitable for tree growth. However, this is a slow process, while deforestation and forest fires are already accelerating at an alarming rate. Tropical rainforest also contains much of the world's biodiversity, with many species not yet discovered, let alone studied – an irreplaceable and essential resource for future medication and biotechnology that is rapidly being destroyed.

Constraining population growth needs to be an integral element of any successful strategy to curb global deforestation. There has been a tenfold increase in global population in the last three centuries, with another 2–3 billion people expected by mid century on present trends, and enormous pressure to clear land for crops and pasture. Fast-expanding GDP levels and consumer habits have all contributed to the current unsustainable rates of deforestation, with China importing increasing quantities of tropical hardwood and soy beans. Providing tradable carbon credits for reforestation and conservation projects can create the right incentives, but the market price for such credits would need to exceed the monetary benefits from deforestation (which increase with food prices and global demand for hardwood).

Multinationals and the Poor

While globalization interconnects the world with increased trade, capital movement and migration, it also opens up new markets to the rich-world multinational corporations. Multinational firms already play an increasing role in developing countries' economies, particularly through foreign direct investment (FDI). China, Mexico and Brazil are some of the major recipients of foreign investment, with multinational corporations now taking advantage of their export-processing zones and low labour costs. In China alone, FDI amounted to $78 billion in 2006. Worldwide more than 65 million people are now directly employed in export-processing zones, in activities linked to multinational corporations.[23]

While multinationals create numerous job opportunities in some of the world's poorest regions, they are by no means philanthropic foundations. They are widely criticized for their overarching priorities – maximizing shareholder value or corporate profits, minimizing wages, and rapidly increasing rewards for top managers, often at the cost of local communities' livelihoods, environmental degradation and other externalities. They often seek pollution havens, where they can initiate production without incurring the costs of environmental regulation. A recent study finds that, on average, a one per cent increase in the costs of required pollution abatement in the US leads to relocation of production abroad and increases net American imports by 0.4 and 0.6 per cent from Mexico and Canada respectively.[24] Multinational corporations often supply products that have been manufactured with environmentally unsustainable methods (and unethical practices including child labour, hazardous working conditions and failure to share profits with local communities). And lack of transparency suggests that consumers are still largely unaware of how products ending up in their homes are manufactured thousands of miles away.

The gradual removal of capital controls has allowed FDI to exit a recipient country as easily as it entered. Acquiring assets in a foreign economy may be costly for multinational companies, and it is not in their interests to relocate shortly after initial investments. But ultimately, multinationals are searching for ways to escape trade tariffs, taxes and regulatory fees, as well as minimize production costs. If opportunities that appear to be more profitable for their shareholders arise in due time, they may relocate their activities, whatever the cost to their former host communities.[25] This also challenges the effectiveness of agreements such as the Kyoto Protocol in curbing carbon emissions in Annex I industrialized nations, if carbon-intensive production is gradually displaced to China or other countries with looser environmental regulations.[26]

Nobel laureate Joseph Stiglitz has severely criticized the role of multinational corporations, and their support by the rich countries, in the economic development of many of the world's poorest nations.[27] Governments in these countries have little bargaining power to negotiate with multinational firms and their highly skilled corporate lawyers. Multinationals generally exaggerate any positive side-effects their activities may have on both the local and national economy. They tend to stress the importance of their operations on local employment and infrastructure and at the same time largely downplay the huge environmental costs their activities frequently impose. These externalities include river and groundwater pollution, deforestation, soil erosion and carbon emissions, and often ruin the livelihoods of surrounding resource-dependent communities. In very few cases are clauses incorporated in FDI agreements that subject multinational corporations to strict environmental regulation and standards, with penalties for non-compliance.

Stiglitz criticizes in particular the role of the American administration and corporations in failing to lead a globally concerted effort to combat climate change. The rejection of the Kyoto Protocol by the Bush Administration gave US corporations a comparative advantage against competitors from those nations that have ratified the treaty. American businesses do not need to pay for the environmental damage of their uncontrolled carbon emissions, and this is equivalent to receiving a subsidy. Stiglitz (and many others) point out that organizations such as the WTO, International Monetary Fund (IMF) and World Bank should include all environmental impacts when judging rules of fair trade or providing aid. Exporters that benefit from energy subsidies or lack of environmental taxes, as in China and the US, should be sanctioned with compensating tariffs to avoid unfair competition at the cost of future climate.

Certainly multinationals are not the only parties at fault. Bribery paves the way for agreements that explicitly ignore environmental impacts. Extensive corruption among often poorly paid public officials suggests that the pursuit of private benefit often takes priority over public duties, social welfare and the environment. Bribes entice public officials and politicians to protect multinationals from whatever environmental regulations may exist, and to block any more stringent constraints. Governments in richer nations and the managers of large corporations have for many years engaged in non-transparent transactions, widely treating bribes as facilitating fees rather than an illegal practice. The stakes are often too high for the voice of local communities and activists to be heard.

In recent years, there has been mounting pressure on multinational corporations to take action on environmental issues. Consumers increasingly demand greater transparency and more detailed information on the production methods and consequences behind the commodities they purchase. Multinationals have thus been forced to take some action for fear of losing consumer support. It often appears that multinational corporations voluntarily take actions that protect the interests of their employees, local communities and surrounding environment, but in most cases, such corporate social responsibility (CSR) is directly or indirectly the result of activism and campaigning by organized consumer groups. Ethical consumerism is on the rise and customers are increasingly aware of the social and environmental implications of their purchase choices. The recent success of fair-trade and eco-labelling schemes reveals that things are changing, even if slowly.

Corporate social responsibility may be driven by other forces as well. Shareholders increasingly scrutinize decisions taken by firms, and try to cooperate with management. Some shareholders and consumers are also putting pressure on firms to invest according to CSR and strike a balance between financial returns to shareholders and social welfare. And pressure does not need to come exclusively from owners or consumers. In Germany, co-determination involves employee representatives taking an active role in the company's management. Together with trade unions, they usually cooperate with management on a range of decisions, and exercise the right to be informed on important corporate issues. Employee involvement in works councils and corporate boards may result in more socially equitable and environmentally friendly policies.[28] On the other hand, while employees and their unions have an active stake in corporate decisions that affect local pollution and working conditions, they are likely to be less concerned about global pollution and carbon emissions.[29] In any case, as environmentalist James Speth and many others have argued, large corporations and multinationals should not be allowed to exercise their often substantial market power for the exclusive benefit of distant shareholders and top managers without social accountability.[30]

Fair or Free Trade?

In our ever more interconnected, global economy, the exchange and mobility of commodities, technologies, funds, labour, ideas and pollution have been increasing rapidly. Many observers – Stiglitz being one of the most prominent advocates – have shown that the rules of the game are far from fair, and that the economic benefits of globalization are distributed quite unevenly. As we discussed earlier, multinationals play a major role in this process, but they are not solely to blame. Governments of developed nations and their international agencies are also largely responsible for shaping international policies that place poorer countries at a disadvantage. Development economist Ha-Joon Chang from the University of Cambridge calls them the 'bad Samaritans' in international policy – international agencies and governments that adopt double standards by forcing on poor countries specific free-market and free-trade policies that are often painful and ill-planned, and prevent new competitors from emerging in particular sectors. Where the irony lies is in the fact that the rich countries preaching 'laissez-faire economics' largely resorted to the exactly opposite policies of protectionism and regulation to support their initial phases of industrialization. In effect, some industrialized nations appear to 'kick away the ladder' by prescribing the opposite policies to those that led to their own economic success in the past.

There is a big difference between unconditionally free and conditionally freer trade, and industrial nations have been so far much opposed to opening up trade in sectors they consider vulnerable to foreign competition (and sensitive for domestic voters). One of the most blatant examples of such unfair, asymmetric trading has been the Common Agricultural Policy (CAP) of the European Union. Around 60 per cent of the current EU budget (which represents approximately 1 per cent of the EU's GDP) is misused for wasteful agricultural subsidies and programmes. On the one hand, this makes it harder for farmers in developing nations to compete with heavily subsidized and tariff-free European commodities (although environmental taxes, rather than trade tariffs, should actually be imposed to reflect the environmental cost of transportation from remote regions, even if this disadvantages to a certain extent farmers in poorer countries); on the other, public funds that should be available for educational programmes, research and development initiatives, conservation agriculture, and environmental protection are captured mainly by a minority of the largest and wealthiest farmers and landowners.

Globalized trade usually opens up markets in developing countries to products from industrialized nations. At the same time, these rich countries, and the international organizations they dominate, have blocked access by poor countries to their own markets, and obstructed their development with unfair conditions. They largely fail to recognize that the poorer nations' infant industries require at least short- to medium-term financial support (through tariffs and subsidies) to attain maturity and compete with long-established foreign companies in richer economies. Governments in industrial nations generally impose higher tariffs on processed agricultural/timber imports compared to raw materials, thus discouraging the development of manufacturing in the poorer nations. They generally preach elimination of trade barriers, but maintain generous subsidies for their own rich farmers and agricultural products, which place millions of poor farmers in the developing countries at a major disadvantage.

The very fact that tariffs and subsidies are mainly eliminated for manufactured goods rather than agricultural commodities and textiles produced by developing nations reflects the weak bargaining power of the latter in trade negotiations and their smaller representation in international organizations. Industrial nations and international bodies need to recognize that developing countries require assistance rather than discrimination. They need greater access to markets for their agricultural products, liberalization of unskilled, labour-intensive sectors and less restriction on labour mobility. As long as developed nations control the trade agenda and largely determine the outcomes of negotiations, globalization will remain a largely uneven playing field for poorer nations.

This is not to say that globalization cannot assist the development process of poorer nations. When trade liberalization is accompanied by government support and redistribution of income from those who gain from trade to those who lose – as the successful examples of East Asia in the last three decades demonstrate – economic progress is likely to follow. However, many countries in the developing world, and particularly the weakest states of sub-Saharan Africa, have little infrastructure, feeble flows of foreign direct investment, and inefficient or corrupt political institutions inherited from their colonial history.

These countries seem unable to help their local producers take advantage of the new opportunities that arise from trade.

Poor Governance

Many developing countries suffer from extensive corruption, weak property rights and malfunctioning government institutions. Of course, weak governance and corruption are problems everywhere, although often more pervasive and frequent in the developing world. In poor countries with chronically underpaid government employees, the misuse of public office for private gain is widespread. Patronage, nepotism and bribery have been a development curse for many of the world's poorest nations. Although much malpractice in developing countries is covered up in the absence of effective democracy and independent media, some cases have been widely reported, although often in the aftermath of the events. The former Congolese dictator Mobutu Sese Seko and Indonesian President Suharto embezzled many billions of dollars during their more than 30 years in power, while brutally suppressing human rights with the full support of Western powers, and the US in particular.

Corruption has also been closely linked to poor environmental management and environmental degradation. Governments in the developing world tend to neglect long-term environmental problems, maintaining ill-defined property rights, weak regulation and unsustainable resource use. Inefficiency in public administration is exacerbated by insufficient resources (lack of expertise, infrastructure and equipment). But this is only part of the story. Much of the current and widespread illegal logging, hunting that threatens endangered species, non-compliance of companies with whatever environmental standards there are, and tax evasion is the result of corrupt practices by governments and their officials in developing countries.[31]

Frequent economic scandals demonstrate how public officials often fail to make decisions in the public interest. Governments under-invest in the provision of environmental assets (and other public goods), and instead allocate a large share of public funds to subsidies for private goods and large corporations, to benefit a wealthy minority of vested interests. Generous tax rebates and indirect subsidies for powerful corporations do not help either, as they are in effect forgone government revenues and therefore reduce the overall public budget. As we discuss in Chapter 6, such mismanagement is likely to be worse in ethnically fragmented countries, where governments often neglect the rights of minorities.

Country-specific examples abound. In many developing countries, Brazil and Indonesia in particular, logging companies regularly violate existing environmental legislation and quotas with impunity by bribing local officials, with the companies themselves often being directly controlled by government members. These countries suffer the greatest extent of tropical deforestation as a result of this extensive corruption, and as a consequence, imported timber at European or American ports of entry often exceeds the exported amount declared at the country of origin.

The consequences of corruption and poor governance extend beyond environmental protection and sustainable resource use. Poorer nations that suffer from weak governance and institutions also forgo economic development as a consequence. In other words, unless they find the means and political strength to address issues of corruption and malpractice, they are likely to find themselves in a prolonged poverty trap. The African Union estimates that corruption already costs the continent a quarter of its GDP.[32] Inefficient institutions generally pose severe obstacles to a country's economic development, entrepreneurship and investment. Foreign investors are deterred, while bureaucracy and bribery increase costs and prices, and public revenues disappear into the pockets of government administrators or are squandered on inefficient investments with very low returns. While developed economies could invest in several projects to reduce emissions in sub-Saharan Africa as an alternative to more expensive emission reductions at home (via the Clean Development Mechanism, which we analyse in detail in Chapter 7), Western investors become extremely frustrated by the high levels of corruption and poor complementary infrastructure.[33] Shang-Jin Wei has provided a long list of case studies and statistical evidence, verifying the negative impact of corruption and poor governance on economic development.[34] And Paul Collier, in his new, much-acclaimed book *The Bottom Billion*, identifies bad governance and corruption as one of the four major under-development traps for the world's poorest populations (along with conflict, natural resource mismanagement and landlockedness).[35]

Mismanagement appears to be particularly insidious in many mineral-rich economies, where resource rents are highly concentrated and hence easily captured by corrupt officials and governments. Many other factors influence the extent of government dysfunction and general economic mismanagement.[36] Culture, religion and openness to trade all play a role in explaining differences in governance. Countries open to trade and with a long history of British rule and Protestant traditions appear to tackle corruption more effectively than others. Income per capita complements the list of explanatory variables. Richer countries enjoy more transparency, a cleaner environment and better governance, because they have more resources to supply these public goods and face greater demand for them by populations whose more immediate, basic needs have been satisfied.

However, it would be at least hypocritical and decidedly unfair to point the finger exclusively at developing nations, and solely blame home-grown corruption and poor governance for their socio-economic and environmental ailments. After all, bribes are determined by demand and supply, as in any other market. Public officials and firms in developing countries demand bribes, when their negotiating partners in 'developed' nations are equally eager to supply them. Western governments often criticize developing nations for their lack of democracy, political instability and continuous conflict, while their arms industries and mineral firms benefit from trade with repressive regimes. The trade in uncertified 'blood diamonds' from conflict areas and unsustainably harvested tropical timber has been largely tolerated if not encouraged by Western nations. Similarly, governments in developed nations criticize developing countries for inadequate environmental policies, while their own multinational corporations impose environmental damage in the remotest parts of the planet.

Western governments are far from committed to transparency and accountability, as their ongoing support of the most notorious tax havens embarrassingly reveals. These offshore tax havens, such as the Channel Islands and Liechtenstein, help to divert hundreds of billions of dollars annually from developing countries – money that could have boosted public spending in many of the world's poorest economies. Most of Britain's overseas territories are tax havens, and, as George Monbiot put it, 'The obvious conclusion is that Britain retains these colonies for one purpose: to help banks, corporations and the ultra-rich to avoid tax.' Britain has campaigned against international attempts to eradicate tax evasion, even while such tax havens are often used for money laundering and terrorist financing.[37]

Public Goods and their Under-Provision

One of the fundamental roles of government is to provide public goods that are under-supplied by the private sector, when appropriate markets, say for clean air, do not exist. Similarly, necessities such as safe drinking water, primary education or medical care may be too expensive for the poorest classes when they are 'privatized'. However, governments in the least developed countries usually fail to fulfil this basic obligation. They often misuse public resources (by allocating them to projects with low returns, or appropriating them for personal benefit),[38] and are generally constrained both by poverty, which is exacerbated by policies of the rich nations and corporations, and by the lobbying power of the latter. Without sound public policies, there is always serious under-investment in education and environmental protection. Social returns on investment in education, health and environmental assets in developing countries exceed private sector returns on most investment. Of course, such investment also provides non-pecuniary benefits to health and overall welfare that are difficult to quantify in monetary terms, but no less important.

Ramón López of the University of Maryland provides a long list of cases where the provision of under-funded public goods yields much higher pecuniary returns than private sector investment, in addition to intangible benefits.[39] Of course, the provision of public goods should not be guided by comparing pecuniary rates of returns alone. But in many developing countries there is such extreme under-investment in environmental and human (education and health) assets that large benefits can be anticipated with minimal increases in public spending. Additional enrolment in primary schooling or some small investment in sewage treatment or pollution abatement in ecologically distressed areas will yield large future benefits in terms of income opportunities, lower mortality and improved health.

At national level, development from a low-income economy to a middle-income emerging market (with average income increasing from a few hundred dollars per person to a few thousand) requires only modest public investment in infrastructure, primary and secondary education, and environmental quality. In contrast, Jeffrey Sachs argues that transition to high-income status requires major policy interventions and public investment. These include widespread tertiary education (30 per cent of the relevant age group), generous public funding of research and development (at least one per cent of GDP), and adequate investment in telecommunications and information technology. At the same time, climate change is expected to undermine the capacity of states to provide these productive opportunities that sustain livelihoods, as a result of forgone production and public revenues and increased cost of public infrastructure.[40]

Governments in the world's poorest nations struggle to finance even the most basic public investment in local infrastructure (for example power grids, transportation networks and effective ports), universal primary education and access to healthcare (for example family planning, improved sanitation, safe drinking water, maternity care and malaria protection). Sub-Saharan Africa's lack of sufficient public investment is sometimes attributed to former colonial rule and priority for short-term extraction policies over long-term development planning, as well as inadequate or misdirected aid. The result has been zero or negative income growth for some of the fastest-growing populations, and the world's worst development record.

While cereal yields doubled, tripled and quadrupled in South Asia, Latin America and East Asia respectively between 1960 and 2005, they remained largely stagnant for sub-Saharan Africa. There is thus a huge potential for agricultural improvement as discussed in Chapter 3. Similarly, inexpensive provision of mosquito bed nets and indoor insecticide spraying can dramatically reduce the incidence of malaria. Public investment in education yields high rates of return by increasing labour productivity, empowering women, reducing birth rates and mortality, and improving health. In sub-Saharan Africa only 70 per cent of children are enrolled in primary school, while the private rate of return on primary education is estimated to be three times higher than the average rate in the OECD countries, where primary schooling is universal.

The World Bank and the IMF: Good Prescriptions or Bad Advice?

There is another explanation of why public goods are particularly under-supplied in developing countries. Ramón López links the under-funding of environmental assets and other public services to the structural adjustment pursued in many developing countries, under the auspices of the International Monetary Fund and the World Bank.[41] Neo-liberal policies advocated by the two sister organizations put much emphasis on trade liberalization, elimination of price controls and privatization of public enterprises, with little attention to the provision of public goods. Governments were regularly encouraged to cut public spending and reduce budget deficits, without consideration of the environment or the distributional effects of major price increases for privatized utility services.

As we discussed above, cuts in public spending (generally a precondition for financial aid by the World Bank and the International Monetary Fund) face only limited resistance from the public, since the initial impact may be small. Under-funded protection for tropical rainforest and reduced environmental subsidies and programmes may hardly be noticed in the short run. On the other hand, any attempt to decrease subsidies to powerful corporations usually faces fierce resistance from well-organized interest groups. For that reason, public transport has been widely neglected, while middle-class motorists are subsidized in various ways (though the steep increase in fuel prices between 2007–2008 and current recession have been reducing car use – and sales – even in the most car-dependent economy of the US). Obviously, such policies exert multiple environmental damages by increasing carbon emissions, local pollution and traffic congestion.

Trade liberalization also imposes additional restraints on public spending. For many governments in developing countries, tariffs and duties on imports are the easiest way to collect revenues. Governments eliminate tariffs without developing a sophisticated value added tax (VAT) system as an alternative source of public revenues. Again, as public budgets are constrained, public goods and environmental programmes suffer.

Conclusions

Any discussion of climate change would be incomplete without devoting sufficient space to the particularities of developing nations. People living in extreme poverty with less than a dollar (or two) per day are highly vulnerable to even small external shocks that may affect their everyday production activities and living conditions. Lack of savings and limited support from the state make these people unable to hedge against risks that disrupt their livelihood security. Climate change will simply reinforce this existing vulnerability of the poorest nations, where individuals, communities and governments have few if any resources to adapt to (let alone prevent) global warming. Addressing their increasing vulnerability to a climate change catastrophe requires us to take a step back and evaluate the domestic and external conditions that have exposed the poorest countries to extreme poverty and environmental degradation, even long before the threat of global warming was recognized.

In a speech to the UN Commission on Sustainable Development in 2007, the UN Secretary General Ban Ki-Moon said:

> *Energy, climate change, industrial development and air pollution are critical items on the international agenda. Addressing them in unison creates many win–win opportunities and is crucial for sustainable development.*

Economic development and sustainability should not be seen as conflicting objectives. Developing nations might not have the resources to mitigate their carbon footprints, but technology and aid transfers from richer nations can make sure their development path is one of both green and fast economic growth. Developing countries like China and India will otherwise soon become by far the biggest emitters of greenhouse gases, as their economies expand and their industries continue to rely heavily on cheap but dirty coal. While a clean revolution in many developing nations is underway, with China adopting its first national plan for climate change in 2007, this would need to be subsidized much more generously by developed nations compared to their current mediocre aid transfers.

The world's poor will bear the largest cost of global warming, as agricultural collapse and water scarcity leads to mass starvation and a rise in infectious diseases. Yet many of the world's poor are still unaware of the imminent global warming threat and consequences. While green investment could provide multiple environmental and health benefits, as the successful urban development of Curitiba in Brazil demonstrates, such initiatives require strong support and public investment by well-functioning transparent governments. Unfortunately, poor governance, corruption and weak property rights in most of the developing world all result in accelerating deforestation, chaotic urban planning and under-provision of public goods that would largely benefit the poor.

Yet it is easy to point the finger at weak governments and corrupt politicians in developing countries. Much of the unsustainable use of local and global environmental resources is a direct result of rampant Western consumerism and the relentless pursuit of profit by multinational corporations and their executives. Western governments have blatantly imposed rules of free rather than fair trade on developing nations, with little concern for the impacts on local communities and their environmental assets. The urgent environmental and development challenges we face in our global village require joint, coordinated efforts by developed and developing partners, with countries shouldering responsibilities to the best of their abilities.

6

Ethics and Climate Change

Ethics of Climate Change for Today and Tomorrow

Climate change does not affect everyone on our planet in the same way. It is well known that the poorest people in the poorest countries – mainly in semitropical and tropical regions – bear by far the greatest risk from global warming. Most of the GHGs have been produced by the rich developed economies of the North, which may even benefit initially from climate change, and this raises important ethical considerations about the distribution of damages.[1] The disproportionate burden of future warming on poorer regions (and poorer people within countries) is exacerbated by the current injustice of extreme poverty for much of the world's population in the most threatened countries. This poverty is likely to persist, and suggests that affected populations will not have the resources to survive agricultural collapse or rapid sea-level rise resulting from climate change without outside help.

An additional ethical problem arises from the fact that the current build-up of greenhouse gases in the atmosphere will have its greatest impact on future generations, adding an intergenerational ethical dimension to the climate change debate. Naturally, the poorest regions today are likely to be the worst victims of unconstrained global warming in the future. While everyone tries to ensure the survival and welfare of their own children, the billions who currently survive at subsistence level have no spare resources to save or invest in 'insurance' for the uncertain future. The developed countries have hitherto failed to alleviate poverty in the developing world, and they continue to threaten the survival of the children of the poorest in a world that will be ravaged by the consequences of their own extravagant consumption. In attempting to catch up with the West, the fastest-growing developing country, China, has been reducing poverty, but also devastating its environment, and now matches US emissions in total, though not per capita.

As discussed in Chapter 3, the greatest threat from global warming in the medium term is to food production in already hot and arid regions, including northern China and much of India and Africa.[2] Rising temperatures and more frequent droughts in these areas will interact with current trends and consequences of industrial agriculture to exacerbate erosion, desertification, and growing shortages of water for irrigation and industry. These developments are likely to dramatically reduce the yields of high-input modern varieties as well as accelerate loss of agricultural land. As we discuss further in Chapter 9, there are many practical measures that could avert these risks at low cost, but as yet no political commitment beyond wishful thinking, inefficient policies and inadequate targets.

Major food shortages and price rises would condemn billions of the world's poorest people to starvation – a scale of disaster that is difficult to imagine today. Precisely this difficulty is blocking the rich nations from assuming the moral responsibility for averting this risk of disaster for the poorest or their descendants in the future. While Northern countries may benefit directly from warming, they are unlikely to escape the consequences of a collapsing global economy and mass starvation in nuclear-armed nations. Selfish concern for our own children should thus support the ethics of caring for our poorest neighbours and their children, and all the coming generations who are unrepresented in current lobbying and political decision-making. Edward Page stresses the merits of what he calls a 'global sufficientarian ethic', where 'as many persons as possible should enjoy a satisfactory level of wellbeing regardless of when or where they live'.[3]

This chapter explains these complex interactions between the ethical, economic and scientific aspects of global warming. Economics as a social science cannot be value-free like physics or chemistry, despite claims to the contrary. Economists not only try to understand how economies function, but also try to design policies to increase welfare. Ethical assumptions and values, regarding what is desirable and what is not, are a central feature of much economic analysis, though not always made explicit. In that context, economists approach problems in a way that reflects (or should reflect) the generally agreed value premises of society. The traditional neoclassical approach to economics has often ignored distributional impacts on the poor and on future generations, and the resulting neo-liberal policy focus on efficiency and aggregate economic performance has dominated current thinking on the economics of climate change. However, there is growing criticism that existing cost–benefit analyses of climate change are fundamentally flawed, a point we develop in Chapter 9.

Economics and Utilitarianism

The utilitarian philosophers of the 18th and 19th centuries (such as Jeremy Bentham and John Stuart Mill) argued that the ultimate goal of all activity should be to maximize the sum total of human welfare or happiness.[4] They saw no intrinsic value in other forms of life or the environment, let alone 'rights' for non-human animals. The neoclassical economics that followed essentially identified welfare with consumption, which could include the use of environmental services or animals, though without any regard for their welfare. Only more recently has it become clear that happiness depends on much more than consumption, once basic needs have been met (as discussed in Chapter 4).

Even the early economists recognized clearly that additional consumption would generally be less important for a wealthy individual than for a poor person. This observation provides strong support for the idea of redistributing income or wealth from the rich to the poor, in order to maximize the sum of all individual welfare levels – the utilitarian goal. It is thus ironic that, as income inequality increases everywhere under globalization and unfettered capitalism, there is less concern with redistribution than ever before. Instead, the priority is to lower taxes for the rich to avoid capital and corporate 'flight', and to reduce wages and benefits for the poor to save jobs from outsourcing. International efforts to alleviate poverty also make little headway, with the US spending just 0.17 per cent of its GDP on (often ineffective) aid for the poor, and smaller states only slightly more.

The utilitarian goal of maximizing total welfare has essentially been forced into the straitjacket of neo-liberal or 'market fundamentalist' economics. This ideology claims that taxation or redistribution always reduces economic performance, usually measured as total output (GDP in money terms), which is, quite incorrectly, taken to be a measure of national welfare. The utilitarian goal is apparently maintained, but now without regard for the real determinants of wellbeing, the distribution of gains or the fate of the losers. At the same time, individual selfishness and greed are assumed to be the main motivators of human activity in most modern neoclassical economics. These motivations are then assumed to produce the greatest possible output and welfare through the 'invisible hand' of sufficiently competitive markets, provided that government interference is minimized.

This view of the world is wrong in almost every aspect, as behavioural economists and others have shown over the last 30 years. Since relative income is much more important than absolute income (above poverty levels) for subjective wellbeing, people in rich countries are motivated to work too hard and compete too much. In the long run, relative gains for some are always accompanied by relative losses for others, while 'social capital' is lost and average wellbeing fails to increase.[5] Taxation provides an incentive to spend more time on leisure and social relationships, with friends and family, which are major determinants of happiness. Some taxation of personal income is thus actually *necessary* to achieve true, Pareto efficiency, and reduce wasteful personal exhaustion and environmental destruction in the competitive 'rat race' to 'keep up with the Joneses'. Furthermore, most people have an inborn sense of fairness and justice which tempers greed in many situations for good evolutionary reasons. Without such instincts, societies based on cooperation and communication could hardly evolve and function.

The evolution of moral sentiments has also left a tribal legacy that is exploited by nationalist politics and the neo-liberal ideology of individualism and consumption. This originally rather natural preoccupation with linguistic or geographical neighbours – now nation-states – makes it too easy to ignore the victims of climate change or globalization in an uncertain future or in far-away places. On the other hand, there is also a growing recognition that tribal ethics or clan solidarity are both inconsistent and dangerously inadequate for the modern 'global village' of our interconnected world. Among those who are well informed about the issues, there is widespread concern about endangered species and environments today, as well as the future effects of climate change. Natural environments and the incredible range of life they contain do have intrinsic value for many individuals, even if they do not expect to benefit directly from them as consumers or tourists. Philosophers of diverse backgrounds stress the urgency, for our very survival, of an encompassing global ethics and morality.[6]

Most economists agree that at least the 'deserving poor' should be supported by society, though not too generously! Opposition to the impacts of technological change and globalization is reduced if the losers in the resulting economic and social upheaval are compensated in some way by the winners. A frequent justification for the utilitarian focus on the sum of individual welfare as a criterion for progress is that the winners *could* compensate the losers when the total or sum of welfare increases. Of course, in practice, compensation is often not paid. This in turn is justified by the claim that, in the long run, every-one will benefit from change and growth as economic mobility – both upward and downward, or 'rags to riches' and 'riches to rags' – redistributes the gains and the losses.

This is yet another neo-liberal claim that has been disproved by recent history. The clearest measures of income mobility have actually been declining in the recent decades of globalization and restructuring, while income inequal-ity has been rising rapidly, not only in the UK and US, but even in traditionally more egalitarian countries like Germany. In an unprecedented historical record, the real hourly wages of the majority of American workers have actually been falling or stagnating for several decades of rapid economic growth. Most of the benefits of growth have been going to the richest classes, in what Nobel Prize-winning economist Joseph Stiglitz calls the 'trickle-up' economy, which has supplanted the 'trickle-down' economy of the past, in which growth in the long run also raised the incomes of the poor.[7]

Even the best-intentioned compensation schemes – and indeed the whole utilitarian idea of adding up individual welfare – break down completely under the major threat from climate change: a large-scale loss of human life. The ultimate victims of runaway warming cannot be compensated, or indeed consulted if they have not yet been born. Risking their lives for the sake of more consumption today (or tomorrow) is equivalent to simply dropping their welfare from the utilitarian sum, and contradicts fairly universal ethical princi-ples of protecting life. In the extreme situation that climate change may ultimately impose upon us, utilitarianism without compensation is reminiscent of the mass exterminations perpetrated by Stalin and other tyrants, supposedly in the interests of a glorious future for the survivors. Of course, future lives are abstract and uncertain concepts today, and thus fail to elicit our sympathy in the same way as the victims of contemporary atrocities, or an earthquake or other natural disaster. As Stalin is reputed to have remarked, 'One death is a tragedy, but a million deaths are a statistic.'

Social Welfare and Externalities

Modern economics defines costs imposed by a producer or individual on the rest of society as 'externalities'. If polluters face a 'green tax' on their emissions, they have an incentive to reduce these externalities, perhaps by investing in cleaner technology, and thus increase social welfare.[8] Dangerous technologies or products that directly threaten lives or health may also be simply prohibited by government regulation when practical alternatives are available. Competitive markets are widely believed to be efficient and maximize utilitarian social welfare, but this classical result only holds when the costs of information and externalities are neglected. In the real world of uncertainty and unregulated speculation, the financial crash of 2008 has revealed the fragility and inefficiency of market economies that run primarily for the benefit of the super-rich. The pervasive externalities of modern economies, including ever-rising greenhouse gas emissions, also reveal the persistent failure of governments to resist industry lobbying and protect the wider society. As discussed in Chapter 7, efforts to curb emissions such as the Kyoto agreement and the EU carbon trading scheme have had little success so far.

Externalities are often described as market failures, and the Stern Review described climate change as the greatest market failure of all. It could also be argued that despoiling the environment and endangering future lives for private profit represent ethical failure as well. If loss of life can be directly attributed to toxic waste emissions, then those responsible can face severe legal penalties. This rarely happens, because the effects are usually delayed, perhaps by many years, as in the case of asbestos, so legal proof is difficult in the face of corporate cover-up and denial. However, the principle of responsibility – sometimes called the 'polluter pays principle' (PPP) – is clearly accepted. It would thus be quite logical to hold individuals and firms morally responsible for their carbon footprint, as one (perhaps small) contribution to future global warming. In fact, a still modest, but growing, number of consumers and businesses are beginning to assume some ethical responsibility for the effects of their individual decisions on the environment, including climate change. As people become better informed about the scale of likely catastrophe under continued 'business as usual', selfish concern about the world we bequeath to our children and grandchildren should strengthen the 'one world' ethics of caring for other species and poorer populations.

Just Society and Unjust Climate Change:
Rawls and his Theory of Justice

As we have explained, 19th-century utilitarianism just adds up all individual welfare; some people usually benefit while others become worse off under any particular policy, but as long as average welfare improves, the policy is justified. This ethical position underpins much modern economic policy, but significantly fails to address the fundamental issues of distribution and equity and is therefore seriously misleading when applied to climate change (and many other areas). One of the most influential philosophers who shaped modern thinking on social justice and environmental ethics, and provided an alternative to utilitarianism, is John Rawls.[9] In his seminal book *A Theory of Justice*, Rawls proposes a social contract for equality of opportunity – where individuals agree to limit their own rights for the sake of achieving this common objective.

Rawls argues compellingly that utilitarian indifference to how welfare is distributed across individuals or generations – and, we may add, how climate change affects particularly vulnerable groups of people and future generations – violates the fundamental human rights of the victims. Equal access to resources (whether this is the right to adequate consumption, access to fresh air or the right to live) can be an achievable social arrangement. And even more important, it does not need to be imposed by an external force. People may voluntarily and freely agree to arrangements that protect a common right and secure equality of opportunity, thus achieving social justice.

Rawls uses a construct which he calls the 'original position'; this is a hypothetical state of affairs which precedes any other social arrangements and agreements. Imagine a situation where we all find ourselves without prior experiences, knowledge or memories, and come together in a room to negotiate for the rights we are entitled to. In effect it would be as if we were all under a 'veil of ignorance', without any information regarding our own personal characteristics, preferences, social status or abilities, expected outcomes, the beliefs and traits of others, society's features, or our position in time. More important, we would not know how to compare ourselves with anyone else in the room at that particular time. By not pursuing particular objectives (influenced by personal interests) individuals would then agree to a social contract with equal access to environmental and other resources.

Under the veil of ignorance, everyone is in the same position. In such circumstances, rational people would unanimously agree on two fundamental principles of justice. First, they would agree that each individual (or generation, if people represented different generations without prior knowledge of their position) has equal access to a range of basic liberties. Since we do not know whether we would find ourselves in a better or worse position in an alternative scenario (of unequal access to resources and rights), the prudent choice is equal access or equality of opportunity.[10]

The second principle (often called 'the Difference Principle') states that deviations from equality are only justified if they improve the welfare of the worst off.[11] In other words, richer nations would be justified in using more environmental or other resources (for example burning more fossil fuels) only if this (permanently) raises the welfare of the poorest countries. Since unhindered climate change will deprive the poorest in future generations of the basic capability of survival, for which there is no compensation, current polluting practices are simply ethically unacceptable. The argument that the current generation is actually poorer than future generations, and hence entitled to use up irreplaceable resources, makes the doubtful assumption that economic growth will continue unabated, and of course ignores issues of distribution. The worst victims of our profligacy will actually be impoverished and starving, rather than beneficiaries of whatever growth does take place.

Rawls's theory of justice builds on socialist ideals and the social democratic tradition of Sweden and other Scandinavian countries. Its main emphasis on distribution and equity is certainly completely absent from neo-liberal economic thinking, where unconstrained private ownership for private profit (particularly of the wealthiest and most powerful) is the fundamental right. Private ownership works perfectly well as an allocation mechanism if the distribution is equitable and markets are functioning competitively (which is far from the case for environmental amenities). In practice, though, the dominance of concentrated owners and their interests not only maintains poverty and destitution today, but also endangers the future of the planet. The current obsession with destructive material growth in the global economy has a depressing historical precedent. Central planning by groups of bureaucrats in the misnamed and non-democratic 'socialist' economies of the former Soviet Bloc also sacrificed environmental quality, and the fundamental liberties emphasized by Rawls, for the sake of wasteful growth.

Equalizing Access to Rights beyond Income: Sen's Capabilities Approach

Another renowned approach to achieving equity and justice is that of Nobel laureate Amartya Sen on capabilities. Sen's conceptual framework is based on the assumption that true development lies in equalizing capabilities, in other words the potential of people to achieve the life they value.[12] Poverty and deprivation imply not only lack of income but particularly the incapacity to achieve such capabilities and objectives that are not necessarily related to material consumption. Those things we truly value in life (which Sen calls 'functionings') may range from elementary needs such as adequate food and clothing to more complex needs such as self-respect, community participation, ability to feel emotional affinity and use of complex imagination. For such reasons, the Human Development Index calculated by the United Nations as a measure of development takes into account both life expectancy and literacy standards, in addition to income levels. This recognizes that income is an input in determining human welfare rather than the final output we should wish to maximize, as confirmed by the numerous surveys on subjective wellbeing or happiness discussed in Chapter 4.

Climate catastrophe, or just unequal access to environmental resources, may also prevent individuals today or in the future from 'functioning'. The philosopher Martha Nussbaum, who has further developed Sen's capabilities theory, provides a list of ten 'central human functional capabilities', many of which are closely related to the status of our surrounding natural environment.[13] Living a long and healthy life, for instance, will undoubtedly depend on food production and food security both within and between generations, which is expected to be at severe risk from climate change-induced soil erosion and water scarcity. Being able to live harmoniously with other plants, animals and our natural world in general, is one of the ten capabilities analysed by Nussbaum, and the most obvious one to be impaired by anthropogenic climate change.

What is important is not necessarily the functioning itself, but the capability or potential for the functioning. For instance, the loss of biodiversity due to climate change is likely to impair discoveries of new medicines, and removing the capability to expand our scientific knowledge is considered unethical, despite the fact that we know little of what is there is still to be discovered. Many farmers in developing countries have been practising unsustainable agriculture for decades, but this does not justify our emissions that are worsening their environment. And we may appreciate that the Great Barrier Reef and its corals still exist, even though we may have no immediate plans to visit the area and may simply never do so.

The Day after Tomorrow (the Precautionary Principle)

There is still much scientific uncertainty about the details of climate change impact and particularly the timing of damage it may inflict on the poorest regions, future generations and the Earth's ecosystems. But we are confident that anthropogenic climatic change is already underway, and it will be too late when everyone realizes that these threats are imminent. If temperature exceeds the threshold level of two additional degrees, the risk of runaway warming and associated cataclysmic events will increase dramatically.

In health and safety regulation, the 'precautionary principle' is meant to be a safeguard against potentially severe or irreversible damage to life and limb. In practice, under the pressure of industry lobbying, regulators usually wait for years or decades until public pressure becomes irresistible before taking action against toxic but profitable substances such tetraethyl lead additives in petrol or asbestos. In these cases, tens of thousands or even millions of victims and their families have to struggle to obtain compensation for the most blatant corporate and government malfeasance. In the case of climate change, restricting use of fossil fuels and switching from industrial to conservation agriculture is necessary to avoid jeopardizing the very existence of future generations.[14]

People tend to be risk-averse, particularly about their own children, and those who are well informed about the dangers of global warming are likely to favour serious abatement measures (despite climate change involving a range of subjective risks that cannot be precisely quantified). As Oxford philosopher John Broome has summarized, there is no ethical justification to 'discount' the value of future lives likely to be lost as a result of catastrophic climate change.[15] So sacrificing these – as yet unknown – victims, to avoid reducing the extravagant consumption of the rich today, is ethically quite indefensible.

Agenda 21 at the UN Earth Summit in Rio in 1992 (where climate change entered the international political agenda as a potential global threat for the first time) explicitly urged participating countries to adopt the precautionary principle in environmental planning.[16] Unfortunately, there was not much political will to implement the principle for an environmental issue with such global dimensions as climate change. At an individual level, we all buy insurance policies for our private property, but coordination failures prevent sovereign states from adopting sufficient precautionary measures, not to 'compensate' for but to avoid the loss of irreplaceable human and natural life.

The 2004 blockbuster movie *The Day after Tomorrow* is based on a hypothetical climate change apocalypse, where global warming causes the Greenland and Antarctic ice caps to melt and interrupt the North Atlantic Circulation, triggering a series of super-storms in the Northern hemisphere that freeze everything in their path in just a few days. Even if all this is obviously science fiction, we certainly know that global warming is capable of causing irreversible disasters (even if we are not absolutely confident about the exact nature of causalities, their magnitudes or statistical probabilities). In perverse contrast, consumers are sensibly keen to insure against accident and theft, but short-sighted and opportunistic politicians cannot agree on the same need for protecting future generations from the risk of cataclysmic events by reducing greenhouse emissions (as the precautionary principle would suggest).

The precautionary principle is often attacked for obstructing 'progress', usually by industry lobbies that try to profit from risky products or innovations that may indeed benefit some individuals but impose severe damage on others. Health and safety regulations often raise costs, as well as saving lives, but of course can never prevent all accidents. Balancing costs and benefits is the topic of Chapter 9, where we argue that the ethical response to climate change, guided by the principles of Rawlsian justice, will not be exorbitantly costly if implemented early enough, and will instead yield major health and welfare benefits in addition to mitigation. Contrary claims are mainly based on lobbying by energy producers and others who stand to lose from carbon taxation, a switch to alternative energy and related measures for abatement. Due in part to this lobbying, and also lack of a determined effort at public education by governments, there is still widespread ignorance among voters about the science of climate change and the likelihood of future catastrophe. This ignorance unfortunately extends to many economists, who predict only trivial damage from another century of rising emissions and temperatures under business as usual.

Risk-Loving, Risk-Avoiding and the Risk of a Catastrophe

Most studies evaluating the costs of climate change underestimate the risks of extreme, catastrophic events by not incorporating runaway warming due to positive feedback mechanisms. Research on many of these feedbacks is only just beginning, and the lack of detailed forecasts makes it much easier to ignore the real threats behind these very complex processes. Yet there is a surprising analogy with private insurance. Few individuals have any idea of their own personal probability of accident in any particular situation. Most car owners think they drive with above average skill and care! While complaining about premiums, most people would also agree that legal requirements for insurance are sensible – a widely accepted social contract under the 'veil of ignorance' concerning one's own luck and care in the accident 'lottery'.

Perhaps a better analogy with climate policy is protective or 'defensive' investment in safety, such as seatbelts or smoke detectors. We rationally spend money, and vote for limitations on our freedom to be (perhaps fatally) negligent, in order to avert unknown but potentially catastrophic risks. Saving the premiums, in order to buy better medical care after the accident, seems absurd. Yet this is essentially the collective response urged by economists and politicians in the richest economies who oppose serious mitigation policies. This response is not consistent with risk-aversion or awareness of the scientific findings on climate change. It also violates the human rights of the poorest members of the current and future generations, who will be the worst-affected victims if increasing water shortages and agricultural collapse lead to mass starvation. Reckless or risk-loving drivers who endanger others directly, or fail to buy insurance, impose externalities on other road users and are subject to prosecution. What is missing today is recognition of the need for similar measures to reduce the risk of future climate catastrophes, externalities that will just as surely be caused by continuing our current reckless emissions.

The Rawlsian ethics of maximizing the welfare of the least advantaged provides fairly clear prescriptions for policy, prescriptions that are obviously nowhere near to being implemented. Anyone whose life is threatened by climate change and its consequences, even if only at some uncertain time in the future, can be seen as one of these least-advantaged members of human society – at that particular point in time. While there is no ethical justification for 'discounting' these future lives, or valuing them less than current victims of natural or other disasters, the temptation to do so is strong. The actions of any one individual today will probably have little effect on future climate, so it is easy to 'free-ride' and wait for collective action, which is certainly needed to ensure that abatement is effective and the burden is fairly shared.

'An Old Man's Grandchildren Are his Crowning Glory' (Proverbs, 17:6). Or Perhaps Not?

As we discussed earlier, as individuals we buy insurance against major dangers that threaten our lives, our health or our property. We are aware of the small probability that these threats will materialize, but nevertheless we prefer to hedge against the risk of them taking place. This can be accomplished through insurance companies: we pay a fee and transfer the risk of loss to them. We often do this implicitly and informally, without the help of insurance contracts. As individuals, we generally wish to see our children enjoying at least the same quality of life as our own. In order to do that, we often sacrifice part of our consumption and invest in our children's education, and we accumulate savings and assets, which we bequeath to them at a later stage. We feel a strong moral responsibility to assist our descendants in their own risk management, to help them once they begin their first business, once they purchase their first property or when they go through hard times. Why are we then so reluctant to provide similar insurance for future generations when it comes to climate change catastrophe? Why does altruism work in some cases but not in others? After all, it should not be the nature of the threat that matters. We would not like to have our children alone at home when a burglar enters the house, and we do not abandon them during extreme weather. But why is it, then, that we do so little to prevent extremes of climate change?

There are often great difficulties in visualizing climate change damages. Certainly the Earth has experienced climate change before and oscillated from one ice age to another (as we discussed in Chapter 2), but we have no memories of a climate change catastrophe. And this makes a big difference in raising awareness for climate change issues and ethical responsibility for those we bring to life. We certainly feel ethically responsible for educating our children and providing food and shelter for them, and developed societies add legal responsibility to parental instincts. In order to be good parents, we build on the past experience of others; we receive help from our own parents and advice from friends and the media. Of course, we may not be sure whether we were good parents or not until we reach the end of the process (and our children become adults).

The difficulty in recognizing a similar moral responsibility with respect to climate change lies in the nature of its impacts; they are not as evident, direct or immediate. And even more important, climate change is a global problem and therefore concern for climate stability is a public good that benefits all, rather than just the concerned individual. Our private actions as parents are not sufficient by themselves to protect our children from the threat; they need to be accompanied by similar sentiments and reactions from all or most other parents.

There may be yet another reason why individuals perversely ignore their ethical responsibility to prevent global warming. Even under business as usual, many believe that it will take decades before the worst impact of climate change is felt. As individuals, we may feel a stronger responsibility for our children than for our great-great-grandchildren, due to 'genetic dilution'.[17] The further we look into the future, the less concerned we tend to be about the damage we may inflict. If a climate catastrophe was obviously imminent, we would probably adjust our destructive behaviour immediately, to protect ourselves and our children. If the worst consequences of climate change under business as usual were delayed until 2100 (as some economists believe, in contrast to the scientific evidence), then this burden would fall on our great-great-grandchildren. Every child has two parents but sixteen great-great-grandparents and so forth. As the time horizon extends, so does the number of our predecessors. We are in effect the great-great-grandparents of those children whose world may be devastated at the end of the century. As parents, we each share responsibility for our children with a partner. As great-great-grandparents we share the same ethical responsibility with (at least) fifteen other people. Perhaps this 'dilution' explains what economists call the 'pure time rate of discount', though this is rejected by moral philosophers as justification for inaction.

The consequences of our current environmental destruction may develop rapidly and unpredictably, just like the financial crisis of 2008. The ill-founded but still common belief that they will only fall on later generations is undoubtedly another obstacle to adjusting our energy-intensive consumption. Nevertheless, most of us want our great-great-grandchildren to think highly of us for what we have achieved and left to them. It is certainly not the first time humanity has caused irreversible damage – we have already destroyed numerous species and habitats, and brought many more to the brink of extinction.[18] We are certainly not proud of our ancestors' environmental record, and few would want to be remembered by their descendants for contributing to a climate catastrophe.

Oh Brother, Where Art Thou?

Many people are aware that unhindered climate change will devastate the lives of billions of people in developing countries, leading to mass starvation and epidemics. Why are we then so slow to react? Part of the explanation may lie in the fact that as individuals we tend to favour welfare and support for people of a similar background to ours (whether ethnic, linguistic or religious). Reciprocity and generosity appear to be stronger among people of the same 'tribe' or group, with differences in ethnicity, religion and language leading to increased socio-cultural alienation.

This suggests that homogeneous societies are likely to function more efficiently. Social capital and trust is usually higher in societies where people belong to the same ethnic group. Even in a highly developed economy such as Belgium, long-standing frictions between the Flemish and Francophone communities and political parties created a major political crisis in 2007–2008. Economists Alberto Alesina and Edward Glaeser have argued that the welfare state is less developed in the US compared to Europe as a result of ethnic heterogeneity.[19] Rich white communities are less likely to support cash transfers and state intervention that largely benefit-poorer black and Hispanic communities. Indices of ethnic fractionalization, capturing the probability that two randomly selected individuals belong to different ethnic groups, have been used to explain disparities in economic development, policies and institutions. Ethnically fractionalized countries lag behind in terms of income levels, political stability and provision of public services. They often suffer from violent conflict between ethnically diverse groups, which destroys local infrastructure and diverts public funds away from education, health and environmental assets.[20]

Could ethnic heterogeneity have repercussions for environmental management? The answer is yes. In Côte d'Ivoire, for instance, the extent of environmental degradation and soil erosion was greater across ethnically heterogeneous than homogeneous agricultural communities.[21] Recent research also suggests that ethnically fractionalized communities in sub-Saharan Africa suffer from more limited access to piped, safe drinking water.[22] As a general rule of thumb, ethnically homogeneous communities are more likely to cooperate and sustainably harvest a common resource base, while mistrust and frictions across heterogeneous groups often results in a 'tragedy of the commons' where resources are exploited unsustainably.

In a largely ethnically fractionalized world, divided into separate entities by political borders and socio-cultural barriers, our limited generosity outside our own borders does not come as a surprise. Governments devote a much larger share of public expenditure to domestic public goods and income redistribution compared to miserly provision for international aid, debt relief and technology transfers. This priority for domestic public goods seems to depend on electoral preferences. We do tend to be much more tolerant of absolute poverty, malnutrition and extensive illiteracy in other countries, or sometimes even in different neighbourhoods in the same city. The feeling of belonging to a nation-state rather than a common planet hence makes policymaking more myopic and self-centred. In order to tackle environmental issues of global dimensions, such as global warming, we will need to extend our social empathy beyond our own geographic and ethnic borders.

Willingness to Pay and Willingness to Accept

Economists use the Contingent Valuation Method (CVM) to estimate the value people attach to non-marketed environmental goods. As we will discuss in detail in Chapter 9, this is a central part of climate change cost–benefit analysis, where costs of climate change mitigation are contrasted with estimates of climate change damages. People are asked how much they would be willing to pay to protect an endangered species or habitat, or to reduce personal risk. This is claimed to provide a measure of the utility people derive from such environmental assets, imperfect as it may be. A major problem is that the answers to such questions depend on how many similar questions are being asked at the same time! All-encompassing and decisive questions such as 'How much would you be willing to pay to prevent further global warming?' depend on so many unstated assumptions that their meaning and interpretation become very questionable themselves.

Sometimes economists can derive a more accurate valuation of environmental services by examining the revealed preferences of individuals (rather than the stated preferences, as in the case of CVM). Home-owners, for instance, may pay higher prices for houses in cleaner environments or closer to nature reserves, with the price premium reflecting the value attached to these environmental amenities. For many environmental services, though, especially in the context of climate change, where benefits are less localized, revealed preferences are difficult to identify.

We have already questioned the interpretation of willingness-to-pay (WTP) surveys. Many economists believe that they underestimate the true value people attach to the environment. When individuals are asked instead for their willingness to accept (WTA) compensation for loss of an environmental asset, they tend to give higher values for the same environmental good. Although the WTP and WTA methods should provide similar estimates, most studies find that this is not the case. People seem to suffer the loss of something much more than they value gaining the same thing, often around twice as much. This psychological paradox, first identified by Nobel laureate Daniel Kahneman and Amos Tversky in the early 1970s, has been verified in many subsequent environmental economics studies.[23] In the context of climate change, it may suggest that people are likely to have a much stronger preference for preserving the environmental status quo, and hence demand a much higher compensation than revealed by WTP methods for environmental damages related to climate change.

Some economists also believe there is a moral dimension to the problem. Willingness-to-accept estimates are higher because people demand a larger compensation for actions they regard as morally wrong.[24] When people feel they have a 'right' to environmental quality, biodiversity and climate stability, they generally require a much higher payment to accept damage or loss that is perceived to be unethical. The WTA transfer resembles in that respect a bribe as compensation for unethical or criminal conduct. Individuals may also require larger monetary compensation for environmental degradation, simply because of the uncertainties involved in how environmental losses might affect them.

Environmental Protection as a Human Right

In recent years, many lawyers have also expressed concerns about the ethical implications of climate change and violation of human rights. They explore how global environmental issues can fall within international environmental law, and make actors and states accountable for their environmental impact.

Global warming violates a broad range of human rights, which are internationally protected by treaties and conventions. Human rights to health, food, water security and decent livelihoods are all at stake, for billions of people in developing countries, in a world of rising temperatures and declining soil fertility. These human rights are already enshrined in the Universal Declaration of Human Rights of the United Nations and the two international conventions that followed, the International Covenant on Civil and Political Rights and the International Covenant on Economic, Social and Cultural Rights. Environmental protection is unfortunately not recognized as a separate human right per se, but nevertheless can fall within international law jurisdiction to the extent that it affects other broader human rights, such as the right to life, health, adequate food and water.[25]

Countries ratifying international human rights treaties commit themselves to respecting and protecting the rights involved. For local (in contrast to global) environmental pollution, the state is generally more proactive in facilitating human rights protection and ensuring legal procedures are in place in case of violation. For environmental issues of global dimensions, the pressure on states to act is usually less formal unless international conventions are incorporated into domestic law. Pressure from other signatory members and international organizations ensure compliance to a large extent, and the International Court of Justice, as the primary judicial organ of the United Nations, also has the jurisdiction to settle legal disputes and provide advisory opinions on legal questions submitted to it by UN member states. Although a special chamber within the International Court of Justice has been established to deal with transnational environmental issues, the chamber has remained generally inactive (on the other hand the European Court of Human Rights, representing the nations participating in the Council of Europe, has examined a few cases of environmental damage, although always at a national level). Strengthening the domestic and international legal framework for human rights protection is particularly needed for low-income countries, where human rights are generally less respected due to weak institutions and lack of public resources.

Climate change is expected to increase environmental displacement, immigration, loss of livelihoods and violent conflict. Despite the primary role of the United Nations as a safeguard of international peace and security, the UN Security Council has not considered climate change as an eminent threat to global stability. The Security Council has generally avoided taking action on international environmental issues, with the sole notable exception being the resolution to hold Iraq accountable for environmental damage inflicted on Kuwait during the 1991 Gulf War. The United Nations Environmental Programme (UNEP) was established in 1971 as a separate UN body specializing in environmental issues, but still remains a UN programme rather than a UN semi-independent agency such as the World Trade Organization or the World Health Organization, hence limiting its political influence. As we discuss in Chapter 9 in more detail, it is extremely difficult to weigh the benefits of current emissions against the risks of climate change, and hence give the concept of 'sustainable development' concrete content within international law. The very fact that future generations will mainly bear the cost of climate change further complicates court decisions, although representative proceedings on behalf of the unborn are common in English law, and could hence be extended to an international level.[26]

Spoiling Nature or Being Spoiled?

So far, we have discussed the rights of the poor and future generations, and how these are violated in the context of climate change. But this approach obviously does not give much consideration to nature itself. Allocating rights exclusively between human beings (whether poor or rich or in the future or present) ignores the implicit rights of other species to coexist with us. We (sometimes) feel ethically responsible for inflicting damage on other human beings, but we usually ignore the fact that we are not the sole species capable of experiencing pleasure and pain. This attitude has been termed 'speciesism', in analogy to the racism traditionally used to justify discrimination and cruelty to allegedly 'inferior' human races by more powerful rulers and conquerors. There is certainly scope, therefore, to extend our altruism beyond human beings when evaluating the consequences of our present behaviour.[27]

We often think of the value of nature in terms of its direct utility to people. And indeed, nature provides a whole range of invaluable services to us in the form of either primary materials or amenity values. Climate change damages many of these services. To some extent, we may try to estimate such damages, either by looking at market values for environmental services if they exist, or more usually by approximating them with the Contingent Valuation Method we discussed earlier.

Are we, though, only ethically responsible for preserving those environmental services that are directly useful to us? Most people recognize that there is also an intrinsic value in nature, a value that is not related to direct benefits we enjoy. For instance, we may feel an ethical responsibility to preserve rare plant or insect species, remote habitats and landscapes, beyond any direct benefits we are likely to enjoy. Some of us may benefit directly by visiting these locations. Many, though, would simply prefer that these ecosystems remain unspoiled, even if this yields no direct benefits to them. Similarly, we often donate money to help the destitute and the vulnerable without expecting anything in return. This altruism does sometimes extend beyond our own species. Unfortunately, when economists try to estimate a monetary value for climate change or other environmental damages, they tend to ignore this inherent or intrinsic value of nature, in part because of the great difficulties in measuring it.

Desacralizing Nature

Moral responsibilities towards nature are largely shaped by our cultural and religious heritage. Tim Jenkins of Cambridge University argues that Western religion and philosophy generally assume nature to be non-sacred, and hence permit its use and exploitation for human benefit.[28] The era of Enlightenment further estranged human beings from nature, with the view that humankind 'owns' the natural environment, rather than being an integral part of it. Enlightenment endorsed critical free thinking and promoted the emancipation of the individual from religious authority, traditions and natural constraints. There was nothing divine about nature, which was simply seen as a means to expand production and improve living standards.[29] On the other hand, the ancient Greeks regarded environmental hazards (such as earthquakes, drought and crop failure) as signs of divine punishment (nemesis). Natural events and disasters were associated directly with the gods – for instance thunder with Zeus and an earthquake with Poseidon.

Our moral responsibilities within the Christian faith deserve particular scrutiny, with Christianity being the dominant religion in the Western world. Sallie McFague, in her new book *A New Climate for Theology*, provides a fascinating study of how global environmental thinking fits within Christian theology.[30] She suggests that our environmentally destructive attitude is a direct result of how we perceive ourselves in relation to God. We largely see ourselves as privileged entities, superior to other forms of life on the planet (and these feelings of personal superiority even extend towards other human beings of different socio-cultural and educational background). We often feel ourselves isolated both from other human and non-human beings, God included. For most Christians, God is the supernatural creator of our planet, but also remains rather distant from our human world by residing and making judgements somewhere 'above' and far away from it. Isolating ourselves from our supernatural creator naturally gives us the perception of superiority in our day-to-day affairs and diminishes our feeling of responsibility towards other individuals and the environment.

McFague suggests moving towards an 'ecological church', which is truly catholic and ecumenical in embracing all human and non-human beings and nature as a whole. The Sunday sermons are, at best, dominated by moral guidance on how to improve human welfare and decrease human suffering (though often more concerned with dogma, such as opposition to contraception, which has the opposite effect). There is little mention of the need for a more encompassing wellbeing of all God's creation, which would be a big step forward from the current anthropocentric messages of the Church. A more wide-reaching and all-embracing Church would then be able to include in its agenda environmental issues of global concern such as climate change and, even more important, relate these issues to the inevitable increase in poverty and human suffering under unconstrained global warming, particularly for those living in poorer regions of the planet.

While environmentalists are likely to welcome such a move, whatever their religious position, McFague seems to miss to miss the key point that even restrictive traditional ethics should be concerned with the threat of a climate catastrophe that in the worst case could cost billions of lives in the future. Christian and other religious leaders have largely ignored the basic warnings from climate scientists, which should have been quite sufficient to put climate change on the top of their agenda. While an ecological church might be seen as a substantial improvement by many observers, such reform hardly seems to be necessary in order to take a decisive stance on climate change.

McFague's criticism of Christian egocentricity is also far from new. A series of essays published in 1904–1905 by the famous German economist and sociologist Max Weber also emphasized the human-centred ethos of the Protestant Church. In his book *The Protestant Ethic and the Rise of Capitalism*, Weber claims that Protestantism, and Calvinism in particular, favoured hard work, economic gain and wealth accumulation by giving them a moral significance.[31] While the Catholic Church assured salvation for everyone accepting the Church's sacraments, Calvinism put forward a theory of double predestination, in which God predetermined which Christians were destined for salvation or damnation. According to Weber, material wealth and related self-confidence provided individuals with a much-needed sign of salvation and God's grace. Donations to the poor were largely frowned upon, for promoting beggary and laziness rather than encouraging the hard-working ethos that was favoured by God. Religious devotion was hence primarily linked to personal economic gain rather than respect for other human beings or nature as a whole.

Michael Northcott, a leading international ethicist from the University of Edinburgh, provides a more outspoken critique when analysing the immorality of global warming within the spectrum of Christian tradition. Human beings require modest carbon emissions to satisfy their food, clean water and shelter necessities, which Northcott calls 'livelihoods' or 'subsistence' emissions. The emissions per person attributed to the poor in the world's most deprived areas often fall short even of this minimum 'subsistence' level, which could prevent human suffering and poverty for millions in the future if adopted universally. This comes in sharp contrast to the 'luxury' emissions needed to sustain the extravagant, wasteful consumerism of the rich, largely based in Europe and North America, but also as minorities in poor countries. These luxury emissions, determined by greed, overshadow the minimal emissions of the world's poor, determined by necessity. The Christian ethos is particularly critical of such pursuit of luxury, especially when common property (such as our global environmental commons) is appropriated for private benefit. The current consumerism and luxury emissions of the rich are immoral, as they will in effect deny the poor the opportunity to meet even their most basic survival needs, as agricultural collapse and water shortages kick in. Accelerating global warming, fuelled by the lavish lifestyle of the rich, is a theft of common resources that should in principle be available to those living in ecologically vulnerable parts of the planet.[32]

The loss of spiritual connection with nature creates the false impression that we can fully control the Earth's ecosystems through advances in science and technology. As we discussed in Chapter 4, economic growth has become the overriding policy objective everywhere, although the average happiness of rich nations in particular is much less affected by material consumption than by intangible aspects of 'social capital' such as trust and democracy. The materialism that is encouraged by constant exposure to commercial TV from early infancy and competition for status by wasteful consumption of 'positional' goods combine with job insecurity to cause unhappiness and even neuroses or depression. In addition, material growth is devastating environments and ecosystems everywhere and accelerating emissions of GHGs that threaten our future, above all that of the most vulnerable, poorest populations. The ethical contradictions underlying growth policy and the lack of serious environmental policy have not yet been widely recognized.

The Broken Link between Consumption and Production

Since the end of the Second World War, the world economy has become increasingly globalized. Countries trade more with each other, based on what economists call 'comparative advantage' or specialization in what they can produce relatively cheaply, as already described in the early 19th century by the English classical economist David Ricardo.[33] Over the last few decades, the World Bank and the International Monetary Fund have included trade liberalization as one of their main policy prescriptions for developing countries, and encouraged them to reduce tariffs, quotas and other trade obstacles.[34] As a result of freer trade, multinational corporations have gained wider access to markets in developing countries. They are now able to purchase primary materials cheaply, relocate production to countries where labour costs are low and transport the final products back to markets in Western nations, all without regard to environmental or 'external' costs. They are also able to flood developing markets with goods that consumers did not even know the existence of a few years back, as well as destroy the livelihoods of local farmers with heavily subsidized exports from industrial agriculture in the EU and the US.

There is of course a fierce debate between economists and anti-globalists on how freer trade addresses the needs of the poor, inequality and exploitation of labour. Irrespective of differing views on globalization, it is indisputable that local small-scale production is shrinking, and our markets are flooded with products flown in from thousands of miles away. Freer trade secured lower prices for a wide range of products, with the average consumer knowing little if anything about the production and transport of the goods. Few customers realize, for instance, that most flowers bought in American and European supermarkets are flown from countries as far away as Ethiopia, Kenya and Ecuador. Even worse, they do not seem to realize or care that low prices for imported products do not include the environmental costs of transportation and production, and that only a few per cent of what they pay actually goes to the producers.[35]

There are some signs of change, however. The Fair Trade movement encompasses a variety of organizations supporting small, local farmers and craftsmen in bargaining with multinationals, and promoting sustainable methods that protect the income and health of growers, workers and consumers. The retail share of Fair Trade products, though still tiny, is growing rapidly, jumping by 47 per cent in 2007. Without such support, small-scale farmers find it virtually impossible to compete against the market power of large multinational corporations.[36]

The (modest) success of the Fair Trade initiative is part of the rise of 'ethical consumption'. Over the past few decades, globalization, increased trade and lower transportation costs have broken the link between consumption and production. Consumers bought products with little knowledge of methods of production, country of origin, or environmental and social consequences, with their choices largely influenced by pricing and marketing. Well-founded health and ethical concerns (though still only among a small minority) have driven rising demand for organically and locally produced food, which supports local employment and reduces carbon emissions. The celebrity chef Jamie Oliver recently wrote a book (*Jamie at Home, Cook Your Way to the Good Life*) that lists recipes according to seasons, so that one can easily plan meals according to local produce available.[37]

Ethical consumption – and indeed any rational and informed choice – requires transparent and honest labelling. Most 'prepared' food nowadays does display a long list of information, though not always the most relevant, but buyers of fresh fruit and vegetables have no information on pesticide residues, nutrient content, or methods of production and distribution. 'Eco-labelling' can help consumers choose environmentally friendly products, although its use is still rather limited. The 'dolphin-safe label', for instance, is used on canned tuna to demonstrate that the fish has been caught without harming or killing dolphins. Improvements in labelling with colour codes for carbon footprint and nutritional value are under discussion, but generally being resisted or 'diluted' by the powerful supermarket chains.[38]

More detailed information would help environmentally sensitive consumers to make choices in accord with their values, and reduce their ecological footprint. This is particularly relevant for industrial meat production, where health hazards for consumers and appalling animal welfare conditions have been systematically concealed by the supermarkets which depend on this industry, as we discussed in Chapter 3.[39] In addition, the meat industry is a major producer of GHGs, in particular methane, and cause of environmental degradation.[40] There are thus several reasons, in addition to health concerns, for ethical consumers to reduce or cease consumption of industrial meat and dairy products, and comprehensive labelling could do much to inform about these vital issues.

Conclusions

Although often not apparent at first sight, ethical values permeate economic thinking and policy. The way we approach social issues with economic theories and policies mirrors our ethical value judgements. Our ethical stance influences the way we answer questions such as the following:

- How much pollution is too much for whom?
- How does social welfare depend on the distribution of social capital and environmental quality, as well as material consumption?
- How do we weigh impacts on future generations against current decisions?

With increasing recognition of imminent environmental threats and a climate change catastrophe, economic analysis needs to recognize moral responsibility to treat the Earth with respect and protect those vulnerable to environmental degradation.

Managing our global commons requires much beyond adopting relevant policy measures, market solutions and technological transfers. Even more fundamentally it is important that we collectively recognize the ethical responsibilities of our current actions towards the present and future poor. Our failure to stabilize GHG concentrations at lower levels will have devastating impacts, particularly for developing nations, but also for our own future. Economists mistakenly consider material consumption as the ultimate determinant of happiness and welfare, thus neglecting the importance of social capital and environmental protection, and helping to justify continuing policy priority for destructive and wasteful growth. The global economic crisis of 2008–2009, combined with threatening deflation, offered a rare opportunity for counter-cyclical investment in labour-intensive, alternative energy and environmental protection, which would also combat rapidly rising unemployment. But this opportunity has been largely wasted.

As we have repeatedly emphasized, mitigation of climate change is a form of insurance against future humanitarian crises, widespread poverty and agricultural collapse. Such defensive investment, supported by the continuously increasing scientific evidence on anthropogenic climate change and its positive feedback processes, is urgently needed. In spite of uncertainty, we need to take precautionary measures to minimize the risk of catastrophe and protect the most vulnerable. To achieve this, we have to extend our moral obligations to our direct descendants to include all future generations, and particularly the poor of the developing world.

As consumers and producers, we need to recognize the threat and look beyond private profit. Broken links between consumption and production, nature and faith, and distant communities of different backgrounds (though sharing a common planet) need to be rejoined. In a world of increasing inequality and ecological crises, the need for international cooperation, to promote both climate stability and social justice, is a moral imperative under the emerging risks of climate catastrophe and mass starvation.

7

Kyoto and Other International Environmental Agreements

Climate Change as a 'Global Public Good' Problem

In August 2005, at least 1800 people lost their lives as Hurricane Katrina hit Louisiana and Mississippi, submerging most of New Orleans with scenes that resembled a catastrophe of biblical dimensions. The 2003 European heatwave was much deadlier, causing the loss of at least 35,000 lives with unprecedented temperatures of around 40 degrees or more for several weeks. In March 2004, Cyclone Catarina (a rare tropical cyclone in the South Atlantic) hit Brazil, causing severe property damages and human injuries. In recent years, Australia, Argentina, northern China and parts of the US have experienced some of their worst droughts ever, damaging harvests and contributing to the dramatic rise in many food prices. As we discussed in Chapter 2, even if these anomalies are not necessarily or exclusively attributed to climate change, it is now well accepted that rising global average temperature will increase the frequency of extreme weather conditions. The geographic distribution of such events makes it apparent that climate change does not concern just a few countries or people; it is an environmental problem of global dimensions and, hence, requires coordinated global action.

By the beginning of the 1990s, it was becoming apparent that global temperatures had been rising and that human interference with the climate system was responsible. The first report, in 1990, of the Intergovernmental Panel on Climate Change (IPCC) – the scientific body operating under the auspices of the United Nations to evaluate the risk of global warming – explicitly linked temperature changes to global greenhouse gas emissions and created momentum for global action. The 1992 United Nations Conference on Environment and Development in Rio tabled an agreement on global warming called 'the UN Framework Convention on Climate Change', building on the scientific evidence of the first IPCC report. Industrialized nations were reluctant to take any strong action against greenhouse gases, and there was no agreement on binding commitments apart from an abstract and modest target of stabilizing carbon emissions at 1990 levels by 2000. This lukewarm response to the threat of climate change was mainly due to American opposition to stronger action (and related reluctance to incur immediate abatement costs). Developing countries were not expected to reduce their carbon emissions, and almost 200 nations signed the convention and left Rio, content with a decision committing them to do very little or nothing!

Since the ratification of the convention, there have been annual conference meetings of its parties, with the first held in Berlin in 1995. Opposition to binding targets by many industrialized nations (the US and Australia among them) remained fierce, but a decision was taken to negotiate a protocol of compulsory commitments and have it ratified at the third meeting of the parties in Kyoto in 1997. In Kyoto, it became apparent once again that there was no will to take strong action against carbon emissions. Participating countries were coming to the negotiations with conflicting objectives in mind. Many developed and most developing nations were simply not happy to sacrifice current or future income for environmental protection, especially since they anticipated no severe damages from climate change to their own economies. On the other hand, some (but few) countries particularly vulnerable to climate change (especially island nations) had a keen self-interest in reaching an agreement on climate change and curbing global carbon emissions.[1] The rather disappointing negotiations in Kyoto ended with industrialized nations (the so-called Annex I countries) committing to a very modest target of reducing emissions by five per cent during 2008–2012 compared to 1990 levels. In March 2001, the Bush Administration withdrew from the protocol, and shortly after Australia followed suit.[2] The protocol finally came into force in February 2005 after the Russian Duma ratified the treaty.

In all 14 United Nations Climate Change Conferences, from Berlin in 1995 till Poznań in 2008 (as well as preceding Intergovernmental Negotiating Committees before 1995), attempts to reach consensus on global action have been a thorny, nerve-racking process. Why is it then so difficult to find common ground and coordinate our actions on climate change? The answer lies in the global nature of the climate change issue. Climate change is a global public good problem, which means that all countries will suffer the consequences, though to varying degrees according to geographical accident. Just how much the climate really will change, and how much any one country suffers, depends on the behaviour of all the main emitting nations, rather than any individual actions to minimize damage. This is not necessarily the case for all kinds of environmental pollution. For instance, we can personally choose how much garbage to leave lying around our house, and how much to bin for collection and (hopefully) safe disposal.

More commonly, though, individuals or countries suffer from environmental problems that have originated as side-effects of the actions of another party (as already noted, this is often called an externality in economists' jargon). When the environmental damage is local (as may be the case for local air pollution or deforestation or in the household waste example above), polluters and victims are neighbours, and it may be easier for the latter to claim compensation from the former (unless, as so often, the polluter is a powerful corporation). For global environmental problems (such as climate change or ozone depletion), the polluter and the victim may be geographically very far from each other. This explains why countries fail to take strong action on averting global environmental damage. Developing countries may suffer from agricultural collapse or increased malaria despite curbing their own greenhouse gas emissions, unless many other states take similar actions. To reverse the argument, countries such as the US, even if they do not commit to any binding targets for CO_2 emissions, will still benefit from the reduced emissions of Kyoto signatories.[3] As a result of this inability to influence outcomes independently and in a predictable way, there is little incentive for individual countries to take firm action on such global environmental issues.[4]

Choosing Strategies: To Abate or to Pollute

Economists often analyse participation in (environmental) agreements with the use of game theory. Game theory is a conceptual tool used to examine choices, when our own decisions (and benefits) depend on the choices made by other individuals or countries. The most common game described in such models of environmental agreements is the so-called 'prisoner's dilemma'.[5] Imagine a simple world of two countries deciding whether to abate emissions (and hence ratify the Kyoto Protocol) or simply pollute and emit GHGs in a business-as-usual manner. When both countries decide to abate, then obviously the long-term benefits of mitigation are quite high and accrue to both of them (after all, environmental mitigation is a global public good). While at first sight this appears to be the reasonable thing to do, often in practice countries choose to act differently.

The decision to abate is perceived to be costly in the short term, particularly by the special interest groups most dependent on fossil fuels. As we discuss in Chapter 9, reducing GHG emissions will do more than slow down warming. Many measures also generate 'co-benefits' and substantial welfare gains, albeit after some redistribution and changes in behaviour that do represent major political obstacles to overcome. In any case, governments generally tend to give greater weight in their policy planning to perceived short-term costs rather than long-term gains (such as the benefits of climate change mitigation). Once the first country decides to abate and commit to binding emission targets, the other country may simply decide to pollute as usual for short-term political convenience and perhaps temporary competitive advantage. The long-term benefits from climate change mitigation will now be much smaller, since only one country abates, but the polluting country benefits disproportionately since it does not need to incur any abatement costs.

In a sense, the polluting country (for example the US avoiding binding targets for CO_2 emissions) simply free-rides on the efforts of other nations to mitigate climate change. Sooner or later, the nation that abates may also change its strategy and either decrease or abandon mitigation efforts if, for example, it loses export markets and jobs to competitors who do not pay the full (climate) costs of their dirty production. If one of the parties does not abate, any unilateral efforts to curb GHGs may be counterbalanced by increased emissions from the polluting nation, and abatement will hence bring about relatively small benefits. Both countries may end up polluting heavily in the long term, despite the fact that they could have both invested in mitigation and achieved a jointly superior outcome.[6]

Perceived differences in pay-offs will necessarily influence the objectives and strategies of individual countries. As developed in discussion of the 'denial industry' in Chapter 2, the Bush Administration had consistently downplayed any long-term costs of climate change, and placed a much larger emphasis on the alleged short-term costs that abatement would impose on the American economy. While denying the benefits of climate change mitigation, energy lobbies in alliance with the previous Bush Administration have also systematically exaggerated the impact that abatement would have on the real economy in terms of reduced investment and increased unemployment. This exaggeration of mitigation costs, with a simultaneous misjudgement of climate change costs (which in the past had been related to the close links of the Bush Administration and family with the oil industry), simply reinforced the American decision to abstain from Kyoto, while the Europeans have at least set targets for abatement, and China has overtaken the US as the leading emitter of GHGs.[7] While the new US administration under Obama has tried to act on climate change and US carbon emissions, ambitious goals needed to compensate for the valuable time lost under the Bush Administration are unlikely to be met in the face of a hostile Congress in the midst of a recession.

In a more complex (and realistic) game with multiple participants, the pay-offs to our own specific strategy will depend both on what other individuals and countries choose and also on how many players choose to follow our strategy or an alternative one.[8] This is exactly why the Kyoto Protocol, in order to come into force, required at least 55 countries to ratify it, including industrialized nations accounting for more than 55 per cent of 1990 global emissions. A smaller number of signatories would create a weak signal for participation, since mitigation efforts by a few countries would have a minimal impact on climate change. Participation in abatement is likely to be self-enforcing when country-specific benefits exceed costs, but this may require some minimum level of collective effort and is likely to be further reinforced as participation expands. If few countries decide to abate, they are likely to gradually revert to pollution one by one. The US (under Bush), for instance, pledged to ratify the treaty and accept binding targets when China and other developing nations stopped being exempted from carbon emission commitments. In a similar vein, Australia under John Howard declined to take part in the agreement as long as the Americans abstained from it.

Clearly, participation in environmental agreements is also largely determined by politics. A change in government in Australia in 2007, with Kevin

Rudd replacing John Howard, created a U-turn in the Australian stance on climate change and the Kyoto Protocol. While John Howard ferociously opposed the treaty, the new government ratified it almost immediately after assuming office. Paul Collier, in his new book *The Bottom Billion*, explains how politics influence participation in another agreement, the Extractive Industry Transparency Initiative (EITI), and his main argument may well extend beyond the EITI to other environmental treaties.[9] When most countries ratify an international agreement, countries resisting ratification for selfish motives often find themselves politically isolated and need to provide increasingly convincing arguments to their electorates for their non-participation.

Carrots and Sticks

Incentives (carrots) and sanctions (sticks) change the pay-offs attached to particular strategies and can encourage participation in environmental agreements. Apart from drawing the US into a new post-Kyoto agreement with binding targets on GHG emissions, we will soon need similar incentives to convince non-Annex I countries (the developing nations with no binding commitments – mainly China and India) to follow suit. Developing nations are simply reluctant to sacrifice economic growth for the sake of preventing climate change, and industrialized nations will need to provide financial transfers if we want to see LDCs curbing their own carbon emissions. Much of this can be based on some kind of technology transfer, where we will simply help poorer states replace dirty polluting technologies with carbon-friendly alternatives. Such transfers are needed urgently, particularly as China's emissions of carbon dioxide already match US levels, thanks to extensive reliance on coal. Of course, this technology transfer is already happening via the Clean Development Mechanism (CDM) – which we discuss in detail in the next section – where Annex I countries meet their Kyoto targets by investing in carbon-saving projects in developing countries, but targets should also be urgently extended to developing nations. Some progress has taken place over the last year in strengthening the Adaptation Fund already established in 1997 alongside Kyoto, which will help poorer nations to improve their infrastructure and gradually prepare for changes in climatic conditions.[10] As an alternative, once developing countries agree on binding targets for their carbon emissions, we could simultaneously extend carbon trading schemes to LDCs and hence offer a market for them to sell their saved carbon emissions.

While carrots tend to be most popular, sticks are rather difficult to implement. There is no supranational authority authorized to sanction non-cooperative countries that either refuse to ratify the Kyoto Protocol or do not meet their commitments. Although no specific measures have been proposed for Kyoto signatories failing to meet targets over the 2008–2012 period, large deviations will certainly create much political embarrassment.[11] Nobel laureate economist Joseph Stiglitz has long argued for trade sanctions against US exports of fossil fuel-intensive products, particularly in his book

Making Globalization Work. Gabrielle Walker and Sir David King, in their new book *The Hot Topic*, suggest that most sanctions are likely to take place via the World Trade Organization (WTO). Russia, for instance, ratified the Kyoto Protocol (a move needed in order for the Protocol to come into force at the time) in order to gain European support for its WTO membership.[12] The WTO is probably in the best position to impose sanctions in the future, since failure to abide by CO_2 emissions targets will create an advantage in international markets for those energy-intensive industries that fail to comply with their commitments. Most urgently, some mix of carrots and sticks to combat tropical deforestation, responsible for about a fifth of total GHG emissions, requires international agreement to fill one of the most glaring omissions in the Kyoto Protocol.

Joint Implementation and the Clean Development Mechanism

The Kyoto Protocol created two facilitating mechanisms to assist the industrialized nations to meet binding targets on reduced GHG emissions. Joint Implementation and the Clean Development Mechanism (CDM) are quite similar in concept and allow Annex I countries to meet their targets by reducing emissions outside their territories. This obviously increases cost-efficiency. If it is cheaper to reduce carbon emissions abroad rather than at home, then industrialized nations can simply pay for reduced carbon emissions elsewhere and receive carbon credits in return. In the case of the Joint Implementation scheme, industrialized nations usually receive carbon credits by funding carbon-saving projects in another relatively affluent Annex I nation. This created investment opportunities for carbon saving in Eastern Europe in particular, where there is large potential for improvements in energy efficiency. Russia alone benefits from almost half of all carbon credits from projects falling under the Joint Implementation umbrella, with Ukraine capturing approximately another 20 per cent.

The Clean Development Mechanism works in a similar way, by having developed (Annex I) countries invest in carbon reduction in developing countries. Gabrielle Walker and Sir David King call this mechanism the 'Robin Hood effect', since the scheme in effect transfers funds from developed to developing nations, without the latter making any concrete efforts. Developing nations offer opportunities for energy efficiency due to the poor standards and production conditions found in abundance within their local economies.[13] This bears a close resemblance to the idea put forward by Eric Neumayer, who sees mitigation efforts by industrialized nations as an aid mechanism to protect the most vulnerable, poorest nations and populations from climate change catastrophe.[14]

One feels almost tempted to say that the Clean Development Mechanism is the ideal solution to climate change: we reduce our carbon emissions, we do it in a cost-effective way, and we also transfer technology and funds to the poorest countries of the globe, all in one move. Nevertheless, the mechanism has received quite a lot of criticism in recent years, and we need to be cautious about the extent to which we should rely on it to mitigate climate change. One criticism is that it is simply a very easy short-term solution to a complex long-term problem and makes governments in industrialized nations ignore the development of new technologies as well as neglect investment and sustainability at home. The Clean Development Mechanism may hence provide a solution in the short run, but still fail to ensure the long-term survival of the planet. For instance, we may simply reforest an area in the Amazon and receive carbon credit in return, instead of investing more in the development of solar panels or wind power at home.

The most important criticism, though, arises when we invest in emission reductions abroad that would have happened anyway. There has been a lot of speculation that much carbon credit has been granted to developed nations for investing in projects in developing countries that had already been planned. The very fact that developing nations have not committed themselves to any binding targets on CO_2 emissions makes the situation even more problematic. While a rich country may, for instance, simply invest in reforesting a particular area in a developing country to increase global carbon sinks, the same forest may be cut down a few years later, as destruction of tropical rainforest continues unabated in many areas without any penalties being imposed. Even more perversely, developing nations have an incentive to delay any domestic measures on climate change mitigation while waiting for a Clean Development Project that will pay for it. Melanie Jarman also emphasizes how bureaucratic the procedure behind CDM projects can be, including several approvals from many different bodies (from local organizations to the UN) and legal fees, which push up the cost of the overall project (and even if it might have been still more expensive to achieve the same reduction of GHGs at home, this does not prove that CDM is the most cost-effective scheme among alternatives). At the same time, CDM projects are often allocated with an overemphasis on the extent of carbon credits earned, downplaying the role of benefits to local communities and poverty reduction.[15]

For all these reasons, there are limits to how much countries can reduce their emissions by investing abroad. For the UK, for instance, this has been limited to only eight per cent of its emissions cap, so that most of the efforts to reduce emissions do need to take place at home. These restrictions have certainly not been easy to agree upon. While the US was still negotiating the Kyoto Protocol in the mid 1990s, they ferociously opposed a minimum limit for domestic abatement, and would not even accept generous proposals by the EU to achieve only a minimum of 50 per cent of emission reductions at home.

Carbon Trading

Apart from the Joint Implementation scheme and the Clean Development Mechanism, a third way to reduce carbon dioxide emissions and meet binding targets is via purchasing emission-reduction credits from elsewhere (these three procedures are often jointly called 'flexible mechanisms'). The way carbon trading works in practice is the following. Developed nations that have ratified the Kyoto agreement have a binding cap on the level of carbon emissions they are allowed to emit. This cap is simply divided into permits, quotas or allowances, in tonnes of carbon, so that we can trade each other's products.[16] A developed country faces two options or strategies in order to reduce carbon emissions and therefore comply with Kyoto targets. It may simply reduce emissions at home or, if the price of permits is low enough, decide to enter the carbon market, go over its limit for CO_2 emissions, and buy permits that compensate for this excessive pollution from another (presumably developing) country or producer that has emission permits to spare.[17] An emissions trading scheme of some kind is usually preferred to carbon taxes by environmentalists, since it is a direct policy instrument for constraining emissions. Of course, industry obviously prefers free permits – which effectively reward the biggest polluters – and has lobbied intensively against auctioning permits. But without taxes or auctions, governments lose an important policy instrument, as we discuss in detail in Chapter 8.

The trading of pollution permits functioned successfully even before the implementation of the Kyoto Protocol. In the US in the mid 1990s, an emissions trading system for sulphur dioxide quotas had been set up to reduce acid rain.[18] The first voluntary carbon emissions trading schemes were implemented in the UK and Denmark, which quickly became merged in 2005 into the European Union Emissions Trading System (EU ETS), which is currently the largest carbon trading programme globally.[19] Participation in the EU ETS is already compulsory for a number of carbon-intensive industries (such as power plants, and paper and cement factories), but excludes transport and households.

There is still, though, much scope for improvement in how the EU ETS programme operates. The ETS has been much criticized for the way permits are allocated to industries. So far, individual EU governments decide how to distribute permits across sectors and firms, a process that is often called 'grand-fathering' (where permits are given out for free rather than sold in an auction, usually to those sectors with historically high levels of emissions).

The EU ETS trading market operates similarly to any other market with a demand and supply side. Initially, demand and supply conditions determined the price of carbon emissions per tonne (between €10 and €20 in 2005). In 2006 the price of permits plunged, because too many permits had been distributed, with supply greatly exceeding demand. After this disastrous experience, the EU took the initiative to reduce emission caps and push up the price of carbon permits (with plans but no firm commitments yet to auction permits in the future). Although EU states are meant to decide on their national caps and allocation of permits across industries (according to so-called National Allocation Plans), the EU Commission scrutinizes member states' proposals to ensure they are compatible with their Kyoto commitments. Thus the Commission suggested in 2006 that approximately a seven per cent reduction below the 2005 carbon allowances would be needed for the second phase of the EU ETS (2008–2012). A reduced supply of allowances and an expected increase in demand (partly due to the inclusion of the aviation industry under the scheme from 2011) are likely to reverse the trend in carbon prices. Unless more radical reform take place, though (such as the proposal to gradually increase the share of allowances to be auctioned up to 60 per cent by 2013 – when the ETS will enter its third phase – and replace the National Allocation Plans with a centralized EU system of emission caps), no drastic changes in carbon prices should be expected.

Beyond 2020 (coinciding with the beginning of the fourth phase of the ETS), even more radical measures have been proposed, such as an auctioning of all carbon permits (with no grandfathering allowed), a reduction of carbon allowances by 21 per cent from 2005 levels, and the inclusion of nitrous oxide and perfluorocarbons (PFCs) in the scheme.[20] Any price fluctuations (which often create market uncertainty and discourage investment in renewables) can be further smoothed out with a combination of taxes and transferable allowances between periods (which we discuss in more detail in Chapter 8). What still remains contentious, though, is how efficiently governments will utilize the public revenues they earn from auctioning carbon allowances, and whether a substantial share will be allocated to investment in energy efficiency and renewable energy.

As we discuss in Chapter 8, the new US President Barack Obama has committed to a similar US carbon cap-and-trade scheme, which in time could become harmonized and linked to the EU ETS (or even merge with it). Irrespective of President Obama's commitment to such a scheme, momentum in this direction has been already building for some time, with ten north-eastern US states setting their own regional CO_2 cap-and-trade system (the Regional Greenhouse Gas Initiative or RGGI), which became operational in late 2008. Although US politicians may have warmed up to the idea of adopting a similar national cap-and-trade scheme, encouraged by the prospects of increased public revenues from auctions (rather than saving the planet),[21] this is certainly a first step in the right direction. An American cap-and-trade scheme is likely to follow a similar evolution to the European one, with an initial generous free distribution of permits, which will be gradually phased out in stages.[22] Other regional carbon trading schemes may follow suit (Japan is currently initiating a similar scheme), which will soon need to merge to avoid multiple pricing of carbon in fragmented markets. A more radical (and hence less politically realistic) carbon-trading proposal is based on the 'contraction and convergence' framework proposed later in this chapter. Allocating permits according to population would in effect disproportionately benefit developing countries and result in generous flows of funds from richer nations for the purchase of carbon permits.[23]

When the Kyoto Protocol came into force, it also became possible for all countries that ratified it to trade emissions permits. This is again quite problematic, since Russia, Ukraine and other Eastern European nations have emissions targets above their actual emissions levels and therefore can easily create an oversupply of tradable permits (with little effect on real climate change mitigation). The Kyoto Protocol also allows developed countries to sponsor carbon-saving projects in developing countries via the CDM scheme and generate in return tradable carbon credits. Once again, investment in developing countries under the CDM may end up in projects that do not guarantee a large and permanent sequestration of carbon (such as investment in reforestation), with little real impact on climate change mitigation.

The Montreal Protocol – A Rare Success

A rare glimpse of hope in the history of international environmental agreements is the success of the Montreal Protocol, an international treaty designed to protect the ozone layer by gradually eliminating the production of ozone-depleting chlorofluorocarbons (CFCs).[24] The agreement was reached in 1987 and implemented in 1989; this is in stark contrast to the Kyoto Protocol, which took more than seven years to ensure broad participation and hence come into force. The production of CFCs under the treaty had to be halved by 1999 compared to their 1986 levels. The rate of phase-out of CFCs was in practice much faster than initially expected. By 1990, industrialized countries had already achieved a 20 per cent reduction in the production of CFCs. In the fourth meeting of the parties in Copenhagen in 1992, binding targets became tighter, requiring more to be done in a shorter period of time. The number of restricted substances increased and a gradual implementation of a total ban on CFCs was agreed (with most CFCs being phased out by 1996). Even more remarkably, participation is almost unanimous. The treaty is now ratified by all major industrialized nations (and was endorsed by the US from the very beginning), with only five countries with minimal contributions to CFC abstaining.[25]

To some extent, the inspiration for a treaty on climate change came from the earlier, striking success of the Montreal agreement in restricting CFC production. The outstanding difference, of course, was that the costs of replacing CFCs were minimal, and only affected a few specialized producers. From its inception, it was quite clear that countries were keen to take strong action against CFCs. There was little controversy about the effects of accumulating CFCs in the atmosphere on ozone depletion. Since the discovery of the Antarctic ozone hole in the mid 1980s, a series of satellite pictures proved that ozone depletion was an actual threat to humanity rather than an uncertain theory yet to be proven.[26] The fact that a thinning of the ozone layer would result in increased exposure to ultraviolet (UV) radiation and hence higher risk of skin cancer was not considered controversial or denied by any major industrial lobby.

Part of the success of the Montreal Protocol certainly had to do with extensive media coverage, undisputed scientific evidence, and a very fast public reaction and broad support. But the other part had to do with economics. Industrialized countries such as the US had an incentive to reduce CFC production even unilaterally, because the cost was relatively low. Action by one country would certainly not prevent ozone depletion to the extent that a simultaneous global effort would. But nevertheless, even a small reduction of cancer incidences was considered sufficient to outweigh the rather low abatement cost. As countries started implementing their binding targets, the cost of alternative technology and abatement fell further, making compliance easier. At the same time, a Multilateral Fund for the Implementation of the Montreal Protocol was established to provide funds to developing countries to eliminate CFC production. Projects focusing on modernizing manufacturing processes, encouraging technology transfer and training relevant personnel were financed by the fund. In this way, developing countries were given a financial 'carrot' in order to participate. For those who did not want to take the offer, there was also a financial 'stick', an explicit threat of trade sanctions, which certainly made non-signatory countries think twice.[27]

What Next?

It is obvious that there is a long way to go before we can hail the Kyoto Protocol as even a successful beginning, especially when we compare it with the Montreal treaty on ozone depletion. It would certainly be unfair to regard Kyoto as a total failure, and it is probably of some use as a starting point. But it could have been a much better starting point if binding targets for emission reductions had been closer to IPCC recommendations for the more drastic cuts that are realistically needed to stay below the two-degree threshold discussed in Chapter 2.[28] The very fact that industrialized nations such as Australia and Norway were even allowed increases in their carbon emissions suggests that there has been little enthusiasm to take strong action against climate change. The European Union, which is often considered the most enthusiastic supporter of Kyoto, only agreed to a modest decrease of carbon emissions of 8 per cent, while allowing poorer but still relatively industrialized EU countries, such as Portugal and Greece, to increase their emissions by more than 25 per cent. Perhaps even more important, as renowned environmental economist Dieter Helm puts it, Kyoto would have been more successful in tackling global GHG emissions if it were based upon carbon consumption rather than production, as the current emphasis shifts responsibility away from the richer nations, particularly the major importers of energy-intensive products from China and elsewhere.[29] Of course, if participation in the treaty was unanimous, such a distinction between consumption and production (or fears of firms losing competitiveness due to the costs of environmental regulation) would have been irrelevant.

Whatever a post-Kyoto treaty will look like, it is essential that more radical reductions of carbon emissions are attained, as well as a more active involvement of developing countries. The current binding commitments for specific reductions from 1990 levels favour those industrialized nations with high emissions. It would be unfair if developing countries with low emissions per person had to commit to the same *percentage* reductions as rich countries that have emitted most in the past. This would simply reward those nations that managed to industrialize earlier and faster, and hence pollute more. Countries that have produced most of the existing stock of GHGs in the atmosphere do need to make a comparatively larger effort for the sake of a global environmental problem such as climate change.

For reasons of equity, there is much support for a 'contraction and convergence' scheme, which as we mentioned earlier would provide allowances for carbon emissions to all countries in proportion to their population.[30] This also requires agreement among the main emitters that global emissions should be capped, by issuing a total number of permits which represents *less* than current global emissions. The cap should then decrease over time (so that we can ideally reduce our global emissions by 80–90 per cent by 2050 or earlier). Developed countries would receive fewer permits than their current emissions, and would thus have to buy excess allowances from poor states that emit less than their allocated permits. This would generate a flow of aid from rich to poor countries, declining inequality and convergence of per capita income levels, though without any implication that actual equality would be reached in the foreseeable future.

Another radical scheme, which secures rights to development in a carbon-constrained world, is the Greenhouse Development Rights framework proposed by the Heinrich Böll Foundation and Christian Aid among others. The main idea is that rich nations should face disproportionately larger obligations for reducing carbon emissions for two reasons. First, because they have greater *capacity* to collect green taxes and finance environmental mitigation, since the majority of their populations have already satisfied their basic needs (by earning above a 'development threshold level' of $20 per day). And second, because they have larger *responsibility* for the climate change threat, having produced most of the cumulative GHG emissions. The capacity and responsibility of individual countries would then jointly determine the obligatory financial contributions per country to an international fund financing mitigation and adaptation, with low-income nations left virtually off the hook until they develop sufficiently.

Although such schemes may appear to be overly generous to developing countries, they do give them appropriate incentives for abatement, and also provide for large transfers to the least industrialized nations. Under Kyoto, on the other hand, non-Annex I developing countries face no penalties for growing emissions, or incentives for mitigation. The schemes, though, however appealing in terms of achieving equity and preventing climate change, appear to be politically unrealistic at the moment.

The United Nations Climate Change Conference in Copenhagen in December 2009, to negotiate a post-Kyoto, was preceded by a European initiative. In December 2008 the European Union unilaterally set a goal to reduce greenhouse gas emissions to at least 20 per cent below 1990 levels by 2020, as well as to increase the share of renewables in energy use by the same amount and time (this is often referred to as the '20-20-20 EU climate plan'). While Europeans may even try to push for more ambitious targets during the post-Kyoto negotiations in Copenhagen, a truly effective international agreement will need much more than stricter emission caps.

Scott Barrett, a renowned expert on international agreements from the John Hopkins University, links the effectiveness of a post-Kyoto treaty to three essential elements.[31] First, a new protocol needs to ensure *broad participation* in a global concerted effort to curb GHGs. Targets need to be specified for all countries (with stricter ones applied for the industrialized economies) to minimize the relocation of carbon-intensive industries to regions of looser regulations. Unless emission caps are specified for all countries (corresponding to a global emission target), 'clean' economies are likely to meet emission targets simply by importing carbon-intensive products from China, India and other developing nations. Instead, relatively poor but fast-growing countries, such as China and India, should be expected to reach the same final end-points along with industrialized nations in the very long term with the help of monetary and technology transfers.

Second, a new protocol needs to provide *incentives for compliance*. So far, many Annex I countries appear to be far behind meeting their Kyoto targets for 2008–2012. Canada, for instance, is already experiencing a 30 per cent increase in GHG emissions above the 1990 levels, with little hope for achieving their 6 per cent reduction target within the few years remaining.

And third, a new treaty would need to focus more on *long-term expected outcomes* and necessary policies, rather than specifying very modest targets for a small number of countries and for a short period of time. So far, Kyoto has focused too much on technical details and targets rather than on how to realistically achieve climate stability. Even if Annex I countries achieved their five per cent reduction by 2012, this would by no means guarantee a decrease in global emissions, even as a first step towards stabilizing average temperatures.

All three conditions would need to be met for a new treaty to be successful. Specifying new stricter targets for all economies, the US and China included, will have little effect unless countries comply fully with their specified obligations.

While trade restrictions can provide the 'stick' for participation and compliance (either in the form of carbon taxes or trade sanctions) and financial and knowledge transfers the 'carrot', action may well need to be taken at a more micro level. Climate change is a much more complex environmental problem than ozone depletion, depending on multiple greenhouse gases (carbon dioxide, methane, nitrous oxide, hydrofluorocarbons and more) emitted across numerous sectors. Scott Barrett proposes that rather than having a single treaty regulating the production of all GHGs in all sectors, a more decentralized approach would be more effective. Sectoral agreements could focus on relevant greenhouse gas emissions across sectors (as in the aluminium and steel industry), with a better chance for full participation and compliance among few producers.

Whatever the shape of a post-Kyoto agreement, it will be a painstaking task to bring both the US and fast-industrializing nations such as China and India on board. High energy prices (with oil above $100 per barrel, as in early 2008) will encourage a gradual shift towards renewable energy and carbon abatement, but without really far-reaching new agreements and policies, changes will come too late to avert the high risk of catastrophic climate change. Funds to assist developing countries have been established, but the focus is often on adaptation rather than mitigation (such as the Adaptation Fund financed by levies on Clean Development Mechanism projects). It is critical that developed nations accept responsibility and assist poorer countries to embark on a carbon-friendly development track. Levying carbon taxes on products and imports (and hence overcoming WTO objections), while simultaneously offering easy access to existing carbon-saving know-how, would level the playing field. Whether governments will be politically brave enough to overcome special-interest opposition for the sake of long-term survival goals is, of course, something that remains to be seen.

Conclusions

Climatic stability is a global public good: the Earth's climate is shared by everyone on the planet, which decreases individual incentives for its protection. As a result, we face a tragedy of our global commons, with the Earth's climate subject to overexploitation. Each country's and individual's polluting behaviour contributes to the increase in GHG concentrations, and unilateral clean-up actions, if not followed by broader participation, normally entail higher costs than benefits. Cooperation among countries is vital for avoiding the climate catastrophe towards which we are heading, but the right balance of economic and political instruments need to be in place to minimize free-riding and maximize compliance.

So far, climate change negotiations have revealed the conflicting interests of participating countries rather than any strong will for concerted action. Many countries (both developed and developing) have been reluctant to commit to drastic cuts of their greenhouse gas emissions. Fears of trade leakage (relocation of industries abroad) or reduced economic growth for the sake of abatement prevented setting ambitious long-term goals capable of preventing a climate catastrophe. The Kyoto Protocol, with its modest emission targets, has been a first (if insufficient) step in the right direction. Its Joint Implementation scheme, Clean Development Mechanism and carbon trading system have provided innovative, cost-effective ways for emission cuts. Nevertheless, with emission targets specified only for a few industrialized countries, and no sanctions for exceeding them, global GHG emissions can in practice increase without limit.

A post-Kyoto treaty needs to ensure that all countries share responsibility in stabilizing global GHG concentrations in the atmosphere. This needs to be a common but differentiated responsibility, with industrialized nations committing to more drastic emission cuts and generous transfers of funds and technology to developing nations. Countries that decide to abstain from a concerted effort against climate change should face trade restrictions, as compensation to carbon-saving producers. Similar retaliatory measures would need to be in place for countries failing to comply with their targets. Having everyone on board is crucial for a treaty to be successful. Climate change is a global public problem, and only action at a global level can prevent the climate catastrophe towards which we are currently heading.

Incentives for Mitigation – Carbon Taxes and Emissions Trading

Market Forces Are Not Enough

Carbon emissions will not be reduced by international agreement, government declarations or even commitments unless there are clear economic incentives for abatement, or alternatively credible legal penalties for failure to comply with appropriate regulation. As we saw in Chapter 7, all these have been conspicuous by their absence in the Kyoto Protocol. Rising prices for fossil fuels for the decade up to mid 2008 provided an incentive in the right direction, but, together with related food price inflation from 2006, also caused hardship for poor people everywhere, and a massive transfer of income to the oil-producing states. Their growing wealth increased the power of authoritarian rulers in countries such as Russia and Saudi Arabia. This has changed dramatically with the global recession of 2008 and collapsing commodity prices, though economic recovery will doubtless renew the upward trend. However, market prices of fossil fuels have not been persistently high enough (yet) to generate the really large-scale investment in alternative energy that is needed to reduce the risk of catastrophic climate change.

When the Organization of the Petroleum Exporting Countries (OPEC) first dramatically and suddenly raised oil prices in 1974, there was a severe, world-wide recession in consequence. Energy saving was encouraged, and efficiency improved in the following years, but oil exploration and development of new fields also received a major boost. Oil prices declined steeply over the next decades, as new fields were developed and production expanded, particularly by non-OPEC countries. While conventional oil output may well peak in the near future, high prices also stimulate the exploitation of hitherto uneconomical – and much more polluting – tar sands and oil shales in North America and Venezuela.

The price of coal, the most abundant and 'dirtiest' fossil fuel, has followed oil prices to rise more than fivefold since 2003, and then drop precipitously in late 2008. Both coal and oil reserves have probably been seriously overestimated for political reasons, and rising prices will eventually accelerate the shift to renewables – such as wind and solar – which have been growing at 30–40 per cent annually, albeit from a very small base. However, most of the world's electricity is still generated by fossil fuels, including 6 billion tonnes of coal per year. Many environmentalists believe that 'carbon capture and storage' (CCS), which can remove perhaps two-thirds of the carbon emissions from burning fossil fuels, needs to be developed for commercial use, and encouraged by appropriate carbon pricing or taxation. However, recent evidence (reviewed in Chapter 9) suggests that CCS (and nuclear power) are much less cost-effective ways of reducing emissions than investment in efficiency and renewable energy.

Emissions from fossil fuels not only have devastating effects on urban health, but will also lead to catastrophic climate change if they continue unchecked. Lack of policies to correct this greatest of all market failures and curb emissions represents what may ultimately be recognized as the most disastrous government failure in history. Even more perversely, fossil fuels (and nuclear power) continue to enjoy gigantic public subsidies compared to very limited support for renewable energy, under the influence of their powerful and well-established lobbies.

The main policy options for reducing emissions are well known: carbon taxes, related tradable permits for emitting carbon, regulations such as limits on vehicle emissions and building insulation standards, public-sector energy-saving investments, and subsidies for alternatives – which will be discussed in detail below. All have been tried and tested in many different contexts, though not, of course, on a scale sufficient to have had much effect on the global problem of climate change. Any of these measures will reduce the demand for fossil fuels, and hence slow down the rate of price increase. Any form of carbon pricing will, of course, raise the price of fuel – and of energy-intensive products – for the final consumer, so government investment in alternatives – such as cheap public transport and alternative energy – is an essential component of mitigation policy. Revenues from carbon taxation (or from auctioning carbon permits) can also be used to reduce taxes on labour for lower income groups – or subsidize clean technology – which in turn will reduce unemployment, and help to gain political acceptance. Simply returning the revenues from a carbon tax to all citizens as a uniform lump-sum transfer might again be popular with low-income households, who would directly benefit, but would be less efficient than a reduction of distortionary taxes. The huge income transfer from the rest of the world to the fossil fuel-producing countries, and its various negative consequences, will obviously also be reduced by carbon taxes.

Regulation

Mandatory requirements, such as insulation and efficiency standards for buildings and appliances, cannot cater for differences in individual tastes or technology, and are therefore often criticized by economists as 'command-and-control' measures. With a high enough tax on carbon, it might be argued,

'Why not leave energy consumption decisions to private individuals?'. There are various arguments against this position. There is much potential for energy saving – both by households and industry – that would have been privately profitable at pre-recession prices, but these opportunities are frequently neglected for several reasons. Poorer households usually lack both the knowledge and funds and access to credit required for investment in energy saving and efficiency which would save money given likely future fossil fuel costs, in addition to reducing emissions. This problem has, of course, become much more severe with the credit and banking crisis of 2008. Furthermore, the considerable market power of traditional electricity suppliers, with large, centralized power stations, is threatened by the entry of small, decentralized units with combined heat and power (CHP), which can yield twice the energy efficiency of large, centralized units. The big producers have thus used their considerable influence to hinder the development of competing, decentralized and alternative power generation. These suppliers do not profit from energy saving, and so often do not encourage investment by customers that would reduce their sales.[1]

Safety standards for buildings, vehicles, toxic emissions and industry are widely accepted (though invariably resisted by lobbyists initially), so there is a need for public education about the role of energy saving in reducing the risks from continued global warming under business as usual. One component of this education would be to require explicit and transparent labelling that reveals the carbon 'footprint' of all products. This would help the growing number of environmentally responsible consumers to make their decisions accordingly, and perhaps alert others to the consequences of their irresponsibility. There is increasing evidence that price 'signals' on their own do not generate optimal decisions when economic actors are not completely informed about all the effects of their actions. Consumers are, for example, generally quite uncertain of their energy consumption and carbon impact from domestic, travel and other activities, and respond more to given financial or other incentives when they know the effects of their actions on the environment. 'Smart meters', which display the rate and cost of domestic energy use at any time, similarly encourage economy.[2]

Any kind of environmental regulation invariably faces vehement opposition from the biggest polluters, who have the most to lose. The benefits of lower emissions are generally spread over a large population and, in the short run at least, may be small or difficult to identify. Each of many individual beneficiaries has less reason – and fewer resources – to campaign for the regulation than the major polluters have for opposing it. The shifting of jobs and industry to a less regulated (and more polluted) environment is a common threat by businesses lobbying against environmental regulation, though there is little evidence that such regulation has so far been an important factor in outsourcing decisions.

Some types of emissions come from many widely dispersed sources, such as vehicles, household appliances and buildings, which would be difficult to monitor and attribute individually. Hence it is more sensible to tax fuel inputs, but mandatory standards for efficiency or average car emissions per kilometre can also help to accelerate the introduction of new and cleaner technologies, albeit in the face of customary protest from the affected manufacturers. When polluters, such as motorists, are actually a majority of the population, the political obstacles to serious mitigation measures are enormous. Major investments in public education, as well as in the alternatives of public transport and cycle facilities, are preconditions for progress. Simply banning inefficient incandescent light bulbs, pioneered by Australia, is a less controversial, long-overdue example that reduces both private costs and GHGs.

To realize the full potential of declining costs of alternative energy, new grid and other infrastructure will be needed, together with the appropriate regulatory framework, as discussed in Chapter 9. Efficiency standards can also provide an important incentive for innovation. Investment in research and development (R&D) to produce new energy-saving products and processes is often hampered by uncertainty about future prices and demand. Standards, on the other hand, provide a definite (and sometimes costly) target to meet if the firm is to stay in business, so appropriate innovation becomes a necessity, rather than a risky gamble on future market conditions. Precisely for this reason, business lobbies typically claim that new standards, such as planned EU limits on car emissions of CO_2, cannot be met in time without major losses of jobs and market share. Campaigns for weaker requirements, or postponement of their introduction, are usually successful. In particular, the German manufacturers of the largest and most polluting cars, and their political allies, blocked proposed tough new restrictions on carbon emissions for new cars in 2007, after the industry failed to meet voluntary targets.

Serious threats to health from substances – such as asbestos in buildings, tetraethyl lead in petrol or smoking in public rooms – have finally led to widespread bans in many countries, after decades of deceptive lobbying and false claims by the industries.[3] Lung cancer sometimes only emerges after decades of exposure to carcinogens, similar to the timeframe in which rising emissions of GHGs under business as usual will have disastrous effects on the poorest and most populous countries. Though most people in Europe, at least, believe that climate change is a serious problem, there is little awareness that non-toxic CO_2 is actually a lethal threat to many in the long run, endangering far more people than the worst of the traditional pollutants ever affected. And of course, there is no widespread support, as yet, for far-reaching and effective mitigation policies that do require changes in lifestyle and consumption patterns.

Another objection to tougher standards for energy efficiency is that low-income families may be unable to afford the initial investments required. Regulation may thus need to be supplemented with a programme of subsidies or tax relief for poorer households, to avoid inequity and increased inequality. Similar problems arise when oil prices rise dramatically, as they were doing until July 2008, or from carbon 'pricing' through taxes or permits.

There are many examples of well-intentioned but entirely counterproductive regulation. EU legislation requiring that five per cent of petrol and diesel consists of biofuel by 2010 (and 10 per cent by 2020), along with huge subsidies for first-generation biofuels in the EU and the US, are actually increasing carbon emissions – as well as food prices – and also accelerating tropical deforestation. We discuss biofuel costs and benefits in more detail in Chapter 9, and show how directly destructive – and expensive – current policy is, while diverting valuable resources from development of improved biofuels that do have a real potential for making a major contribution to mitigation.

Taxes and Permits

Establishing an appropriate price for carbon emissions is essential to provide the right incentives for abatement. Taxing all fossil fuels in the same way as petrol is taxed in the EU would be the simplest approach, one which individual countries could initiate independently and ultimately harmonize to achieve the ideal of a uniform, global carbon tax. Revenues from such a carbon tax could be used to reduce taxes on 'goods' such as labour, and hence avoid economic disruption and boost employment, without raising the total tax burden. Or, as noted climate scientist James Hansen has suggested, revenues could be returned in the form of equal shares to all citizens, in order to gain majority political support. However, this would be less effective economically (though perhaps easier to understand for many) than tax reform. A steadily rising carbon tax would provide a predictable planning framework, without the problems caused by fluctuating permit prices under a cap on emissions, as in the EU ETS. Though most economists favour shifting taxes from 'goods' to 'bads' such as emissions, there is very little public understanding of the benefits, and much irrational prejudice against any new tax.

As explained in Chapter 7, free distribution of carbon allowances (and subsequent trading) in the first phase of the EU ETS has allowed huge windfall profits to be made by the biggest polluters and had little effect on emissions. If permits were auctioned, as is planned for the second phase – instead of being freely allocated according to past emissions (grandfathering) – revenues would accrue directly to government, as in a tax system. Issuing too many permits and setting the cap on emissions at too high a level in the EU has meant that the price of carbon has been too low to provide much incentive for abatement so far. In the long run, the cap can be reduced from year to year, and the rising price of (fewer) permits over time would mimic the effects of an increasing carbon tax. However, a fundamental disadvantage of emissions trading is that by capping the quantity of emissions in any period, permit prices may fluctuate excessively with unforeseen shifts in demand. This uncertainty naturally increases the riskiness of investment.

These problems can be mitigated by combining features of taxes and emissions trading in 'hybrid' systems. For example, the fluctuation of permit prices can be restricted by 'banking' and 'borrowing' permits: supplying extra permits when the price exceeds an announced 'ceiling', and withdrawing permits when the price falls below a 'floor'. The extra permits are essentially 'borrowed' from future allocations, and caps in later years have to be reduced accordingly to maintain the target declining trend in emissions. Of course, these modifications would increase complexity and administrative cost, but also offer insurance to users and allow more efficient planning.

In a (pure) tax system, by contrast, the price of carbon is fixed in the short run – between pre-announced increases in the tax rate – and emissions fluctuate with changes in demand. Since the total stock of GHGs in the atmosphere is hardly affected by the flow of emissions in any short period of time, this is harmless provided that the long-term, target downward trend in emissions is maintained. However, the response of the economy to a particular path of rising carbon taxes is very difficult to predict, and also depends on a host of other complementary and regulatory measures. There is likely to be political pressure to raise a planned carbon tax if emissions are declining more slowly than anticipated, so uncertainty over the price of carbon can never be entirely eliminated. Carbon trading is often seen to be vulnerable to industry lobbying for free distribution, which is certainly eroding EU plans for permit auctions. However, any attempt to impose carbon taxes would also be subject to lobbying for tax breaks and exemptions by major energy users, so neither system is corruption-proof.

EU carbon trading is here to stay, and will no doubt be improved and extended over time. Perhaps even more important, new US President Barack Obama has committed to a national carbon cap-and-trade system, in a radical departure from the policy of his predecessor. Shortly before the election of Obama, economist Robert Stavins argued for a carbon cap-and-trade scheme that combined auctions with grandfathering as the only politically feasible route to realistic carbon pricing in the US.[4] Initial free distribution of half the permits issued (for the scheme to gain political acceptance) should be gradually reduced until all permits are auctioned. Stavins also favours a hybrid system to limit permit price fluctuations, and – in contrast to the EU ETS – a comprehensive, 'upstream' point of regulation, where all primary energy producers will require appropriate carbon allowances, as will importers of carbon-intensive products from countries without a similar scheme, such as China.

As EU politics are dominated by recession priorities in 2009, the US example and new leadership may play a key role in persuading other countries to adopt cap-and-trade systems of their own, though serious measures will probably be delayed everywhere by the recession. In the long run, various national or regional cap-and-trade systems should, of course, be harmonized to allow efficient international carbon trading, with the same carbon price in all markets. Such an evolutionary development from initially independent systems will provide governments with growing auction revenues to help gain public acceptance. This route seems to be politically much more realistic than plans which depend on far-reaching and comprehensive international agreement in order to implement an ideal, harmonized global cap-and-trade (or carbon tax) system. In the meantime, and post-recession, fossil fuel prices will surely rise again, which will have at least some of the effects of appropriate carbon pricing (though with obvious disadvantages). Of course, more rapid alternative energy development will also slow down the increase of fossil fuel prices.

Many variants of global cap-and-trade have been proposed, usually based on the idea of fair or equal per capita distribution of allowances to all countries or individuals. Rich nations with high per capita emissions would then have to purchase extra allowances from poor countries, so carbon trading would be coupled with large flows of funds or aid from the developed to the developing economies. Politically, this represents a major additional obstacle to attaining significant carbon reduction in the advanced economies. These proposals are reviewed by environmental writer Oliver Tickell in his book *Kyoto 2*; it appears that there is little prospect of their realization at the moment.

Unfortunately, the same problem arises for Tickell's preferred alternative, which is a global auction of permits to primary energy producers. This would be administered by an international authority that would also distribute the proceeds to help the victims of climate change and invest in alternative energy. Such a body would require enormous powers and the full cooperation of national governments to avoid cheating, and, with around a trillion dollars of annual income to distribute worldwide, would also be subject to immense lobbying pressure for allocation of the funds. Given the weakness of today's United Nations, and the strength of international divisions, it seems utopian to expect national governments to relinquish control of such gigantic permit auction revenues from their domestic energy producers.

Conclusions

Despite the theoretical advantages of carbon taxes, other countries are more likely to follow the example of the US and EU, and develop their own carbon trading systems, that are more acceptable for the industries most affected with at least some initial free distribution of permits, and a gradual extension of auctioning. Harmonizing differing national cap-and-trade systems in the course of time – as more countries introduce carbon trading – is likely to be much easier than attempting to install 'top–down', global cap-and-trade in the aftermath of Kyoto. What is needed to contain climate change is a meaningful carbon price that complements other measures, such as shifting subsidies from fossil fuels to alternative energy, and appropriate regulation and education.

The Costs of Climate Change and the Benefits of Mitigation

Cost–Benefit Analysis

Economists have made many attempts to compare the costs of reducing greenhouse gas emissions with the expected benefits of limiting damage from climate change in the long run. This kind of 'cost–benefit analysis' generally assumes only relatively minor monetary costs of warming (a few per cent of GDP), in a much richer – and far distant – future, and claims that more conventional investment yields greater benefits to future generations than major mitigation efforts today. Thus American economist William Nordhaus, one of the first to use cost–benefit analysis in a climate change context, recommends a slowly rising carbon tax starting at about $30 per tonne of carbon, adding only three per cent to an oil price of around $100 per barrel (which was the average price in 2008). This is very little compared to oil prices that have risen several times over in recent years, and thus amounts essentially to 'do nothing now' (the global recession in 2008 brought collapsing prices, but the upward trend will probably continue when the economy recovers).

Nordhaus claims that this minimal tax is 'optimal' and will result in a CO_2 concentration of around 550ppm and a temperature increase of 2.6 degrees by 2100. Since he neglects carbon and albedo feedbacks, however, these numbers are actually far too low (they were based on now out-of-date science from the IPCC's third report). Nordhaus offers no discussion of the ethics of an 'optimality' which is likely to impose starvation on billions of the world's poorest people, though he does admit to ignoring regional impacts, where most of the damage to developing countries would be done. He seems to be unaware of all the scientific evidence for the rapidly rising risks of runaway warming and future catastrophe unless drastic mitigation policy is started very soon. Indeed, he makes the entirely absurd claim that business as usual for the rest of the century, which would render much of the planet uninhabitable as mean temperatures rose by five degrees or perhaps much more, would only 'cost' around 2.5 per cent of global GDP! Crucially, Nordhaus and most other economists completely neglect the most obvious ethical and distributional issues of large-scale loss of life from catastrophic climate change and agricultural collapse under continued business as usual.[1]

Though using a similar basic framework, the first official government review of the economic costs of climate change came to very different conclusions. Named after its lead author Lord Nicholas Stern, a former chief economist of the World Bank, the Stern Review generated extensive publicity with its warning of major damage to the future world economy from continued business as usual. Stern argues for urgent mitigation policies, including a substantial carbon tax three to four times higher than that advocated by Nordhaus. The latter, like other economists in the do-nothing-now camp, claims that Stern's methodology is inconsistent and his results unconvincing. Ironically, however, these critics have actually missed the most serious weaknesses and inconsistencies of the Review, which in many respects follows their standard methodology.

As in previous attempts to model the economics of climate change, Stern uses the usual utilitarian approach to social welfare that we discussed in Chapter 4, adding up just the utility of the *average*, and growing, consumption of future generations. However, he departs from earlier work by arguing on ethical grounds that these future generations should all be treated essentially equally, or given almost the same 'weight' in current decisions about mitigation. This assumption of almost equal treatment of infinitely many future generations has the very odd implication that most of the costs of climate change (due to just a slightly lower consumption for our much richer descendants) occur after 2200. Thus, like his critics, Stern thinks the economy will grow for ever at similar rates to the past, but differs in being concerned about our immeasurably richer, far distant descendants losing some of their astronomical incomes because of climate change.[2]

In his 2008 Ely Lecture summary and update of his Review, and in his 2009 popular book *A Blueprint for a Safer Planet*, Stern tentatively admits the implausibility of some of these results, and suggests giving more egalitarian weight to the cost of climate change for earlier generations because they are poorer (but *not* just because they are born earlier). He emphasizes the necessary ethical dimension of climate policy, which is noticeably lacking in the work of Nordhaus and others, but then proceeds to ignore the most serious ethical implications of a disastrous fall in world food supply. In one of his last footnotes he remarks, 'Emissions deeply damage and sometimes kill others.'[3] However, loss of human life in particular is systematically neglected in the body of the lecture, and only briefly mentioned in the *Review*, in contrast to frequently emphasized ethical concern for the consumption of all unborn future generations. In his *Blueprint*, Stern sees large-scale migration as the main human cost of climate change.

Stern and other economists are well aware that the poorest countries in tropical or southern latitudes will bear the brunt of climate change, which we discussed in detail in Chapter 5. Nevertheless, Stern assumes that the worst possible case of climate disaster (which he claims is very unlikely) is just a permanent loss of 20 per cent of average global GDP, and this beginning only in a distant future, when people will still be much richer than today, even after such losses. The Review mentions 'non-market' impacts on health and the environment, and offers some discussion of increased mortality in poor countries due to disease and malnutrition as warming reduces agricultural productivity. However, the loss of life is assumed to be on a very small scale, leading to only minor adjustment of the welfare measure based on average global consumption.

There is thus no recognition of the possibility that climate change under business as usual could interact with already serious – and worsening – problems of water shortage and soil erosion, and cause a truly catastrophic collapse of food production in many developing countries. Given the current precarious state of agriculture and water supply in many hot and arid regions, without major policy changes this is likely to happen long before the mid-century target date for substantial emission reductions proposed by the UK and other EU governments. Billions of the world's poorest people (in a much larger future population) would then face starvation, as we explained in Chapter 3. Major disasters of this kind do not fit into the utilitarian framework, as we discuss below. Stern and others have admitted the abstract possibility of catastrophic outcomes, but only as the result of very unlikely, extreme climatic events, and without relating them to the currently developing, real threat to global food supply. Most seriously, neither Stern nor his many critics seem to realize how even his 'strong' policy proposals virtually guarantee a *very high* probability of catastrophic events, rather than the 'insurance' against worst cases that he claims.

Like most economists, Stern assumes that material economic growth will continue indefinitely, so that average global GDP and consumption will be around 12 times the present level by 2200. He expects China's real income to grow by 'a factor of ten to fifteen' already by 2050. This is ecologically totally implausible in a world where many of the ecosystems most important for our survival are already close to collapse as a result of human activity. GDP and other measures of economic growth make no allowance for the use or destruction of natural resources, and the conventional projection of past growth rates into the future depends on unlimited substitution of knowledge and capital for environmental services and resources. Occasionally Stern mentions in passing that continued business as usual with growing emissions might *reduce* future incomes, or cause negative growth, but he never really develops this, although the scenario is so much more plausible than his conventional growth assumptions.

Stern also follows traditional economics that assumes happiness (utility or subjective wellbeing) will increase indefinitely with individual consumption. This completely ignores the huge body of evidence from the last 30 years – discussed in Chapter 6 – that economic growth alone does little to increase average happiness or life satisfaction in developed countries. Even in China, average subjective wellbeing has declined over two decades of double-digit growth.

On this evidence, reducing the rate of GDP growth in rich economies by investing more in sustainable technologies (including energy-saving measures), would safeguard, rather than lower, future welfare (by helping to avert the risk of future disaster), in contrast to conventional political and economic wisdom. In addition, such investment is generally more labour-intensive than traditional use of fossil fuels for labour-saving technologies, and would thus create jobs and help to counter the effects of the global financial crisis and economic downturn that erupted in late 2008. Even in recent periods of prolonged growth, about 10 per cent of the labour force in highly industrialized economies have remained jobless but wanting to work (though not all are officially unemployed), which is a major determinant of unhappiness.

In developing countries, on the other hand, growth can raise average wellbeing, and improve the lives of the poorest people in particular, though most of the benefits are often appropriated by the rich. Thus more aid and 'greener technology' transfer from the rich countries could foster sustainable development, with both short-term welfare gains from poverty reduction and environmental improvements and long-term benefits from reduced warming. Though the 'co-benefits' from many greener technologies are widely recognized, Stern and many economists underestimate their potential to reduce the assumed high costs of a rapid, large reduction of carbon emissions. As we show in detail below, much of the investment required for rapid mitigation would actually have major short-term welfare and employment benefits, in addition to slowing warming in the long run, if political obstacles could be overcome.

If no new mitigation policies are implemented, business as usual is likely to increase the use of coal and dirty, non-conventional oil from tar sands, which may well double emissions of GHGs by mid century (and also double the stock of pre-industrial greenhouse gases in the atmosphere somewhat earlier). Stern mainly considers a 50 per cent reduction of current emissions by 2050, which he claims could stabilize atmospheric GHGs at 500ppm carbon dioxide equivalent (including other GHGs – about 450ppm of just CO_2). According to his Ely Lecture, this is almost certain to raise global mean temperature above the crucial two-degree threshold (over the pre-industrial level). In fact, the latest science suggests that carbon and other feedbacks neglected by Stern are likely to generate runaway warming with much higher temperatures under his weak and late target for cutting emissions.

Recent models[4] predict that the two-degree mark will ultimately be breached even at the current level of nearly 390ppm CO_2, so the prudent level required to largely eliminate the risk of catastrophic damage and loss of future life should eventually be substantially less, particularly when the role of aerosol cooling is included, as we develop below. The risk also depends on the rate of mitigation – delay could easily trigger irreversible feedbacks and runaway warming – so the essential target for minimal risk is widely agreed (by many scientists and environmentalists, though not by most economists) to be a cut in global emissions by about 80–90 per cent by 2020–2030. Stern's preferred 'strong mitigation policy' of a 50 per cent cut by 2050 thus seems more like a recipe for runaway warming, planetary disaster and assured destruction of the world's poorest peoples.

The wealthy Northern nations might indeed enjoy milder winters and longer growing seasons in a rapidly warming climate. But they would hardly be able to avoid the resulting chaos and conflict unscathed in an extensively nuclear, chemically or biologically armed world, as not just millions but billions of the poorest inhabitants starved. Refugee and international security problems on an unprecedented and unimaginable scale are likely to dwarf the much-vaunted benefits of technological progress in the advanced economies. Reducing such threats – as well as large-scale loss of future lives in the poorest countries – to a percentage of average global GDP has no ethical or economic justification, and Stern's calculations follow previous attempts that avoid these issues by giving little weight to the regional and distributional impact of catastrophic warming.

Stern repeatedly dismisses the target of stabilizing greenhouse gases at close to present levels as prohibitively costly, although there is a substantial probability that various feedbacks could – even after stabilization at the current level – still push temperatures more than two degrees above pre-industrial levels. Above this threshold, the dangers of further carbon and ice-albedo feedbacks causing runaway warming rise rapidly. Stern actually emphasizes in his Ely Lecture that 'key positive feedback from the carbon cycle ... has been omitted from the projected concentration increases quoted here'. This is an extraordinary admission, as the crucial importance of carbon and other feedbacks has been well understood (though not quantified) for some time. Thus Stern is effectively admitting that even his minimal targets for emissions reduction by 2050 are very unlikely to achieve his objectives for stabilizing atmospheric greenhouse gases – targets that, by his own admission, carry a very high risk of catastrophic outcomes.[5]

Stern does deserve considerable credit for emphasizing that major economic costs of climate change are inevitable under continued business as usual, though many other writers had done so before him, and their pioneering work is largely ignored in his writings. In spite of the problems with his methodology, the publicity received by this first official review of the costs of climate change has surely helped to ensure that the threat is now widely acknowledged, at least in developed countries. Stern also emphasizes the urgency of serious carbon pricing and other, complementary mitigation measures and the huge costs of the delay entailed in waiting for new evidence or technology. These recommendations stand in stark contrast to the minimal and useless tax measures proposed by Nordhaus and others, who understand neither the full implications of current climate science nor the current threat to food supply, and discount future disasters to trivial present values. In his *Blueprint*, Stern also provides clear and scathing critique of these economists as 'fundamentally misleading and often simply incorrect in both their application of economics and representation of the conclusions of the science' (p77).

It is thus all the more surprising that Stern fails to support the more ambitious policies that are needed to avoid the risk of agricultural collapse in the medium term, a failure which he justifies by far too high estimates of the cost of radical mitigation policies. In his *Blueprint*, Stern recognizes that scientists such as James Hansen have made 'strong and serious arguments' for much lower targets than his own. However, his ultimate defence seems to be that 'to push harder for a lower target could disrupt the possibility of agreement in the very near future' (p150). He goes on to claim that his weak target is actually 'very strong in terms of action necessary to achieve it', and with the discovery of new technologies could later be revised down. In fact, the technologies for energy saving, conservation agriculture and planting trees are simple, labour-intensive, already available and ideal for low-cost employment-generation in the global recession. Ironically, Stern has himself made a strong case for a 'green fiscal stimulus' to combat both the economic crisis and climate change, but unfortunately misses some of the most promising components.

Stern and other economists who claim that drastic measures would incur huge economic costs simply ignore the evidence that switching vast existing subsidies from industrial agriculture and fossil fuels to conservation agriculture, afforestation and alternative energy would generate massive cost *reductions* under expected future fossil fuel prices. Thus environmentalist Lester Brown, President of the Earth Policy Institute in Washington, DC (never cited by Stern), has repeatedly outlined a practical though radical, low-risk and low-cost global mitigation strategy to reduce emissions by 80 per cent by 2020. The latest version, 'Plan B 3.0', calls for large-scale 'mobilization' to mass-produce available alternative technologies, which does depend on a major shift in public opinion and political awareness. These programmes have much in common with our recommendations here, though we put more emphasis on the role of agriculture, the economic fundamentals and incentives, and the short-term co-benefits to health and welfare from abatement measures, in addition to slowing global warming.

Lack of Interest and Rates of Interest

One might have expected that Stern's neglect of catastrophic climate change impact and loss of life in the poorest regions would have attracted critical attention. Instead, symptomatic perhaps of limited interest in the welfare of the poorest and the ethics of global redistribution, most of the response by economists has focused on what they see as his exaggerated concern for the welfare of future, richer generations. Stern follows ethical philosophers in refusing to 'discount' the welfare of future generations according to market-based interest rates. By contrast, many economists believe that even very large costs of climate change in the distant future, say 100 years hence, do not justify much expenditure on mitigation at the moment. Instead, they claim, conventional investment (at current rates of interest) would have a greater pay-off after 100 years than the same expenditure on abatement, yielding larger returns (in the form of higher output) than the expected costs of climate change.

On these assumptions, it would be possible to compensate those who suffered the costs of future warming, and even have a surplus left over for the lucky rest of the world's population in cooler Northern climes. How this is supposed to work when many future lives are lost, not just a few per cent of average incomes or GDP – so that the losers cannot be compensated – is never even mentioned, let alone explained. All this assumes that close to present rates of material growth and interest will be maintained by the magic of technological progress over the next 100–200 years – which is itself preposterous under any consideration of ecological constraints, even without the threat of climate change. It makes even less sense to suppose that the most vulnerable inhabitants of the future world – probably descendants of today's poorest peoples – will all survive climate catastrophes to enjoy their compensation.

Stern does recognize that ethical concern for all members of all (much richer) future generations – and not just for our own direct descendants – is hardly consistent with the almost complete indifference shown by rich countries to the fate of billions of people in extreme poverty today. As economist Eric Neumayer has pointed out, mitigation policy by the most developed countries today is not only about protecting the consumption of our (even richer) descendants tomorrow. More fundamentally, our investment in mitigation today is also a form of deferred foreign aid, for the benefit of the poorest countries and populations that will suffer most from future climate catastrophe.[6]

Economists' models of climate change assume that all costs can be evaluated in money terms, so future damage can be compensated by higher incomes. Furthermore, relative prices remain constant, because there is essentially only one 'output', representing average global GDP, in the models used by Stern and others. While this approach obviously fails when loss of life results from warming, it also quickly breaks down for simple economic reasons when relative prices change.[7] Thus Stern notes that agriculture accounts for about 24 per cent of global GDP, and as a simple example to illustrate the importance of food prices relative to other goods, we next consider a world twice as rich as ours in terms of average income, with the same share for agriculture. Suppose now that higher temperatures, desertification and droughts reduced food production by half, for a number of years in succession. If prices were to remain constant, our hypothetical descendants who lose 12 per cent of twice our income would still be much richer than we are – to be precise, 76 per cent richer.

It should be immediately obvious what is wrong with this calculation. Wheat prices nearly trebled from late 2006 to early 2008, and other grain prices nearly doubled, for a number of reasons. Demand in the big developing countries has been growing rapidly, as middle-class consumers adopt Western diets and switch to meat and dairy products, requiring much more grain to produce than vegetarian diets. There have been droughts and harvest shortfalls in Australia and other exporting countries, and a third of corn output has been diverted to heavily subsidized ethanol production in the US.[8] If the world's total grain harvest were drastically reduced, say cut in half by accumulating adverse effects of runaway warming and water shortages in the major producing countries, following business-as-usual economic growth, then food prices would rise many times over, eroding the real purchasing power of average incomes.

Adaptation by extending cultivated areas in temperate zones, switching from grain to higher-yielding potatoes if blight-resistant varieties were developed and reducing meat consumption could obviously mitigate the impact. However, really large-scale and prolonged droughts in the hot and arid growing areas that feed the most populous countries would still have catastrophic outcomes. The poorest urban populations, who will probably still be living at subsistence levels, and unable to grow much for themselves, would depend on food aid to survive. Even the middle classes would have to spend most of their income on food and so would have little left over for other purchases, and thus aggregate demand and sales everywhere would collapse. As business revenues plummeted, most employees could no longer be paid, and unemployment would soon spiral out of control. Falling incomes and purchasing power would ultimately limit price rises, but not before almost everything edible had become unaffordable for the poorest urban populations everywhere. Many people would have to spend most of their time searching for – and trying to grow – basic foods for survival. Even if wasteful, intensive stock-rearing – and overeating by the rich – stopped in a world where few would be able to afford meat, a disaster of this magnitude would almost certainly condemn the poorest inhabitants of the poorest countries to mass starvation.

It is important to emphasize that this scenario does not depend on very improbable, extreme warming outcomes, or even just a more likely, long period of rising emissions and collapsing ice-caps. Agricultural productivity in much of the world is already unsustainable with current methods, as 'water mining' steadily lowers water tables in most irrigated areas. If warming continues unabated, climate models predict water shortages will gradually worsen, accelerating soil erosion, and leaving farmers in arid regions increasingly vulnerable to ever more frequent droughts and other extreme weather events. The Fourth Global Environment Outlook (GEO 4), published by the United Nations Environment Programme (UNEP) in 2007, sums up the evidence for expected dire effects of unmitigated warming. The UN's 'synthesis report' summarizes the IPCC's Fourth Assessment Report of early 2007, but follows the most recent science in warning of 'impacts that are abrupt and irreversible' and 'very large'.[9]

Such clear language had been missing in the earlier reports, which omitted the most threatening possibilities for which numerical probabilities could not be calculated. In particular, the possible collapse of the polar ice sheets is admitted in the synthesis, though it was excluded from the earlier chapter on climate science under pressure from the major polluting nations. Just when the crucial 'threshold' is reached, at which point catastrophic conditions destroy a substantial proportion of the world's already threatened harvests, cannot be forecast. However, the present trend of rapidly worsening water shortages in many of the hotter growing areas suggests that the recent doubling of wheat and other grain prices until the financial crash of 2008 is just the first portent of impending storm in the world's food markets.

The Value of Life

Economic models of the cost of climate change typically ignore the likely species extinctions and loss of life in the future, though Stern claims to include such 'non-market' impacts in his worst case – the 'permanent' loss of 20 per cent of future GDP, though still on a path of unlimited growth. He gives no hint on the extent of future loss of life – human and non-human – included in his damage estimates, nor how these fatalities and extinctions are evaluated, while also failing to realize just how serious the threat to agriculture really is. The probability of the worst kind of catastrophic outcome is assumed to be very small by Stern and other economists who have considered such cases. In fact, a careful reading of the evidence reviewed in Chapter 3 suggests that, under continued business as usual, major food crises are virtually inevitable in the not too distant future, though their precise timing is likely to remain beyond the reach of forecasting models.

Most economists agree that willingness to pay (WTP) for investment to reduce a small risk of fatality can be interpreted as a measure of the 'value of a statistical life' (VSL), provided that full and transparent information is available to all affected parties. Thus, suppose a community of 10,000 people suffers on average two random fatalities from an environmental hazard every year. A partial clean-up could reduce the risk to one annual fatality, thus saving one statistical life every year, at the cost of an additional tax of $500 to be paid by each individual annually. Realistically, eliminating the hazard entirely would be much more costly, and require an extra annual tax burden of, say, $2000 per person. Assuming similar incomes and preferences in the community, a 'reasonable' result of democratic voting might be the decision to save one (statistical) life per year, at a total cost of $5 million (500×10,000), rather than spending $20 million to save two lives. Our community is thus valuing one statistical life at more than $5 million, but less than $10 million (while remembering that the risk faced is very small, comparable to the risk of, say, a traffic fatality).

This decision is reasonable, because it roughly accords with real examples of local, democratic decision-making, common in Switzerland, and with results from detailed questionnaires that ask people about their WTP to reduce small risks in hypothetical but plausible situations. These results, of course, depend on income, and in poor countries most people simply cannot afford to spend much on life-saving investments, even to reduce very high levels of risk to life and health or ensure such basics as cleaner air or potable water. It follows that the 'value' (in this sense) of their statistical lives is much smaller than in rich countries.

Although it is widely recognized by all ethical systems that human survival chances should not depend on income, this principle is almost universally violated by the strong positive relationship between relative income and survival chances in all countries and at all ages. Thus in developed countries with the most unequal distribution of income, such as the UK or US, average life expectancy varies by 10–15 years or more between the most deprived and the most affluent areas, with large differences in infant mortality.[10] As the income gap between rich and poor in these (and many other) countries has grown in recent decades, under the combined impact of neo-liberal policies and globalization, so the discrepancy in health, life expectancy and educational outcomes between the deprived and the privileged has also increased.

As discussed in earlier chapters, some (though still insufficient) attention has been paid to the plight of the poorest nations, where most of the world's nearly 3 billion poorest people live on less than two dollars per day, and suffer high rates of mortality and debilitating disease. Economists such as Jeffrey Sachs have explained that a relatively modest aid effort by the rich nations could remove the worst poverty, and drastically reduce mortality rates.[11] Yet neo-liberals oppose aid for the poorest countries and populations, many voters appear to be indifferent to their fate, and Western governments have failed to raise aid for developing countries to meaningful levels.

This indifference has no more ethical justification than overt racism, but it still remains the dominant attitude to the fate of the world's poorest inhabitants and their descendants under unabated global warming. Part of this indifference is undoubtedly due to widespread lack of knowledge about the dire consequences of climate change, for Southern agriculture in particular. Current poverty in the developing world has been given extensive publicity, but with little enduring response. Altruism and empathy have evolved as essential for social cooperation, but largely in the context of communities that share ethnic or linguistic heritage, which is an inadequate basis for social justice in our global society.[12]

Climate Catastrophe and the Precautionary Principle

Continued business-as-usual emissions of GHGs (and other activities) threaten the survival chances of billions of the most vulnerable members of present and future generations, and violate the most basic principles of justice and human rights. Rawlsian justice, as discussed in Chapter 6, implies that the *welfare* of the worst off (which obviously includes survival) should be maximized. This is, of course, a long-term goal, and one which appears to be unattainably utopian under current lack of concern in the rich countries and resulting political constraints. Economics can help to minimize the costs of achieving this goal, but cannot replace the ethical judgements required. Economic models of 'optimal' intergenerational welfare based on *average* income per head, as used by Stern and others, make only minor adjustments for the huge and growing inequalities in income and welfare, both within and between countries. These models are thus really not relevant to the crucial distributional issues of life-saving aid for the most vulnerable, both currently and in the future.

The ethics of priority for saving life cannot say precisely how much of our consumption we should sacrifice today in order to alleviate current poverty and to reduce emissions to protect future lives. The answer depends on how much 'weight' we give to the welfare and the lives of the poor, compared to our own consumption, and on how we evaluate their future survival chances. The social context is also highly relevant. Collective action is obviously much more effective than anything that a few individuals can achieve in the short run. However, political commitment and consensus on originally controversial issues is usually built upon the pioneering efforts and initiatives of individual campaigners who are brave enough to defy majority prejudice and, frequently, defamation. The ethical ideal of offering equal opportunities to the currently most deprived and most vulnerable is obviously constrained in practice by political feasibility and personal commitments, habits and perceptions.

The argument for reducing emissions much more rapidly than suggested by Stern or current government targets is strongly supported by enlightened self-interest. Runaway warming poses less well-defined dangers to the rich Northern nations than to the poor South, but to expect continuing growth, peace and prosperity while the poorest starve, failing states proliferate and world order collapses is a dangerous delusion. The potential for destructive – and ultimately even global – conflict inherent in climate change is now being increasingly emphasized by international organizations such as the United Nations Environmental Programme.[13]

The award of the Nobel Peace Prize in 2007 to former US Vice President Al Gore and the UN climate panel IPCC, for their work in disseminating the scientific findings about climate change, underlines the national and international security issues involved. Most who favour little or no action on climate change now have wildly optimistic views on survival under runaway warming, based on seriously inadequate understanding of the science of feedbacks and consequences for agriculture in developing countries. Indifference to the plight of the poorest countries is rarely admitted directly, but rather camouflaged under protestations to the contrary, and buttressed by complaints about the ineffectiveness of aid to countries suffering under weak government, failing institutions or corrupt dictatorships.[14]

While the possibility of a large-scale collapse of food production in hot and arid areas has been largely neglected, a few economists such as Frank Ackerman (whose book *Can We Afford the Future* offers a much better guide to policy than Stern's *Blueprint*) and theorist Martin Weitzman have begun to take seriously the risk of truly catastrophic, runaway warming that scientists have long emphasized. This could be triggered by carbon and albedo feedbacks, particularly if the crucial two-degree threshold were exceeded, leading to irreversible break-up of the ice caps and release of most of the carbon currently sequestered in permafrost and peat bogs. In the very worst case, warming oceans would destabilize the huge offshore deposits of frozen methane hydrates, ultimately releasing many times the current atmospheric content of GHGs and raising global mean temperatures by 10 degrees or more. The last similar event, 55 million years ago, caused the extinction of most species, while the ice-free poles enjoyed tropical temperatures. Much of the Earth would be inundated or otherwise uninhabitable, and civilization as we know it would cease to exist.

This is a longer-term threat than the much more immediate dangers to agriculture that we have been emphasizing, but it is nonetheless realistic. The 'precautionary principle' favoured by most environmentalists has also been proposed by Ackerman (and more tentatively by Weitzman) as the appropriate response to the possibility of catastrophe. This essentially means that the overriding policy priority should be to eliminate catastrophic risk altogether, whatever the current cost, and without worrying about unknown or allegedly small probabilities of catastrophe. Similarly, trying to put a monetary value on the lives of large numbers of people in future generations (who cannot participate in these decisions), and then trying to calculate their present value in order to decide how much to spend (or not to spend) on saving their lives, is both nonsensical and thoroughly unethical.[15] Furthermore, as we show next, the money costs of 'buying insurance for the planet' are far from being prohibitive, but instead will yield long-term monetary and welfare benefits, in addition to insuring against climate catastrophe.

The Co-Benefits and Political Costs of Mitigation

While Stern is aware that the co-benefits of mitigation might substantially reduce (or even outweigh) some of the direct costs of reducing emissions, he insists that stabilizing the stock of atmospheric greenhouse gases at close to their present level would be prohibitively expensive. Stern and the IPCC show little understanding of the sheer scale of these co-benefits. Economist Dieter Helm, who criticizes Stern, as we do, for underestimating the costs of climate change and incorrectly equating GDP with welfare, also claims that Stern underestimates the costs of mitigation by neglecting the political obstacles or 'policy costs' which we have also been emphasizing. However, all these authors neglect the potential for mitigation and co-benefits in agricultural reform.[16]

As we shall see, cutting current emissions by half or more through a global switch to conservation and no-till agriculture, energy saving, and halting the burning of biomass would not only stabilize greenhouse gases for the near future, but also yield huge present and future direct welfare gains to the poorest populations. One of the largest anthropogenic source of emissions is biomass burning, most of which also causes severe local environmental damage and health problems.[17] While some biomass is replaced, the often illegal burning of mainly tropical forest for agriculture (often for export to developed countries) is believed to generate about 20 per cent of global carbon emissions. Deforestation also destroys invaluable resources of biodiversity with many long-term uses, while generally only yielding very short-term profits from logging or agriculture.

A major source of emissions is biomass burning for domestic cooking (and some heating) in poor rural populations throughout the developing world. The resulting (mostly indoor) air pollution causes at least 1.5 million premature deaths per year, according to the World Health Organization. In addition, collecting firewood and other biomass occupies much of the working time and energy of the poorest people, time that is diverted from productive activity in subsistence agriculture. Much organic matter that would improve soil fertility is burnt instead, and already sparse tree cover and other vegetation is constantly depleted for use as fuel.

Cheap solar-powered cookers, such as the new prize-winning 'Kyoto box' costing only five dollars, could replace most of this wasteful and destructive activity throughout the Southern developing countries. These simple cookers could be manufactured locally with small initial Western assistance. Since the poorest households do not have the resources even for such a small investment, though it would yield huge private benefits in time-saving and better health, there is a need for modest aid to disseminate this technology, which is entirely justified by the resulting global reductions in carbon emissions. Cultural attitudes often hinder the transition to new techniques, so education has to be part of the programme.[18]

The second innovation that would have massive co-benefits as well as substantial abatement effects is regenerative, low-tillage organic agriculture, or conservation agriculture. As explained in Chapter 3, soils under industrial agriculture are everywhere suffering progressive erosion and becoming net carbon emitters, while 'water mining' for irrigation is depleting irreplaceable aquifers. This process can be reversed if traditional ploughing is abandoned (or reduced) and replaced by cover-cropping with a legume that fertilizes the soil by fixing nitrogen, prevents erosion of exposed surface soil, retains water and smothers weeds. Remaining weeds are controlled by rolling the cover crop, followed by directly planting into uncultivated topsoil. Extensive trials at the Rodale Institute in Pennsylvania show that fuel, energy and chemical inputs are all dramatically reduced, yields increase, and erosion is halted by this technique. At the same time, organic material from the cover crops accumulates, and soils will thus sequester carbon, and become net 'sinks' for many decades into the future. Around one tonne of carbon per hectare can be captured annually by 'organic no-till', twice as much as under conventional no-till with substantial chemical inputs, while soils become more resistant to both drought and flooding. Composting biowaste can substantially increase the amount of carbon sequestered. Depending on local conditions, complementary agroforestry, with trees or bushes in rows between conventional crops, can amplify all these benefits.

A large-scale programme of education is required to convince farmers around the world of the many benefits of no-till and other conservation methods. As well as the deeply ingrained habits of traditional ploughing practices, there is strong opposition from agribusiness to overcome, as lucrative markets from currently expanding, high-input industrial agriculture are threatened. Similarly, there are large profits from illegal logging and deforestation to create new agricultural land, though efficient sustainable management would yield much greater returns in the long term. To overcome these obstacles, a concerted international effort and substantial aid flows are needed, but this expenditure would generate far greater, direct economic co-benefits. In addition, energy saving through more efficient appliances and standards, the general adoption of no-till agriculture, and avoidance of most biomass burning could together reduce carbon emissions by at least half.[19]

Since about half of our carbon emissions are still being absorbed by natural sinks, even partial implementation of these measures, most of which are relatively cheap and easy to implement, could thus stabilize the stock of atmospheric greenhouse gases at around current levels. Fairly complete implementation of this programme would bring emissions down to *below* the rate of absorption by natural sinks. Thus the total amount of GHGs in the atmosphere could actually begin to fall, provided that these sinks do not deteriorate too rapidly. Adding really large-scale agroforestry and sustainable reforestation of non-agricultural land could remove billions of tonnes of carbon annually from the atmosphere as trees matured. Timber, biogas and biochar production could yield further benefits, as discussed below, so the net cost of sequestering carbon in growing trees is likely to be far below the cost of still-undeveloped technology for carbon capture and storage from coal power.

Our focus on the neglected role of agriculture and biomass shows that instead of the very high costs claimed by Stern and other economists, simple and practical mitigation policies would yield huge net economic and welfare gains, after some modest redistribution from rich to poor countries. In particular, the adoption of conservation methods will raise the resilience of food supply in the face of the more frequent extreme weather conditions that are unavoidable in the medium term, however rapidly we reduce emissions. With sufficient international agreement, all this could be achieved quite rapidly in view of the relatively small new investments required, thus giving the world a little more time for the substantial investments required to reduce the remaining emissions from transport and power generation.

Just how important this further reduction is becomes clear from the latest modelling of ocean carbon-cycle feedbacks, which shows that even if emissions are reduced by 90 per cent by 2050, the critical two-degree threshold will eventually be exceeded. The authors of this simulation conclude that avoiding this risk will require further carbon extraction from the atmosphere and subsequent sequestration.[20] The surface waters of the oceans, which form the main natural sink for CO_2, may be close to saturation, so the current natural rate of removal of about half our emissions may decline rapidly. This also shows just how inadequate are the official abatement targets of the EU and UK Government, as well as Stern's preferred paths of emissions reduction. Going beyond the relatively high risks of exceeding the threshold already found by previous climate models under proposed targets, the new results imply that the critical temperature threshold will almost certainly be reached sometime this century unless a major programme of rapid mitigation is started very soon.

We have argued that more than half of current emissions could be cut with the help of modest aid flows to the developing countries, general adoption of conservation agriculture, energy saving, and halting deforestation and biomass burning. This would also yield major net financial, welfare and ecological benefits to the world, even in the short run, as well as stabilizing atmospheric GHGs. A rapid switch to no-till agriculture could probably be implemented with a small fraction of the 200–300 billion dollars of subsidies currently going annually to the richest farmers in Europe and North America and supporting destructive industrial agriculture. Similar sums of taxpayers' money captured by fossil fuel lobbies represent potential *savings* in state expenditures that would substantially reduce emissions in the medium term. Subsidies for bioethanol production in the US and biodiesel in the EU are helping to push up food prices, and probably increase net carbon emissions, because the process is so inefficient and depends on high-input industrial agriculture.[21] Gradually shifting taxation from labour to carbon, or extending cap-and-trade schemes, would obviously accelerate reform.

Similar arguments apply to the transport sector, which produces around 15 per cent of the carbon emissions in modern economies. Most urban trips are less than five kilometres and easy to cycle, particularly if cycle lanes are provided and motorized traffic is restricted by large-scale pedestrian areas. Congestion charging, as in London, has reduced traffic by only about 20 per cent, and is thus an inadequate alternative to the extensive pedestrian areas and switch from cars to bicycles which have transformed cities such as Amsterdam, Florence and Freiburg in mainland Europe. Cycle rickshaws have been spreading from Asia to Western capitals, growing rapidly in popularity in London after the congestion charge reduced traffic. Together with the cheap, street-based cycle rental facilities that are expanding in many European cities, these modes could replace motorized traffic for most short trips. Hybrid vehicles with extra batteries that could be charged overnight from alternative or 'clean' generating capacity, which is under-utilized during such off-peak periods, could provide further, emission-free urban transport.

In addition to substantial energy savings and less pollution, a large-scale shift from cars to cycling and walking would have major health benefits in fighting what is ever more frequently described as the global obesity epidemic. Thus a report by the UK Government think-tank Foresight predicts that 60 per cent of the male population will be obese by 2050 if present trends continue, with devastating consequences for health and the costs of care, and there are similar trends in many other countries.[22] As well as the health benefits from more exercise, a drastic reduction of urban traffic would alleviate much of the local air pollution, which is estimated to cause about 40,000 premature deaths in the UK, over 200,000 in the EU and probably millions worldwide.[23] Furthermore, higher summer temperatures interacting with vehicle emissions will increase ozone formation and both exacerbate these health problems and reduce crop yields in densely populated and motorized areas.

Using the conventional value of a statistical life discussed above, the willingness to pay to avoid these fatalities might amount to several per cent of GDP if people were well informed about the risks, though the health effects of urban air pollution are systematically downplayed by media, car lobbies and governments. Aviation is one of the fastest-growing sources of emissions, encouraged by massive subsidies amounting to over £10 billion annually in the UK alone and tax-free aviation fuel worldwide. Switching these subsidies to improved rail services would have a significant impact on slowing the growth of emissions.

Substantial energy saving in the short run is also possible by using existing equipment more efficiently, or with modest investment, for example in energy-saving appliances and house insulation, which yields a very high private return. These measures obviously become even more attractive when the expected trend of rising fossil fuel prices after the recession is included. Estimated energy savings that would be privately profitable in the long run, as fossil fuel prices increase, are usually estimated to be in the range of 20 to 40 per cent in advanced economies. While a carbon tax would further discourage waste and promote alternatives, these extensive, existing profitable opportunities for energy saving are often neglected through ignorance, force of habit or financial constraints. Poor or already over-indebted households may simply have inadequate cash flows for such investment, and also lack access to (additional) credit, particularly in recession. Government funding, appropriate regulation and standards for energy efficiency thus all have an important role to play.

The financial collapse and beginning global recession of late 2008 offered a rare opportunity for 'green fiscal policy', or public investment to combine energy saving with job creation, at a time when both employment and prices were falling steeply. The construction sector was particularly hard hit everywhere, while retrofitting buildings for energy efficiency uses seven times the labour required for a similar investment in new coal-fired generation, saves more energy than would be produced and of course reduces emissions.[24] This opportunity was largely missed, as governments rescued the banks that caused the crash with huge increases in borrowing and money creation, but no adequate new regulation. At the same time, credit and funding for alternative energy projects and small business in general has been dramatically curtailed by banks lacking the confidence to lend, and with a very short-term focus on the recessionary fall in fuel prices.

A prime example of waste on a gigantic scale is military expenditure amounting to 2.5 per cent of global GDP, about half of which is the US military budget. If even a small proportion of this expenditure were diverted to supporting alternative energy development, the mitigation effect would be enormous, with no net cost to the world economy. Nuclear energy has been the largest civilian recipient of public R&D funding for the last 50 years (initially related to military programmes in several countries, and totalling around a trillion dollars), but the costs of new nuclear power stations have been rising faster than alternatives in recent years. Commercial construction still requires major government involvement in funding, guarantees, disaster insurance, security and waste disposal. Most nuclear waste is still stored in poorly protected, provisional sites, in the absence of any agreement on permanent disposal. The Olkiluoto power station under construction in Finland was billed as a showcase for the latest nuclear technology, but by 2008 it was already two years behind schedule, with a projected cost overrun of at least $2 billion.

The nuclear lobby claims that standardization and mass production of the latest reactor generation could produce 'safe' power at lower cost than renewable alternatives, and a few environmentalists have been persuaded, in spite of all the remaining problems of proliferation, security and waste disposal. These notwithstanding, the UK Government has launched a large-scale programme for building new nuclear power stations, with hidden subsidies but no evidence that this investment is really superior to alternatives. While proponents are enthusiastic about claimed progress in reactor design, they tend to ignore rapid advances in alternative technology, the long lead times for new nuclear power (10 years or more) or comparative cost estimates for different energy sources which suggest that nuclear is the least cost-effective way of reducing carbon emissions.[25]

All of the mitigation measures discussed so far would impose little net financial cost on the global economy. The direct health and welfare co-benefits from these policies in the medium term are likely to add up to several per cent of GDP in many developing and advanced economies. The policy costs – or obstacles to implementation – result from political resistance to the necessary redistribution that is involved in these measures, as well as from ingrained cultural attitudes and habits. In spite of net efficiency gains, a carbon tax or the reallocation of existing subsidies still creates winners and losers, as do all the other policies considered. While the costs, or just the change of habits required, are clearly visible and immediate for well-defined groups, gains such as reduced pollution, mortality and morbidity have less obvious individual impacts on a large population over a long period of time. Opposition to change is thus focused and often vehement, even though general benefits may be recognized by all in the long run.

While these political costs are indeed major barriers to abatement policy, it is important to emphasize that public education and stakeholder involvement in the process of planning and implementation can reduce the opposition and gain converts to sound policies. However, government conviction and initiative, rather than acquiescence to lobby pressure, is required. Special incentives may also be required to encourage initial change of habit in a hostile environment. Thus the car user who switches to cycling on crowded and polluted roads incurs real costs, and only when many others have followed can the health benefits from more exercise be enjoyed, as currently in many European cities.

In summary, perhaps half to three-quarters of current emissions could be cut in the next decade or two, with major co-benefits instead of financial costs in the medium term. This of course depends on political leadership and worldwide mobilization for energy saving, conservation agriculture, tropical forest protection and new plantation, and gradual replacement of economically obsolete capital equipment by cleaner technology – helped by rising carbon taxes and/or fossil fuel prices. Most of the remaining emissions would come from coal power generation. The rapid rise of oil prices up to July 2008, as global demand increased, had begun to have some of the effects of a carbon tax. Though much less well publicized, the price of the most polluting fuel – coal – had also been rising similarly, suggesting that supposedly abundant reserves of easily recoverable coal may have been exaggerated.[26] While this encouraged the rapid expansion of alternative energy, it also implied a huge transfer of wealth to the main oil and gas producers, OPEC and Russia. However, the financial crisis that erupted in the US in the summer of 2008 and then spread throughout the world's interlinked markets – generating a global economic recession by winter – led to a dramatic decline in fuel prices to a quarter of their peak levels due to falling demand.

When the world emerges from recession, the upward trend in fossil fuel prices is likely to continue (encouraged by a slowdown in development of all new energy sources during the recession under current, short-sighted government policies and scarce private funding due to the near-collapse of US and UK banking). The growing environmental and health costs of pollution in China and other developing countries (much of it from coal burning) is likely to accelerate already rapid alternative energy expansion. Prospective new oil and gas reserves are mainly in the Arctic, and will be very costly to exploit. In the meantime, existing technology for 'scrubbing' or removing sulphates and other emissions, but *not* carbon dioxide, from coal-burning power stations (and car exhausts) offers a relatively cheap and tempting interim solution for polluted cities (at much lower cost than long-term development of carbon capture and storage). This would yield substantial *local* health and welfare gains for urban populations in China and many other countries, but at the same time *accelerate* warming by reducing aerosol pollution and its cooling effect, as explained below. First, however, we consider the costs of the most promising forms of alternative energy.

The Costs of More Mitigation: The Future of Alternative Energy

Mitigation measures we have discussed so far would yield major co-benefits in the medium term, as well as reducing emissions by half or more. If political obstacles to the necessary redistribution could be overcome rapidly enough, with large-scale mobilization for 'green fiscal policy', then it should be feasible to stabilize the stock of atmospheric greenhouse gases at close to the present level (remembering that natural sinks still absorb about half of our emissions). And in contrast to repeated assertions by Stern and many other economists, this would not be prohibitively costly, but could be achieved with net economic benefits amounting to several per cent of GDP.

However, there is also a little-discussed downside to even ambitious carbon targets. A drastic reduction of biomass burning and coal emissions would remove much of the smoke and aerosol pollution from the atmosphere. In addition to the huge health benefits from this clean-up (and some local cooling from less soot in the air), there would also be a substantial overall warming effect, as more incoming solar radiation reached the Earth's surface. The existing aerosol cooling effect is probably equivalent to about 50–70ppm of carbon dioxide in the atmosphere (though the figure is subject to considerable uncertainty). Aerosols survive for only about 10 days in the atmosphere before they are washed out by rain, so there is an initial *warming* effect when biomass and coal burning is reduced. Thus additional reduction of carbon emissions would be required to compensate for the loss of the aerosol cooling effect.

It follows that stabilizing total GHGs in the atmosphere at around current levels while also eliminating most of the aerosol pollution would be equivalent to *adding* 50–70ppm of carbon dioxide, enough to ensure that the two-degree threshold would almost certainly be exceeded. Depending on how quickly natural sinks lose their effectiveness, and how the fast-growing developing countries respond, much more drastic policies by the developed countries responsible for most of the existing GHGs in the atmosphere may be required. These more advanced countries, at least, will probably have to reduce their emissions by at least 90 per cent by about 2030 in order to keep global emissions low enough for the stock of atmospheric GHGs to *decline* over time, and compensate for the loss of aerosol cooling.

In their book *Hot Air*, Gabrielle Walker and former Chief Scientific Advisor Sir David King advocate stabilizing total GHGs at a level equivalent to 450ppm of carbon dioxide, at the lower end of Stern's (inadequate) target range. Like most other writers on climate, however, they seem to have forgotten the likely major reduction in aerosol pollution under any serious mitigation effort, which could easily amplify the warming or 'forcing' effect to the equivalent of 500ppm CO_2. Even the lower level of 450ppm of CO_2 equivalent is almost certain to breach the two-degree threshold, perhaps substantially, as Walker and King actually point out, and thus involves a high risk of further – perhaps catastrophic – warming. Despite explicitly acknowledging such risks, Walker and King follow Stern to claim – without any evidence – that this 'is the lowest we can possibly hope to achieve' (p96).

Like almost all writers on climate and mitigation policy, these authors seriously underestimate the potential contribution of conservation agriculture. They do not even mention organic no-till agriculture, which the Rodale Institute has shown can sequester twice as much carbon as conventional no-till farming, while also raising yields. They ignore co-benefits (such as lower unemployment as a result of shifting taxes from labour to carbon emissions) and make no mention of the gigantic subsidies in the UK and other countries for some of the most polluting sectors and destructive activities, which amount to about 700 billion dollars annually worldwide. They praise the UK Climate Change Bill, and climate policy in general, while failing to describe the country's abysmal record on renewable energy and building standards – close to the bottom of the EU league table. Their readers are not informed about the lack of any firm policies (except nuclear power) to achieve Britain's (inadequate) 2050 target, nor is there any mention of strenuous lobbying to undercut the EU's modest 2020 goal for renewable energy.[27]

Surprisingly, Lester Brown's generally much better informed and more decisive *Plan B 3.0* shares two crucial omissions with the inadequate climate policy proposals by Stern and Walker and King. There is no mention of organic no-till agriculture and its potential for carbon sequestration, nor is the warming effect of eliminating aerosol pollution considered. Brown's target of stabilizing atmospheric CO_2 at 400ppm, close to the present level, is similar to the Walker–King target of 450ppm of CO_2 equivalent (including all other GHGs). Thus both targets unaccountably neglect the almost certain loss of aerosol cooling under otherwise far-reaching mitigation plans, which would probably be equivalent to an extra 50–70ppm of CO_2.

Carbon capture and storage (CCS) is a much-discussed response to expanding use of coal, a technology that in principle could be retrofitted to existing coal-burning power plants and remove carbon dioxide from emissions, for storage in exhausted oil fields or elsewhere. While the basic science is well understood, there is only one small pilot coal power plant with CCS in operation near Berlin, and large-scale commercial deployment is believed to be still at least a decade away, with probably very high costs. According to the most comprehensive recent estimates, CCS would require much more coal to produce the same amount of energy, and only reduce total GHG emissions from coal-fired power by perhaps slightly more than two-thirds. Emissions also include methane from the increasingly prevalent open-cast mining, which also has a devastating effect on the local environment, and those of the energy used in transport of coal and CO_2.

In view of the expected rapid rise in the price of coal over the lifetime of new coal-fired power stations that might be retrofitted if CCS was sufficiently developed in the next decades, this technology is likely to be one of the most expensive ways of reducing carbon emissions. Jeffrey Sachs and Nicholas Stern are prominent among the many economists who put great faith in the future of CCS, but their analysis is based on out-of-date cost predictions that neglect the likely continuing rise in the price of coal when the world economy recovers, the unavoidable emissions from open-cast coal mining and the declining cost of the alternatives discussed here. Mark Jacobson provides the most detailed, up-to-date cost analyses of alternative, low-carbon energy sources, and confirms that coal with CCS and nuclear power are the two *least* cost-effective alternatives, while the latest wind turbines in good locations currently provide the cheapest carbon-free energy.[28] In spite of all this, the UK Government plans to support large-scale CCS projects, nuclear power and expensive offshore wind farms, while most of the much more cost-effective onshore wind projects are held up in grotesquely bureaucratic planning procedures.

All experts agree that a cost-effective mitigation strategy must have several components, or 'wedges' as they have been termed by Princeton scientists Stephen Pacala and Robert Socolow.[29] A frequently discussed and obvious first step is energy saving, for example with better home insulation, and replacement of wasteful appliances. Such measures can yield substantial savings for households and business, even without a carbon tax, and particularly when fuel prices rise again. Yet such privately profitable opportunities are frequently neglected due to lack of technical knowledge, or perhaps just force of habit under the pressure of more immediately urgent concerns. A rising carbon tax (or fuel prices) would obviously encourage energy saving, but government regulation – including efficiency standards for buildings and the renovation of older housing – and extensive investment in green fiscal policy are also needed to accelerate the process.

We have discussed the many benefits of a switch to conservation agriculture and reforestation instead of biomass burning, but these measures will not be sufficient to reduce global emissions and the stock of GHGs to safe levels. Replacing the oldest and least efficient conventional power stations with cleaner and more efficient generation would be the most obvious next step, but here there are several different alternatives. Most power stations convert only about 30–50 per cent of their energy output into electricity, and lose the rest as waste heat. Smaller, decentralized 'cogeneration' or combined heat and power (CHP) units, located close to industrial users or residential areas, can double their efficiency by utilizing 'waste' heat. These efficiency gains have usually been opposed by utility companies defending their market power and profits with large centralized power stations. Currently, available CHP carbon emissions per unit of energy may well be only slightly greater than from future CCS technology in large centralized power stations, though the cost of electricity from the latter is likely to be at least 50 per cent higher, reflecting both much greater fuel consumption and higher capital costs.

Most of the cost of wind power comes from the initial construction, or capital cost. However, electricity from the latest 5–7MW wind turbines is already considered to be competitive with conventional power. It is likely to cost much less than coal generation with CCS over a plant lifetime in which the price of coal will probably continue its recent rapid increase – a trend that was only halted by the global recession which started in 2008 (sufficiently rapid expansion of alternatives would, of course, slow down the rate of increase of fossil fuel prices). Decentralized fossil fuel generation with CHP might be cheaper in the short run, as long as fuel prices remain depressed by recession. But large-scale, commercial CCS is at least a decade away, by which time wind and solar will both be almost certainly much less costly than even retrofitting CCS to large coal power stations. Recognition that this prospective technology is likely to be one of the most expensive methods for reducing GHG emissions would also encourage faster development of the much more promising, but hitherto neglected, geothermal and no-till alternatives. Rapid expansion of the currently most efficient alternative power sources – wind and decentralized CHP – to replace the most inefficient coal-fired capacity and decommissioned nuclear plants, would be one of the most cost-effective components of 'green fiscal policy'.

Although alternative energy has attracted relatively little government subsidy in comparison with nuclear, fossil and first generation biofuels, costs have fallen steadily with rapid technical progress, while global demand for wind and solar has grown at around 25–40 per cent a year (though from a very small base). This spectacular growth, together with rising commodity prices up to the financial crash of 2008, generated a surge in prices for wind turbines (and silicon-based PV panels), as manufacturing capacity failed to keep up with expanding demand. With sufficient investment for mass production of the latest wind turbines, the cost of this well-tried technology would undoubtedly fall considerably, and the historical downward trend could be resumed. Wind power could grow even faster than before the recession – with government-supported credit – in contrast to deployment of the new nuclear and CCS technologies, which would require a decade or more for development to large-scale production.

Wind power in Denmark and Germany is an interesting example of co-benefits from the support of an 'infant industry'. While subsidized 'feed-in tariffs' (which guarantee premium prices to producers of alternative energy) were strongly criticized by the fossil fuel lobby, these countries are now the technological leaders in wind generation, and dominate world export markets. Denmark produces about 20 per cent of its electricity from wind, and Germany has by far the largest installed capacity, which produces about six per cent of its power. The UK, and Scotland in particular, with Europe's greatest wind power potential, are lagging far behind, due to lack of support by successive governments until recently. Many promising projects are held up by a cumbersome and bureaucratic planning procedure, and existing subsidies primarily benefit incumbent producers rather than encouraging new investment.

An obvious response for governments to the 'credit crunch' that started in 2008 would have been to provide loans or guarantees for the expansion of wind turbine production (which would reduce their cost as bottlenecks were overcome) and wind farm development (which would also generate employment in recession). Low interest rates – without a commercial risk premium – would allow wind power to compete with coal over a time horizon in which the price of coal is likely to rise well above its average price in 2008. Subsidies, such as feed-in tariffs, may not even be required if the initial credit constraints could thus be overcome, and long-term loans repaid over the extended lifetime of modern wind turbines. The opportunity for large-scale, counter-cyclical, job-creating investment in energy efficiency and wind power has been neglected, however, in spite of all the long-term benefits of lower costs and emissions.

Wind power and other alternatives are often criticized for their intermittent supply, and optimal sites that may be far removed from centres of demand. However, major advances in the technology of high-voltage direct current (HVDC) transmission mean that long distances between generators and electricity users add only moderate cost. The second, and related, crucial point is that winds are very variable across regions, so that national or international (European) grid connections will be required to smooth supply. However, building the required large-scale grid, even just in the UK, will be impossible without major government involvement. A sufficient base-load generating capacity is, of course, still necessary.

It should be emphasized that the variability of wind and other alternatives (as well as the demand for electricity) can be 'smoothed' by energy storage. Most technologies are still expensive, though with potential for development. In appropriate hilly terrain, water can be pumped into high-level reservoirs when excess power is available, and then used for hydroelectric generation to meet excess demand. By far the cheapest form of energy storage, albeit a short-lived one, is the old fashioned 'storage heater'. This decidedly low-tech device was marketed before central heating became popular in the UK and elsewhere, in order to utilize cheap, off-peak or night-time electricity for domestic heating. The storage unit was heated overnight, when there was widespread excess generating capacity, and gradually released warmth throughout the day.

With a large enough wind-generating capacity to exceed night-time demand, the surplus could thus be used to provide cheap and carbon-free heating during daytime hours of peak demand. A related application is to charge the batteries of electric or plug-in hybrid vehicles overnight, to provide cheap and pollution-free motorized transport.[30] Smart metering devices can also switch off non-essential appliances when demand peaks, and lead to better utilization of a smaller generating capacity, thus reducing capital costs.

Occasionally, the wind can drop over an extended region under a large area of high pressure for a number of days. If wind produced more than about 10 per cent of total electricity throughout Europe, even an extended grid connection might not be able to avert shortages in such freak weather conditions, unless there was sufficient storage, complementary solar power or reserve capacity powered by fossil fuels. In the long run, solar power (particularly from North Africa), the cost of which is falling rapidly, should be developed to complement wind, and could itself provide most of Europe's daytime energy, as we discuss in more detail below.

One absurd objection to wind power in the UK, and elsewhere, is the claim that much of the country would have to be 'covered' by wind farms to produce a significant share of electricity. In fact, modern large wind turbines have to be widely spaced, and occupy only one to three per cent of the area of a 'wind farm', so the rest can be used for farming, forestry or whatever, as any traveller through northern Europe can observe.

An interesting and long-neglected alternative in some regions is geothermal power. Rapid advances in the technology of drilling deep wells for oil in recent years have opened up an exciting new potential for extracting geothermal heat from depths of several thousand metres. Engineered geothermal systems (EGS) pump cold water through hot, deep rock formations, and use the resulting steam to power conventional turbines and generators. A demonstration power plant is being completed in Australia, following smaller projects in France, Germany and the US. Government support has hitherto been minimal, although the EGS potential for continuous and relatively cheap power, particularly around the Pacific Rim, is enormous. This technology is also far more promising than nuclear power or CCS, and merits a major, publicly funded development programme.[31]

Hydroelectric power is still by far the most important alternative energy source, though the environmental consequences of large dams such as the Aswan or the Three Gorges in China have been disastrous. There is only limited potential for further development of hydropower, particularly when external costs are considered. On the other hand, there is considerable scope for the development of tidal and wave power in suitable coastal locations.

Biofuels

The most expensive and destructive attempt to produce alternative energy has, ironically, received more support than any other in the US. Motivated by strategic concern over dependence on 60 per cent of oil consumption imported from generally unstable regions, as well as its close ties to agribusiness, the Bush Administration provided massive subsidies (5–6 billion dollars annually) for the production of bioethanol for fuel from maize (corn). The energy-intensive, industrial agriculture on which ethanol is based, and the inefficiency of the whole production process, probably actually increases total GHG emissions, partly from the chemical fertilizers and energy used (discussed below).[32] The rise of world food prices until the recession of 2008 was also exacerbated by the US ethanol policy.

This dismal balance contrasts with the situation in Brazil, the other major producer of ethanol. Here, in tropical or sub-tropical conditions, the production of ethanol from sugar cane is much more efficient, and appears to generate a net reduction in carbon emissions, while supplying about 40 per cent of Brazil's transport fuel. On the other hand, large-scale sugar cane monoculture has devastating effects on the local environment and economy. Furthermore, intensive cultivation of newly cleared savannah or forest land for biofuels releases large amounts of carbon for many years, which more than compensates for the direct reduction of fossil fuel use. Cultivation of biofuel crops on existing farmland displaces food production onto new land with similar effects.[33]

In addition, demand for biofuels to meet EU targets for renewable energy is encouraging the destruction of tropical rainforest. This problem is particularly acute in Malaysia and Indonesia, driven by growing demand for high-yielding palm oil plantations to produce relatively cheap biodiesel, which takes no account of the environmental destruction and loss of rainforest resources. The entire remaining habitats of the orang-utan in Borneo and Sumatra are under serious threat from rainforest destruction for palm oil monoculture to supply biodiesel for the EU. Requirements for 'sustainable' biofuel sources without destroying rainforest will simply displace food crops from existing farmland to newly deforested areas.

Biodiesel is produced mainly in Europe, where the EU has set perversely unqualified targets for 'renewable' shares in total energy use, rising to 20 per cent by 2020, with no accounting for the total environmental impact. Again, high-cost production is heavily subsidized with ultimately destructive environmental effects, while the main raw materials – rapeseed and soybean oil – compete directly with food production. Nobel Prize-winning climatologist Paul Crutzen has argued that the nitrogen fertilizers used to grow feedstock for biofuels generate so much of the powerful GHG nitrous oxide that the fossil fuel emissions which are saved may actually be exceeded by the greenhouse effect of biofuel production.[34]

A far more promising biofuel is biogas (or syngas) made from non-food or waste biomass that would otherwise be incinerated, deposited in landfill sites, or simply left to decay and pollute the environment. Biogas is produced by anaerobic fermentation of biowaste, and consists mainly of methane and carbon dioxide that can be separated and sequestered, though at additional cost. Thus, refined biogas is similar to natural gas, and can also be used to power road vehicles after slight modification. Small-scale bioreactors and biodigesters are working successfully in many countries, and costs should fall as experience is gained and units can be mass-produced. A further advantage of biogas production is that the residue left after fermentation is a valuable, nitrogen-rich organic fertilizer, which can replace energy-intensive chemical fertilizers which damage the environment and soil biota.[35] Indeed, it is usually forgotten that crop residues and much other biowaste is urgently required to replenish the declining amounts of organic matter in much of the world's cropland to stabilize soil structure and prevent erosion.

As discussed in Chapter 3, there is a further refinement of biofuel production that goes beyond merely reducing emissions, or even achieving carbon neutrality, to actually achieving a negative carbon balance, and in fact offers a potentially cheaper method of carbon sequestration than CCS for coal power. In the process of low-temperature pyrolysis, biowaste is heated without oxygen to produce hydrogen and methane biogas and liquid biofuel, leaving perhaps half of the original carbon content as a residue in the form of active charcoal called biochar. This residue, containing the mineral contents and trace elements of the original biowaste, may have beneficial effects on soil fertility, though much more research remains to be done on the precise effects under various conditions.[36] In the 'terra preta', or fertile, dark soils found in parts of the Amazon Basin, biochar seems to have remained stable for thousands of years, though eventually it will oxidize to carbon dioxide. Only a small proportion of the energy or biogas produced is required to heat the biowaste, so this process provides both energy and fertilizer, while effectively removing carbon from the natural cycle.

Lester Brown and many others have proposed large-scale planting of trees on marginal or waste land to absorb atmospheric carbon dioxide. Lester Brown's *Plan B 3.0* reports estimates of around 1 billion hectares of currently unused but reclaimable wasteland – former agricultural or grass land that could potentially be reforested, with an appropriate carbon tax or reward for carbon sequestration. Sustainable mixed forest, agroforestry or small-scale tree planting yield many additional environmental benefits, as well as biofuel or timber harvest. Much of this potential is in developing countries, so international aid and policies to reverse current deforestation for short-term profit will be needed.[37] Some marginal land is used for common grazing by poor farmers, so commercial reclamation should be accompanied by adequate compensation for any loss of traditional rights, in contrast to the theft and eviction that is still all too common in many developing regions.

Fast-growing perennial grasses to produce biogas and/or biochar can rival or exceed the sustainable 'productivity' of forest, in terms of carbon sequestration and co-benefits. These perennials do not require high-quality land or chemical fertilizers, so their opportunity costs in terms of forgone food production, and GHG emissions, are very low. Their deep root systems mean that even newly reclaimed and planted soils in abandoned agricultural areas are likely to accumulate rather than lose carbon (as under conventional cultivation).[38]

Thus there appears to be a huge potential for carbon sequestration combined with timber and biofuel production that enhances rather than reduces food production through the environmental benefits of sustainable reforestation and agroforestry instead of deforestation. Estimates of available land suggest that billions of tonnes of carbon could be captured annually over decades of growth. International mobilization for halting deforestation and for really large-scale reforestation is needed, policies that could help to reduce atmospheric carbon to safe levels in the next decades, while fossil fuels are phased out. Current wasteful subsidies for destructive bioethanol and biodiesel – and expensive prospective cellulosic ethanol – should be switched to the much more promising developments outlined here, which allow sustainable biofuel production without the diversion or degradation of potential agricultural land. 'Agricultural crimes against humanity' (and biodiversity) are the result of current subsidies for hopelessly inefficient bioethanol and biodiesel, motivated by dependency on imported oil and gas, and agribusiness lobbying, rather than climate concerns.[39]

Solar Energy

Solar power is the fastest-growing variety of alternative or 'green' energy, though still with a much smaller share than wind. Relatively modest subsidies in Germany include a 'feed-in tariff' that guarantees a premium price to producers. The result is a world export-leading technology and industry, and over half the installed global capacity for solar electricity, or photovoltaic (PV) generation. As new and more efficient PV cells come into production, installed capacity worldwide is increasing by about 35 per cent annually, and costs have been declining by around 20 per cent for each doubling of output. New, thin-film PV modules cost much less than traditional silicon-based cells, and decentralized generation with these or related new technologies is expected to become competitive with coal when fossil fuel prices start to climb again after the recession. In view of these well-publicized advances, it is astonishing to read the claim by nuclear enthusiasts Gabrielle Walker and Sir David King that alternatives to silicon 'probably won't be available for several decades'.[40] Solar generators using reflectors to concentrate sunlight are also being developed, and again have major potential for further growth and cost-reduction.

These astounding developments open up new perspectives that would have seemed utopian only a few years ago. A few thousand square kilometres of solar panels along the southern or Mediterranean periphery of Europe or north Africa could supply much of the regions' daytime power requirements into an EU-wide grid.[41] Southern winter cloud cover is generally local and short-lived, and accompanied by windy conditions in much of the north, so an essentially continuous, total supply of clean, alternative electricity could be maintained from the solar/wind combination and distributed with the appropriate international grid connections. As explained above, surplus night-time generation from wind (and possibly remaining fossil fuel and nuclear base-load capacity) could then be used for charging electric (or hybrid) vehicle batteries to provide clean motorized transport, as well as storage heaters.

Implementing this final wedge of cost-effective mitigation in the EU will clearly require extensive international cooperation rather than the uncoordinated – and often inconsistent – national policies that are only just beginning to be set up. The European political framework should at least facilitate a coordinated energy policy when a sufficiently strong sense of urgency emerges. National rivalries or hostilities across borders in Africa and Asia provide a less favourable environment for effective mitigation.

The other main solar application, solar thermal or water heating, is led by China, and with other uses – such as solar cooking and water disinfection – is also expanding rapidly as costs continue to fall. Again, a little more government support, by diverting subsidies from fossil fuels and nuclear energy, could dramatically accelerate the rate of expansion of solar energy use. The huge environmental benefits from substituting solar energy for biomass burning in developing countries have already been emphasized.

Solar energy in northern latitudes shares with wind the problem of intermittent supply, and the need for storage as well as a base-load capacity for stable, reliable provision. In the long run, storage technologies offer potential for further development, possibly including the large-scale use of hydrogen produced by solar or wind energy. However, in the short to medium term, the technologies described here are all available and indeed, for the most part, have already been proved to work in practice. They offer cost-effective alternatives to fossil fuels that would allow the world to reduce net emissions of greenhouse gases by around 80–90 per cent by 2020–2030, and minimize the risks of runaway warming at a quite modest financial cost. As we have explained, the obstacles are political and educational rather than economic or technical.

In contrast to the practical solutions discussed here, there has also been some discussion of 'geo-engineering' to sequester carbon by fertilizing plankton in southern oceans, or far-fetched schemes to reflect solar radiation. These yet-to-be-developed technologies are likely to be far more costly than tree planting or making biochar, and fraught with potential dangers, while diverting attention from the political obstacles to cost-effective mitigation.

Conclusions

Our emphasis here on the co-benefits of mitigation suggests that the real, long-term net costs (in narrow economic terms) of even a drastic worldwide reduction of emissions would be very modest. The short-term, perceived costs of changing habits and customs, and the necessary redistribution are, of course, much greater, and form the main psychological and political barriers to change. If natural sinks have not declined too much by 2030, and positive feedbacks not progressed too far, the total stock of carbon in the atmosphere could then be declining. This, and further progress with new technologies, would thus offer a reasonable probability of remaining below the crucial two-degree-rise threshold.

The developed countries will probably have to implement the largest reductions in any international framework that succeeds Kyoto. One of the major political uncertainties most relevant for climate change is the question 'When will progressive environmental degradation and worsening water shortages, in China and India in particular, lead to serious remedial action?'. To the extent that these and other developing countries lag behind the developed world in reducing emissions for the next two or three decades, the advanced economies may have to pursue abatement well beyond the 80 per cent target suggested here.

Finally, it cannot be sufficiently strongly emphasized that this relatively 'optimistic' assessment depends fundamentally on a *rapid* reduction of GHG emissions. As many writers (including Stern) have pointed out, further delay in implementing serious abatement measures will necessitate much more drastic policies later. Already, at present concentrations of GHGs, and with the likely reduction of aerosol pollution under any serious mitigation effort, it will be necessary to *remove* large amounts of carbon from the atmosphere to avoid the risks of runaway warming. Again, as we have shown, this is feasible with existing technology, by using conservation, no-till agriculture and extensive reforestation to sequester large amounts of carbon, while switching to low-carbon energy. However, as argued above, the immediate *perceived* costs and political barriers (in spite of net co-benefits) are likely to remain substantial, until serious impacts of warming become so obvious, after a dangerously long period of further business as usual, that public perceptions change and political resistance also collapses.

Stern has performed a major service by gaining widespread publicity for the serious threats from climate change and emphasizing the need for substantial mitigation policies. Though his conclusions stand in clear contrast to the 'do-nothing-now' response of most economists, they still imply very high risks for the poorest populations in particular. Stern's critics have tried to justify their neglect of future catastrophes – and generations – by pointing out the problems inherent in the conventional welfare function used by Stern, where the wellbeing of (survivors in) future generations is not discounted. This critique misses the most important issue: the fundamental failure of virtually all economic approaches to incorporate likely large-scale loss of human life in the future. Scientific evidence suggests that catastrophic loss of life in the world's poorest regions is not a very unlikely, 'worst case' consequence of continued business as usual (one which is not even considered by most economists). Instead, according to the latest research, runaway warming and irreversible climate catastrophe are almost inevitable unless drastic abatement measures are started soon. The standard welfare function of average income used by both Stern and his critics, which treats future loss of life and biodiversity as a minor correction for 'non-market impacts', thus has no scientific – let alone ethical – justification.

The overwhelming majority of economists who have considered the costs of climate change – from Stern and his team to their numerous critics – have failed to incorporate the latest evidence from climate science on the high probability of accelerating feedbacks and runaway warming if mitigation is too little and too late, as it would be under all official targets. Instead they still assume catastrophic events to be extremely unlikely, and essentially reduce the risks to relatively small reductions of much higher future average income. Historical high rates of material economic growth, which have depended on ruthless and growing exploitation of non-renewable resources, are simply projected or assumed to continue for centuries to come. The future distribution of income and poverty (under the impact of climate change) receives even less attention than these issues do today. The assumption of everlasting material growth, whatever happens to climate and environment, is based on blind faith in technical progress – a science fiction scenario in defiance of all the evidence from climate and environmental science. Ironically, this ideology is shared by neo-liberal economists – otherwise implacably opposed to government planning and intervention – and the Chinese Communist Party. Both have favoured growth at the cost of the environment and sustainability, and the apparent success of the latter has even elicited increasing admiration from the other end of the traditional political spectrum.

Belief in everlasting material growth may also be influenced by wishful thinking and the mistaken idea that consumption growth always increases subjective wellbeing, though average life satisfaction has declined in China and failed to increase in many developed countries. This evidence has been completely ignored in the conventional consensus on material growth as the universal priority for economic policy. Slower but more sustainable growth (that does less damage to the environment and social capital and raises the survival chances of our descendants) is thus perceived to be a welfare cost, rather than a net benefit, in the perverse 'cost–benefit' analysis still widely applied to climate change, and indeed to many other economic issues.

In addition to these problems, the costs of mitigation are overestimated by Stern (and even more so by his critics, who actually accuse him of the opposite tendency). This is because Stern, and most other economists, seriously underestimate the short-term co-benefits to human and agricultural health from a greener economy. Although many of these co-benefits are indeed discussed informally by Stern, he ignores these factors in his repeated but unsupported assertions that any low-risk mitigation policy would be prohibitively expensive.

Stern appears to be torn between a desire to use traditional cost–benefit analysis to make the case for mitigation and occasional awareness that this approach does not capture the biggest problems. His support of a high-risk policy with very slow reduction of emissions is contradicted by recognition of the potential dangers of positive feedback effects, as well as by the published estimates of climate sensitivity that he frequently quotes. More usefully, a few economists such as Frank Ackerman and Martin Weitzman have begun to consider the consequences of catastrophic, runaway warming, which cannot be ruled out if atmospheric carbon doubles under business as usual in the next decades, though the probabilities are essentially incalculable. The rational collective response by humanity should be to do whatever it takes to avert the *possibility* of catastrophe, and to ensure our survival, without wasting time trying to calculate the (unknowable) 'optimal' mitigation path. Persuading individuals and nations to abandon free-riding, and support collective survival strategies, remains the fundamental political challenge.[42]

Almost all discussion of the economics of climate change has been hamstrung by a misplaced focus on growing *average* consumption of a non-declining world population. Most economists in developed countries have little interest in agriculture, perhaps because this sector is now so small a part of advanced economies. Thus there is little awareness of just how great is the threat to food supply in the developing world from further warming and progressive water shortages under current policies. The second result of this neglect is that the huge potential of conservation agriculture and reforestation (for combining mitigation with short-term economic co-benefits) has been missed.

The inadequate targets adopted by the UK and EU, and supported by Sir David King and Lord Stern, involve a high probability of dangerous warming according to even the optimistic IPCC climate modelling forecasts, which they themselves cite. The results of these too-high targets are likely to be catastrophic for the poorest and most overcrowded countries, and spill over to the rest of the world, long before ultimate temperature extremes are approached. Climate predictions are becoming more pessimistic with rapidly shrinking Arctic sea ice, which, together with the extensive co-benefits of far-reaching mitigation measures emphasized here, should raise both the urgency and feasibility of such policies.[43]

10

From Economic Crisis to Mobilization for Mitigation

In the two years of writing this book, predictions from climate science have become steadily more pessimistic. The IPCC Fourth Assessment Report in 2007 predicted a sea-level rise of only around 50cm over the coming century, and a slow decline of Arctic sea ice cover. These predictions were far too optimistic. Now, a summer ice-free Arctic in a decade or two seems likely, and if the break-up of the Greenland ice cap accelerates, sea levels could rise by metres per century, to match the dramatic pace of rising at the end of the last ice age. As sea ice and snow cover in the northern hemisphere recede, albedo, or reflectivity of land and water surfaces, declines, so they absorb more solar radiation and warm faster during lengthening summer seasons. Already rapid northern warming will accelerate, releasing ever more methane from thawing peat bogs in an additional carbon 'feedback', which in turn generates still more warming. While the oceans are warming much more slowly than the atmosphere, their capacity to absorb carbon dioxide is also likely to decrease. The probable doubling of pre-industrial concentrations in the next few decades, under current, weak abatement plans based on the IPCC Report, could easily trigger irreversible methane release and collapse of the ice caps. This in turn could push temperatures to the top of (or beyond) the IPCC range of up to five or six degrees over pre-industrial levels. The result would be the collapse of our civilization, leaving much of the Earth's surface uninhabitable and displacing or destroying most existing species, including the human population.

In the years preceding the 'crash' of 2008, energy, food and other commodity prices had been rising rapidly, raising hopes that this trend would partially simulate a steadily increasing carbon tax, and accelerate the switch to renewable energy (though at considerable cost to the poor, as wealth was transferred to oil producers). When prices fell precipitously with global recession in late 2008, so too did funding for energy and other investment. At the same time, governments struggled to implement gigantic bailouts for the banks that had caused most of the problems, creating corresponding long-term liabilities for taxpayers who were losing their homes and jobs. When the global economy recovers, energy and food prices will doubtless resume their upward trend.

Food supply in developing countries is already threatened by rapidly declining water reserves and soil erosion. Climate change will increase the frequency and severity of extreme weather events, including droughts in hot and arid regions, while higher temperatures and tropospheric ozone pollution will further reduce yields. The high-yielding varieties of the Green Revolution depend on high inputs of water, energy and chemicals, and hence are particularly vulnerable to these developments. Industrial agricultural monocultures also encourage emerging epidemics, such as the new black stem rust Ug99, which is spreading from Africa and which no modern commercial wheat is immune to. Intensive animal farming for meat production provides the ideal breeding ground for even more deadly potential threats to the human population such as avian flu, and the current swine flu pandemic. Long before rising seas inundate the world's coastal cities, major droughts and depleted aquifers are likely to devastate agriculture in many of the poorest and most populous countries. In the worst case, the most impoverished billions (of a still rapidly growing world population) would face starvation, and the global economy would collapse, as most incomes were spent on astronomically priced basic foods. Already in early 2009, major food-producing regions – such as northern China, parts of the US and Argentina – were suffering from their worst droughts for decades, with predictions of severely reduced grain harvests. Food prices, which have not fallen from their 2008 peak as fast as other commodity prices as the recession worsened, are also expected to start rising again when demand picks up and already low grain stocks are further depleted by poor harvests.

In contrast to this grim scenario, a major theme of this book has been that a large-scale shift from industrial to sustainable or conservation agriculture, and from biomass burning to reforestation, could simultaneously protect food supply and sequester much of the remaining carbon emissions. This would provide time for the necessary transition from fossil fuels to renewable energy, and also reduce the costs of energy and chemical inputs, costs which are likely to rise rapidly when the global economy starts to grow again. Large-scale transition to sustainable, conservation agriculture would also create rural employment everywhere when labour is substituted for chemical and energy inputs. In addition to all the other benefits, this would help to staunch the flight to the cities that is creating rapidly growing slums and huge social problems in most developing countries. Economic studies of climate change which neglect the huge potential of conservation agriculture, such as the famous Stern Review, fail to appreciate how short-term cost-reduction can be combined with more sustainable food supply and GHG abatement in the long run. These studies thus exaggerate the financial cost of drastic mitigation, and hinder the educational effort needed to gain broad public acceptance and facilitate decisive political action.

A related topic, which urgently requires corrective public education, is the still prevailing obsession with economic growth and GDP as the prime indicators of individual welfare and national performance. Decades of research by economists and other social scientists show that average levels of subjective wellbeing in advanced countries have little relationship to real income per capita, though *relative* income is one of many factors that do affect wellbeing. These results are only slowly being disseminated, and so far have had little influence on public policy discussion. However, the ugly downside of 'market fundamentalist' economics – growing poverty, inequality and deprivation in some of the richest countries and declining social mobility for the majority, while most of the benefits of growth are captured by the highest earners – is attracting increasing attention in a time of deep global recession. It is also becoming clear that neo-liberal or market fundamentalist policies of excessive deregulation – primarily for the benefit of the super-rich in unfettered, 'casino capitalism' – were the fundamental cause of the crash of 2008. These policies, which had started under Reagan and Thatcher in the 1980s, were pillars of economic orthodoxy right up to the crash, in spite of all the obvious imbalances and the fundamental unsustainability of 'credit bubble'-fuelled growth.

After the years of climate change denial by the Bush Administration, new US President Barack Obama has struck a very different tone, in this as in most other policy areas. While the Kyoto agreement failed abysmally to slow down rapid growth of GHG emissions, non-participation by the US, and their obstructive stance at a succession of UN climate conferences, did help to draw attention to the problems. With a successor to Kyoto due to be negotiated in December 2009, there are hopes for US cooperation, particularly following Obama's commitment to a comprehensive 'cap-and-trade' or carbon emissions trading system. Though EU emissions trading has primarily generated huge windfall profits for the biggest polluters, a better designed, more comprehensive US system, where at least some permits were auctioned rather than freely allocated, could encourage similar reform in Europe. Equally important, other major polluters, such as China and India, might be tempted to follow these examples, and raise revenue through carbon pricing under a cap-and-trade system, as well as reducing extreme levels of pollution in their cities and rivers. Less local pollution would improve urban health, as well as reducing GHG emissions. Finally, national or regional carbon trading systems would be relatively easy to integrate internationally, to achieve the uniform carbon price necessary for minimal-cost abatement worldwide.

The evolution and imitation of national carbon pricing systems does not require the kind of comprehensive international agreement that more ambitious, 'top–down' plans for global systems of permit trading or carbon taxation and revenue redistribution depend on. Political barriers to the latter are likely to remain insurmountable for a long time, whereas initially uncoordinated efforts can inspire imitation and gradual integration as benefits become apparent.

Existing national and EU targets for emission reductions are all 'too little, too late', with very high risks of dangerous or runaway warming going far beyond the often-cited threshold of two degrees above pre-industrial global mean temperature. As we have emphasized throughout, even really ambitious mitigation targets will not entail the absurdly high welfare costs claimed by some economists, and in the medium term will generate major co-benefits in terms of human and animal health. However, there are unavoidable political or policy costs of changing behaviour and overcoming the powerful vested interests of the fossil fuel and agribusiness lobbies.

Environmentalists such as Lester Brown of the Earth Policy Institute have argued persuasively that large-scale mobilization of public opinion and national resources, of the kind last experienced during World War II, is required to meet the challenge of climate change in the next few years. Such a reaction requires extensive public education on the urgency of the current threat from runaway warming under business as usual, without which far-reaching abatement measures would lack legitimacy. Despite a well-publicized scientific consensus, numerous government expressions of concern and various targets (though few policies) for GHG reductions, in Europe at least, such education has hardly begun. The problem is particularly acute in the big developing countries, where discussion of even acute local pollution and its health impacts is widely suppressed, and in the US, where denial dominated public and media discussion of climate change until President Obama's appointment in 2009.

The recession that started in 2008 has diverted attention from what is still widely perceived to be only a vague threat from far off, future climate change, to the more urgent priority of stabilizing the economy. The 2008–2009 economic downturn actually offered an unprecedented opportunity for really large-scale government investment in alternative energy and efficiency – a 'green fiscal stimulus' – with huge potential for job creation in labour-intensive sectors, and little danger of generating future inflation or 'crowding out' of private investment. Instead, most funding in all the various national plans to combat the recession has gone to the banks that originally caused the problems, or to populist tax reductions that will either be saved by consumers in uncertain times or, in part at least, spent on imported goods. As philosopher A. C. Grayling aptly put it in the *New Scientist*:

> *If you cannot pay your mortgage you will be out on the street, but if you are a banker who has lost billions the government will bail you out. ... Occasionally there is mention of the impending end of the planet as we know it, but somewhat in passing, as if it did not quite matter or were not quite true.*[1]

Serious mobilization to mitigate climate change and counter the worst recession since the 1930s needs several components. Collapsed construction sectors (the first and hardest hit in several economies) could be rejuvenated by mass employment of their idle workers for refurbishing homes and commercial buildings to modern standards of energy efficiency. Reduced expenditure on unemployment and other benefits, and major future declines in energy consumption, would represent an enormous social return on such investment, both in money terms and in GHG abatement. In pathetic contrast to what is needed, the UK Government of Gordon Brown only plans to start large-scale refurbishing of homes by around 2012, when the recession will probably be over, and finish by 2030, when it will be too late avert dangerous climate change.

Complementary measures include utilizing waste industrial heat and building decentralized combined heat and power (CHP) generators – highly effective and short-term projects compared to the decade or two before complex new technologies such as large-scale carbon capture and storage (CCS) or improved nuclear could be developed and commercially installed. The largest single component must be a new 'smart', high-voltage direct current grid to transport wind and solar power from the best sources to centres of demand. Since the latest onshore wind turbines in good locations are competitive with centalized coal generation, if there are adequate grid connections, and with expected rising costs of fossil fuels in the long run, the next step should be expanded mass production of the latest generators and sufficient subsidies to overcome the perverse (but temporary) incentives of recession-depressed fossil fuel prices. Dramatic technical progress in solar energy would also be complemented by adequate grid connections to the sunniest regions across the EU and Mediterranean periphery and in other regions. Such large-scale infrastructure needs international support, but would create gigantic market opportunities for private investment in new solar technology, which is likely to be competitive long before commercial CCS or 'cheap and safe' nuclear energy.

In depressing contrast to all these opportunities, the global economic crisis in 2008–2009 has led to falling investment in alternative energy, due to funding problems and declining prices of fossil fuels. As pioneering climate scientist James Hansen has emphasized:

> Coal is the single greatest threat to civilization and all life on our planet. ... The dirtiest trick that governments play on their citizens is the pretence that they are working on clean coal.[2]

Yet coal still receives major direct and indirect subsidies, with no accounting for even local and immediate devastating pollution, let alone long-term climate effects. CCS is still seen by many as an important component of mitigation, without people realizing that, together with nuclear power, it is likely to be the most expensive way of reducing carbon emissions. The influential motor lobby has also succeeded in obtaining huge public subsidies in several countries, as the economic crisis hit their overcapacity for production of highly polluting and overpowered vehicles using outdated technology. These 'scrappage' schemes encourage motorists to go into more debt than they can comfortably afford, by buying new cars that may be more polluting than their old ones! Again, government intervention to rescue a depressed industry has missed the chance of enforcing a major shift to modern, green technology – in this case, plug-in hybrid and electric models, with much lower emissions and energy use.

When the world emerges from recession and credit flows more freely again, fossil fuel prices will resume their upward trend, and alternative energy with further improved technologies will become increasingly attractive for private investment once more. But valuable time will have been lost before growing public perception of the threats from local pollution to current health, and from climate change to the future of civilization, finally generate appropriate political response. New US leadership, food shortages and natural catastrophes could all help in this process, particularly when job loss or insecurity is no longer the overriding concern of so many voters and workers.

Notes

Chapter 2: Basic Science of Climate Change

1   See Stern, N. (2007) *The Economics of Climate Change*, Cambridge University Press, for a comprehensive review. This work has been updated and summarized in Stern's Ely Lecture (2008) 'The economics of climate change', *American Economic Review: Papers and Proceedings*, vol 98, no 2, pp1–37. We discuss this and related work in detail in Chapter 9.

There are several excellent accessible introductory surveys of the current state of climate science, such as Calvin, W. (2008) *Global Fever*, University of Chicago Press; Strom, R. (2007) *Hot House*, Copernicus Press; Lynas, M. (2007a) *Six Degrees*, Fourth Estate, London; Pittock, B. (2009, second edition) *Climate Change: Turning up the Heat*, Earthscan; and Pearce, F. (2006) *The Last Generation*, Eden Project. Perhaps the best is Archer, D. (2008) *The Long Thaw*, Princeton. Sir David King and Walker, G. (2008) *The Hot Topic*, Gower, is good on the science, but weak on policy, as we explain in Chapter 9, which is perhaps not surprising from a former chief scientific advisor to a UK Government that has the worst record on climate-related policy in Western Europe. The superb website www.realclimate.org provides non-technical summaries of the latest developments by an international team of leading climate scientists, as well as precise demolition of the absurd claims still appearing by the 'denial industry'.

2   Rather confusingly, a carbon dioxide ppm *equivalent* measure (ppme) is sometimes used, in particular by Stern; this includes the effects of the other greenhouse gases such as methane, which has a much stronger warming effect in the short run, though it eventually decays into CO_2. Stern and many other writers often neglect the cooling effect of aerosols, which is believed to roughly cancel out the influence of the 'other' GHGs, so that net warming or 'radiative forcing' can be simply ascribed to just the increase in carbon dioxide of about 110ppm since pre-industrial times.

3   Lockwood, M. and Fröhlich, C. (2007) 'Recent oppositely directed trends in solar climate forcings and the global mean surface air temperature', *Proceedings of the Royal Society A*, vol 463, pp2447–2460.

4   The programme title, 'The Great Global Warming Swindle', (inadvertently) well describes the treatment of the topic in the programme, as analysed and exposed in all the shabby detail of this low point of recent British broadcasting on www.realclimate.org. Claims by various deniers that current warming was 'natural' rather than anthropogenic (caused by solar activity) had long been known to be false, even before the recent final, conclusive proof by Lockwood and Fröhlich (Note 3 above). These issues are further discussed below.

5   The sequence began about 2.8 million years ago, initially with the 40,000 year cycle in the Earth's axis of rotation. For unknown reasons this later switched to the 100,000 year Milankowich Cycles in the Earth's orbit that seem to have precipitated the last eight ice ages.

6   Hansen, J. (2007) 'Special Report Earth', *New Scientist*, 25 July. Hansen is director of NASA's Goddard Space Center in New York. Since the 1980s he has been an outspoken advocate of serious policy to mitigate climate change, and more recently a strong critic of the Bush Administration's frequent attempts to gag climate scientists. Monbiot, G. (2008a) 'One shot left', *The Guardian*, 25 November, summarizes the evidence on Arctic warming and ice loss.

7   See Ravilious, K. (2007) 'Asia's brown clouds heat the Himalayas', *New Scientist*, 1 August; Seinfeld, J. (2008) 'Atmospheric science: Black carbon and brown clouds', *Nature Geoscience*, vol 1, pp15–16.

8   Wooster, M. (2007) 'Progress in quantifying biomass burning contributions to the global carbon cycle', presented at Royal Geographical Society Annual International Conference, London, 29–31 August.

9   It is important to remember that the IPCC's Fourth Assessment Report, which appeared in 2007, had to present complete agreement among hundreds of scientists, including delegates from the US, China and Saudi Arabia. Reports are reviewed – and commented on – by governments, so lead authors may come under more or less subtle pressures to avoid controversy and conform with majority views. In the meantime, accelerating Arctic ice loss has confounded several IPCC predictions, though these are still cited in support of dangerously inadequate targets by governments and economists.

10   Lynas, M. (2007a) *Six Degrees*, Fourth Estate, London, p218.

11   Baer, P. and Mastrandrea, M. (2006) *High Stakes*, IPPR, London.

12   Like all forecasting models for such complex systems as the global climate (or even national economies), climate simulations can only provide a distribution of more or less likely outcomes. Various plausible parameter assumptions then generate the range of modelling predictions.

13   Hansen, J., Sato, M., Kharecha, P., Beerling, D., Masson-Delmotte, V., Pagani, M., Raymo, M., Royer, L. D. and Zachos, C. J. (2008) 'Target atmospheric CO_2: Where should humanity aim?', *The Open Atmospheric Science Journal*, vol 2, pp217–231.

14   Stern causes some confusion by usually including non-carbon dioxide greenhouse gases in his carbon dioxide equivalent measure (ppme), while neglecting the fact that aerosols have a roughly similar global cooling effect, so the standard carbon dioxide measure in ppm is an adequate approximation for net warming. Stern also refers to tonnes of carbon dioxide in the atmosphere, instead of tonnes of carbon used here (the former can be obtained from the latter by multiplying by 3.67).

15   In his Ely Lecture, and in his *Blueprint*, Stern has admitted that his Review 'underplayed the risks of global warming and should have presented an even bleaker view of the future'.

16   Burke, J. E., Brown, J. S. and Christidis, N. (2006) 'Modeling the recent evolution of global drought and projections for the twenty-first century with the Hadley Centre Climate Model', *Journal of Hydrometeorology*, vol 7, no 5, pp1113–1125.

17   Monbiot, G. (2006) *Heat*, Allen Lane, London, Chapter 2. This book is another good introduction to aspects of climate change, though mainly focused on policies for mitigation in the UK.

18 UCS News, 3 January 2007, at www.ucsusa.org/news/press_release/ ExxonMobil-GlobalWarming-tobacco.html. The full UCS report, 'Smoke, mirrors and hot air: How ExxonMobil uses big tobacco's tactics to "manufacture uncertainty" on climate change', is available at www.ucsusa.org.

19 Monbiot, G. (2006) *Heat*, Allen Lane, London, p37.

20 Connolley, W. and Schmidt, G. (2007) 'Swindled', *RealClimate*, 7 March, www.realclimate.org. See also the summary (2008) 'Climate swindlers excused', *New Scientist*, 26 July, p7.

21 Mann, M. and Schmidt, G. (2007) 'Lindzen in *Newsweek*', *RealClimate*, 17 April, www.realclimate.org. Because of the light it throws on the style of the scientist once considered the most 'respectable' of the sceptics, we present their complete analysis below:

As part of a much larger discussion on 'Learning to live with global warming' in Newsweek *recently, the editors gave some space for Richard Lindzen to give his standard 'it's no big deal' opinion. While we disagree, we have no beef with serious discussions of the costs and benefits of various courses of action and on the need for adaption to the climate change that is already locked in. However, Lindzen's piece is not a serious discussion. Instead, it is a series of strawman arguments, red-herrings and out and out errors. Lindzen claims that because we don't know what the ideal temperature of the planet should be, we shouldn't be concerned about global warming. But concern about human-driven climate change is not because this is the most perfect of possible worlds – it is because, whatever its imperfections, it is the world that society is imperfectly adapted to. Lindzen is well aware that predictions of weather are different from climate predictions (the statistics of weather), yet cheerfully uses popular conflation of the two issues to confuse his readers.*

Lindzen claims that the known amount of 'forcing' on the system proves that CO_2 will only have a small effect, yet makes plain in the subsequent paragraph that the total forcing (and hence what the planet should be reacting to) is quite uncertain (particularly before the satellite era). If the total forcing is uncertain, how can he say that he knows that the sensitivity is small? This issue has been dealt with much more seriously than Lindzen alludes to (as he well knows) and it's clear that this calculation is simply too uncertain to constrain sensitivity on its own.

Among the more egregious of Lindzen's assertions is this one: 'Ten years ago climate modellers also couldn't account for the warming that occurred from about 1050 to 1300. They tried to expunge the medieval warm period from the observational record – an effort that is now generally discredited'.

It's remarkable that Lindzen is able to pack so many errors into two short sentences. First of all, doubts about the global scale of warmth associated with the 'medieval climate anomaly' date back well over a decade and certainly precede any known attempts to use climate models to simulate medieval temperatures (see, for example, Hughes and Diaz, 1994, 'Was there a "medieval warm period", and if so, where and when?'; there are even earlier conference proceedings that were published coming to similar conclusions). To the best of our knowledge, the first published attempt to use a climate model and estimated forcing histories to simulate the climate of the past millennium was described less than seven years ago in this Science *article by Tom Crowley, not 10 years ago – (a 43 per cent error). Crowley's original study and the other similar studies published since established that the model simulations are in fact in close agreement with the reconstructions, all of which indicate that at the scale of the northern hemisphere, peak medieval warmth was perhaps comparable to early/mid 20th century warmth, but that it fell well short of the warmth of the most recent decades. Not only has the most recent IPCC report confirmed this assessment, it has in fact extended it further back, concluding that the large-scale warmth of recent decades is likely anomalous in at least the past 1300 years. So we're puzzled as to precisely what Lindzen would like to have us believe was 'expunged' or 'discredited', and by whom?*

Finally, we find it curious that Lindzen chose to include this very lawyerly disclaimer at the end of the piece: '[Lindzen's] research has always been funded exclusively by the US Government. He receives no funding from any energy companies'.

Richard, one thinks thou dost protest too much! A casual reader would be led to infer that Lindzen has received no industry money for his services. But that would be wrong. He has in fact received a pretty penny from industry. But this isn't for research. Rather it is for his faithful advocacy of a fossil fuel industry-friendly point of view. So Lindzen's claim is true, on a technicality. But while the reader is led to believe that there is no conflict of interest at work behind Lindzen's writings, just the opposite is the case.

It should hardly be surprising to learn that Lindzen was just chosen to share the title of 'false counsellor' in the list of leading 'environmental sinners' compiled in the May issue of Vanity Fair *on the news-stands now (article 'Dante's Inferno: Green edition'; unfortunately, this sits behind the subscription wall, so you'll have to purchase the magazine for further details). Incidentally, several other frequent appearers on RC, such as Fred Singer, Willie Soon, Sally Baliunas, James Inhofe and Michael Crichton, share in the award festivities. For a time, Lindzen set himself apart from this latter sort of contrarian; his scientific challenges were often thoughtful and his hypotheses interesting, if one-sided – he never met a negative feedback he didn't like. Sadly, it has become clear that those days are gone.*

22 Lynas, M. (2007b) 'Neutrality is cowardice', *New Statesman*, 3 September, p21.
23 Pearce, F. (2009) 'Arctic meltdown is a threat to humanity', *New Scientist*, 28 March.

Chapter 3: Prospects for Agriculture

1   See a study for the Soil Association by Andersons (2008) 'The impact of rising oil prices on organic and non-organic farm profitability', August, www.soilassociationscotland.org.
2   See UNFPA (2007) 'State of World Population 2007: Unleashing the potential of urban growth', www.infpa.org/swp and UN-Habitat (United Nations Human Settlements Programme) (2003) *The Challenge of Slums*, Earthscan, London.
3   See books by environmentalist (and President of Earth Policy Institute, Washington, DC) Brown, L. (2008a) *Plan B 3.0*, Norton, and Brown, L. (2005) *Outgrowing the Earth*, Earthscan. These provide useful surveys and detailed references to the original scientific literature.
4   Brown, L. (2008a) *Plan B 3.0*, Norton, and Brown, L. (2005) *Outgrowing the Earth*, Earthscan; see also Morton, O. (2007) *Eating the Sun*, Fourth Estate, for discussion of plant reaction to CO_2, but no reference to evidence that leguminous

cover crops can replace artificial nitrogen under organic no-till, as we explain below.

5   See MacKenzie, D. (2009) 'Resistant wheat to tackle destructive fungus', *New Scientist*, 20 March.

6   See Benjamin, A. and McCallum, B. (2008) *A World without Bees*, Guardian Books, and Jacobsen, R. (2008) *Fruitless Fall: The Collapse of the Honey Bee and the Coming Agricultural Crisis*, Bloomsbury.

7   Stiglitz, J. (2006) *Making Globalization Work*, Allen Lane, p86. Stiglitz was formerly Chief Economist at the World Bank, and is now at the Earth Institute at Columbia University and the Brooks World Poverty Institute, University of Manchester. His book provides a scathing critique of institutions of globalization designed to benefit rich countries and corporate interests at the cost of the poorest.

8   See Stiglitz J. (2006) *Making Globalization Work*, Allen Lane, p86, and the following references in Note 9.

9   There are many useful surveys of aspects of the world food system, including Albritton, R. (2009) *Let Them Eat Junk*, Pluto Press; Weis, T. (2007) *The Global Food Economy*, Zed Books; Rajotte, T. and Tansey, G. (eds) (2008) *The Future Control of Food*, Earthscan; Harvey, G. (2008) *The Carbon Fields: How our Countryside can Save Britain*, Grass Roots; Lawrence, F. (2008) *Eat Your Heart Out*, Penguin, London; Patel, R. (2007) *Stuffed and Starved*, Portobello Books; Nestle, M. (2007) *Food Politics: How the Food Industry Influences Nutrition and Health*, University of California Press; Buttal, F. H., Foster, J. B. and Magdoff, F. (eds) (2000) *Hungry for Profit: The Agribusiness Threat to Farmers, Food, and the Environment*, Monthly Review Press. These authors explain how the market power of a few large multinational agricultural and retail corporations is fostering unhealthy food and unsustainable farming, while driving small farmers out of business in both developing and developed countries, with the support of the World Trade Organization and their associated governments.

10   Pollan, M. (2008) *In Defense of Food*, Penguin, London and Albritton, R. (2009) *Let Them Eat Junk*, Pluto Press, London review the extensive literature on the devastating health effects of modern industrial agriculture and processed food production, particularly sugar and refined carbohydrates. The Organic Center (TOC) (www.organic-center.org) commissions scientific studies on these issues, including detailed rebuttal of recent claims by the UK Food Standards Agency (FSA), that organically grown products are not nutritionally superior to organic produce. TOC reports how the FSA ignores pesticide residues, in spite of growing scientific concern about 'cocktail' effects of ingesting numerous chemical residues, and actually reports findings that contradict their own conclusions. More rigorous and wide-ranging TOC studies find additional nutritional benefits from organic food. (www.organic-center.org/science.nutri.php?action=view&report_id=126).

11   Pollan, M. (2008) *In Defence of Food*, Penguin, London.

12   See Mason, T. and Singer, P. (2006) *The Way We Eat: Why our Food Choices Matter*, Rodale, and Pollan, M. (2007) *The Omnivore's Dilemma: A History of Four Meals*, Penguin, London. Pollan makes a compelling case for the sustainable production of animal products that complements mixed farming and delivers much higher quality. Their prices do exceed the quite unrealistic market prices for industrially farmed products that exclude environmental and health costs, but are much lower than any reasonable estimate of the total social and private costs of intensively reared animal products.

13 Pachauri, R. (2008) 'Global warning: The impact of meat production and consumption on climate change', Peter Roberts Memorial Lecture, Compassion in World Farming, London, September. See also Notes 8–11 above and Compassion in World Farming (2007) 'Global warming: Climate change and farm animal welfare', www.ciwf.org/resources/publications/environment_sustainability/default/aspx. See also Harvey, G. (2008) *The Carbon Fields,* Grass Roots, for a well-researched account of how industrial, grain-fed meat and dairy production has been driven by cheap oil and government subsidies with devastating environmental, health and social costs. He also shows how switching to sustainable, grass-fed meat and dairy production would benefit consumers with more nutritious products, sequester large quantities of carbon, and increase efficiency, particularly when oil and grain prices continue their upward spiral after the recession.

14 See Montgomery, D. (2007) *Dirt: The Erosion of Civilizations*, University of California Press, for a detailed history and prescient review of the neglected menace of soil erosion.

15 See Franz, J. and FitzRoy, F. R. (2007) 'Desertification and climate change: Global and regional impacts of degradation in the Aral Sea basin', paper presented at Royal Geographical Society Conference, London, August.

16 See Montgomery, D. (2007) *Dirt: The Erosion of Civilizations*, University of California Press; Brown, L. (2008a), *Plan B 3.0*, Norton; Brown, L. (2005) *Outgrowing the Earth*, Earthscan. Roberts, M. and Schlenker, W. (2008) 'Estimating the impact of climate change on crop yields: The importance of non-linear temperature effects', NBER Working Paper No 13799, predict up to a 79 per cent fall in average yields in the US by the end of the century under rapid warming. By contrast, the smaller estimates of future climate impact on agriculture by Cline, W. (2007) *Global Warming and Agriculture*, Center for Global Development, are based on far too optimistic predictions of climate change under business as usual, which have been overtaken by recent developments, as discussed in Chapter 2.

17 Brown, L. (2008a) *Plan B 3.0*, Norton, and (2005) *Outgrowing the Earth*, Earthscan.

18 These issues are discussed in detail by Tansey, G. (2008) 'For good or for greed', *Ecologist*, November, and by Rajotte, T. and Tansey, G. (eds) (2008) *The Future Control of Food*, Earthscan. Geoff Tansey is a Joseph Rowntree Visionary for a Just and Peaceful World, and received the Derek Cooper Award for best food campaigner/educator in 2008.

19 Biofuels are discussed in detail in Chapter 9. 'First-generation' ethanol and biodiesel production from industrial agriculture or tropical deforestation for palm oil plantation probably increases net GHG emissions.

20 Evans, A. (2009) *The Feeding of the Nine Billion*, Chatham House.

21 Brown, L. (2008a) *Plan B 3.0*, Norton; and Brown, L. (2005) *Outgrowing the Earth*, Earthscan, London.

22 See Brown, L. (2008a) *Plan B 3.0*, Norton; and Brown, L. (2005) *Outgrowing the Earth*, Earthscan, London.

23 Harvey, G. (2006) *We Want Real Food*, Constable, and Pollan, M. (2007) *The Omnivore's Dilemma: A History of Four Meals*, Penguin, London, provide detailed references.

24 Montgomery, D. (2007) *Dirt: The Erosion of Civilizations*, University of California Press, p213. As he points out, heavy clay soils, for example, do require some tillage to avoid compacting.

25 MacKenzie, D. (2008) 'Let them eat spuds', *New Scientist*, 2 August.

26 MacKenzie, D. (2008) 'Let them eat spuds', *New Scientist*, 2 August.

27 These issues are reviewed by Harvey, G. (2006) *We Want Real Food*, Constable, and Montgomery, D. (2007) *Dirt: The Erosion of Civilizations*, University of California Press.

28 See Notes 8–12 above and Blythman, J. (2004) *Shopped: The Shocking Power of British Supermarkets*, Fourth Estate, and Schlosser, E. (2001) *Fast Food Nation*, Allen Lane/Penguin, London. These authors describe the devastating impact on consumer (and animal) health resulting from the concentrated market power of the food and retail industries, in symbiosis with industrial agriculture and unconstrained by any meaningful public regulation. This impact is most visible in – but by no means restricted to – the current obesity 'epidemic', which is predicted to overtake smoking in its long-term disability and death toll. Monbiot, G. (2008b) 'Small is bountiful', *Guardian*, 10 June, summarizes the evidence that smaller farms produce higher yields per hectare, probably due to greater labour-intensity and the better motivation of family members, who provide much of the workforce on small farms.

29 LaSalle, T. J. and Hepperly, P. (2008) 'Regenerative organic farming: A solution to global warming', Rodale Research Paper 07-30-08, Rodale Institute, PA, www.rodaleinstitute.org; LaSalle, T. J., Hepperly, P and Diop, A. (2008) 'The organic green revolution', www.rodaleinstitute.org.

30 See Earley, J., Niggli, U. and Ogorzalek, K. (2007) 'Issues paper: Organic agriculture and environmental stability of the food supply', International Conference on Organic Agriculture and Food Security, FAO, Rome, Italy, May; Douds, D. et al (2005) 'Environment, energy, and economic comparisons of organic and conventional farming systems', *Bioscience*, vol 55, no 7, pp573–582; and many other references in Ho, M. W., Burcher, S. and Lim, L. C. et al (2008) *Food Futures Now*, ISIS, London, and LaSalle, T. and Hepperly, P. (2008) 'Regenerative organic farming: A solution to global warming', Rodale Research Paper 5-28-08, Rodale Institute.

31 This idea, which contrasts with strong opposition to GM by most organic farming experts, is developed by Adamchak, R. and Ronald, P. (2008) *Tomorrow's Table: Organic Farming, Genetics, and the Future of Food,* Oxford University Press.

32 The most detailed and up-to-date account of Cuban agriculture is Wright, J. (2008) *Sustainable Agriculture and Food Security in an Era of Oil Scarcity*, Earthscan. See also New Economics Foundation (2008) *A Green New Deal*; Ho, M. W., Burcher, S. and Lim, L. C. et al (2008), *Food Futures Now*, ISIS, London; Rosset, P. M. 'Cuba: A successful case study of alternative agriculture', in F. Magdoff (ed) (2000) *Hungry for Profit: The Agribusiness Threat to Farmers, Food, and the Environment*, Monthly Review Press. The decline in mortality and obesity following the drastic reduction in calories consumed after the collapse of Soviet aid is documented by: Franco, M., Ordunez, P., Caballero B., Tapia Granados, J. A., Lazo, M., Bernal, J. L., Guallar, E. and Cooper, R. S. (2007) 'Impact of energy intake, physical activity, and population-wide weight loss on cardiovascular disease and diabetes mortality in Cuba, 1980–2005', *American Journal of Epidemiology*, vol 166, no 12, pp1374–1380.

33 See Lehmann, J. (2007a) 'A handful of carbon', *Nature*, 10 May; Mann, C. (2008) 'The future rests on soil. Can we protect it?', *National Geographic*, September; Lehmann, J. and Joseph, S. (2009) *Biochar for Environmental Management*, Earthscan. A highly critical analysis is offered by Ernsting, A. and Rughani, D. (2008) 'Climate geo-engineering with "carbon negative" bioenergy', www.biofuel-watch.org.uk. We discuss the costs and benefits of biofuels in Chapter 9.

Chapter 4: Economic Growth, Wellbeing and Sustainability

1 Charles Jones makes the point that annual world income per capita grew by just 0.08 per cent between 1500 and 1750. The corresponding growth rate between 1950 and 1990 is equal to 2.20 per cent. See Jones, C. I. (2002) *Introduction to Economic Growth*, Norton, New York.

2 There is a tendency for middle-income countries to converge towards the richest ones in income terms, whereas the lower-income countries tend to converge to a much lower income level. This has been described as an income distribution with 'twin peaks'. See Quah, D. (1996) 'Twin peaks: Growth and convergence in models of distribution dynamics', *Economic Journal*, vol 106, no 437, pp1045–1055.

3 In the AOSIS Barbados Declaration in 1994 and subsequent five-year programmes of action, climate change and sea-level rise appeared first in the list of sustainability concerns. Of course the AOSIS states focus primarily on monitoring sea-level rise, mapping vulnerable areas and assessing damages rather than taking any proactive measures. The declaration can be downloaded from the website of the alliance (www.sidsnet.org/aosis/index.html).

4 The Environmental Kuznets Curve (EKC) is likely to hold, though, when considering national carbon dioxide emissions per unit of GDP rather than per capita reflecting improved energy efficiency, but increasing total emissions due to economic growth. See Roberts, J. T. and Grimes, P. E. (1997) 'Carbon intensity and economic development 1962–1991: A brief exploration of the Environmental Kuznets Curve', *World Development*, vol 25, no 2, pp191–198.

5 John Pezzey suggested that the plethora of definitions of sustainability necessarily contributes to confusion. See Pezzey, J. C. V. (1997) 'Sustainability constraints versus optimality versus intertemporal concern, and axioms versus data', *Land Economics*, vol 73, no 2, pp448–466.

6 See Malthus, T. (1798) *An Essay on the Principle of Population*, Oxford University Press (reprint 1993), Oxford, UK.

7 See Boulding, K. (1966) 'The economics of the coming spaceship Earth', in H. Jarrett (ed) *Environmental Quality in a Growing Economy*, John Hopkins Press, Baltimore, MD, and Carson, R. (1962) *Silent Spring*, Houghton Mifflin, New York.

8 World Commission on Environment and Development (1987) *Our Common Future*, Oxford University Press, Oxford, UK.

9 A convention on biological diversity and a statement on forest principles also emerged out of the negotiations at the Earth Summit.

10 See Ehrlich, P. and Holdren, J. (1972) 'One-dimensional ecology', *Bulletin of the Atomic Scientists*, vol 28, no 5, pp16–27. For a recent overview on how the IPAT identity has evolved and been used over the last 30 to 40 years, see Chertow, M. R. (2008) 'The IPAT equation and its variants', *Journal of Industrial Ecology*, vol 4, no 4, pp13–29.

11 For global population trends, see the latest report on 'World population prospects' of the United Nations Population Division, www.un.org/esa/population/unpop.htm.

12 The same point is also made by Jeffrey Sachs; see Sachs, J. D. (2008) *Common Wealth: Economics for a Crowded Planet*, Penguin Books, London.

13 See Smyth, R., Mishra, V. and Qian, X. (2008) 'The environment and well-being in urban China', *Ecological Economics*, vol 68, nos 1–2, pp547–555.

14 The Easterlin Paradox is due to the pioneering work of American economist Richard Easterlin; see Easterlin, R. A. (1974) 'Does economic growth improve the human lot?', in P. A. David and M. W. Reder (eds) *Nations and Households in Economic Growth: Essays in Honour of Moses Abramowitz*, Academic Press, New York. Important recent articles and surveys include Blanchflower, D. G. (2007) 'Is unemployment more costly than inflation?', Working Paper 13505, National Bureau of Economic Research; Inglehart, R., Foa, R., Peterson, C. and Welzel, C. (2008) 'Social change, freedom and rising happiness: A global perspective (1981–2007)', *Perspectives on Psychological Science*, vol 3, no 4, pp264–285; Brockmann, H., Delhey, J., Welzel, C. and Yuan, H. (2008) 'The China puzzle: Falling happiness in a rising economy', *Journal of Happiness Studies*, doi: 10.1007/s10902-008-9095-4; Frey, B. S. (2008) *Happiness: A Revolution in Economics*, MIT Press, Cambridge, MA; Aldred, J. (2009) *The Skeptical Economist*, Earthscan, London; Easterlin, R. A. and Angelescu, L. (2009) 'Happiness and growth the world over: Time series evidence on the happiness–income paradox', IZA, Bonn, DP 4060.

15 Similarly, people *underestimate* their happiness when they were younger, because they evaluate memories of their objective past situation against current aspirations; see Easterlin, R. A. (2005) 'Building a better theory of well-being', in L. Bruni and P. L. Porter (eds) *Economics and Happiness*, Oxford University Press, Oxford.

16 See Beath, J. and FitzRoy, F. (2008) 'Public economics of relative income', Mansholt Lecture, University of Wageningen, The Netherlands, September.

17 Easterlin, R. A. and Angelescu, L. (2009) 'Happiness and growth the world over: Time series evidence on the happiness–income paradox', IZA, Bonn, DP 4060. See also Stevenson, B. and Wolfers, J. (2008) 'Economic growth and subjective well-being: Reassessing the Easterlin Paradox', Brookings Papers on Economic Activity No 1, pp1–87, which confuses short-term correlations and long-term trends, as discussed by Easterlin. When both the trend and cyclical component of real income is included in a West European panel, short-term cyclical income has a strong effect on average happiness, and trend income has little effect. Relative income, and perceived relative income, have negative effects on individual SWB of about the same magnitude as own income, as shown by Layard, R., Mayraz, G. and S. Nickell, S. (2009) 'Does relative income matter? Are the critics right?', SOEP papers on multidisciplinary panel data research, DIW Berlin.

18 Luttmer, R. F. P. (2005) 'Neighbors as negatives: Relative earnings and well-being', *Quarterly Journal of Economics*, vol 120, no 3, pp963–1002.

19 Helliwell, J. F. (2006) 'Well-being, social capital and public policy: What's new?', *The Economic Journal*, vol 116, no 510, pp34–46, and Helliwell, J. F. and Huang, H. (2005) 'How's the job? Well-being and social capital in the workplace', Working Paper 11759, National Bureau of Economic Research. See also Konow, J. and Earley, J. (2008) 'The hedonistic paradox: Is *Homo economicus* happier?', *Journal of Public Economics*, vol 92, nos 1–2, pp1–33.

20 Many authors have documented these tendencies in great detail; see, for example, Jackson, T. (2009) *Prosperity without Growth*, Earthscan, London; Offer, A. (2006) *The Challenge of Affluence*, Oxford University Press, Oxford; Lane, R. E. (2001) *The Loss of Happiness in Market Economies*, Yale University Press, New Haven, CT.

21 Denmark usually comes top in international rankings of SWB, and this is probably related to high levels of trust and social cohesion.

22 Michaelson, J. (2009) 'National accounts of well-being: A new measure of success', www.neftriplecrunch.wordpress.com/2009/01/26/national-accounts-of-well-being-a-new-measure-of-success. French President Nicolas Sarkozy has commissioned a team of prominent economists to consider ways of improving the measurement of economic performance, to include environmental and social aspects; 'Report by the Commission on the Measurement of Economic Performance and Social Progress', September 2009, www.stiglitz-sen-fitoussi.fr.

23 See Wackernagel, M. and Rees, W. E. (1996) *Our Ecological Footprint: Reducing the Human Impact on the Earth*, New Society Publishers, British Columbia.

24 WWF has issued a biennial report containing footprint estimations since 2000. The most recent one is the 2008 Living Planet Report downloadable from the WWF webpage, www.panda.org/about_our_publications/all_publications/living_planet_report.

25 See Weber, C. L. and Matthews, S. H. (2008) 'Quantifying the global and distributional aspects of American household carbon footprint', *Ecological Economics*, vol 66, nos 2–3, pp379–391.

26 See Hartwick, J. M. (1977) 'Intergenerational equity and the investing of rents from exhaustible resources', *American Economic Review*, vol 67, no 5, pp972–974.

27 Hanley, N., Moffatt, I., Faichney, R. and Wilson, M. (1999) 'Measuring sustainability: A time series of indicators for Scotland', *Ecological Economics*, vol 28, no 1, pp53–73, and Lange, G.-M. (2004) 'Wealth, natural capital and sustainable development: Contrasting examples from Botswana and Namibia', *Environmental and Resource Economics*, vol 29, no 3, pp257–283.

28 See Rowe, J. (2003) 'Grossly distorting perception', *The Ecologist*, 1 February, www.theecologist.org/pages/archive_detail.asp?content_id=400, accessed 15 February 2009.

29 See Stiglitz, J. (2006) *Making Globalization Work*, Allen Lane, London, Chapter 3.

30 See Daly, H. E. and Cobb, J. (1989) *For the Common Good: Redirecting the Economy towards Community, the Environment and a Sustainable Future*, Beacon Press, Boston, MA. Recent data on the Genuine Progress Indicator can be downloaded at the webpage of Redefining Progress, www.rprogress.org. See also Costanza, R., Erickson, J., Fligger, K., Adams, A., Adams, C., Altschuler, B., Balter, S., Fisher, B., Hike, J., Kelly, J., Kerr, T., McCauley, M., Montone, K., Rauch, M., Schmiedeskamp, K., Saxton, D., Sparacino, L., Tusinski, W. and Williams, L. (2004) 'Estimates of the Genuine Progress Indicator (GPI) for Vermont, Chittenden County and Burlington, from 1950 to 2000', *Ecological Economics*, vol 51, nos 1–2, pp139–155.

31 Friends of the Earth and New Economics Foundation (2006) 'The Happy Planet Index', www.neweconomics.org/gen/uploads/dl44k145g5scuy453044gqbu11072006194758.pdf, p8.

32 For a concise analysis and history of the links between the tobacco industry's falsification of the scientific evidence on the health effects of smoking and climate change deception which still continues despite a scientific consensus that is equally overwhelming, see Bazerman, M. H. (2006) 'Climate change as a predictable surprise', *Climatic Change*, vol 77, nos 1–2, pp179–193 and Monbiot, G. (2007) *Heat*, Allen Lane, London.

Chapter 5: Development in a Changing Climate

1 See Sahn, D. E. and Stifel, D. C. (2003) 'Progress toward the Millennium Development Goals in Africa', *World Development*, vol 31, no 1, pp23–52, and Clemens, M. A., Kenny, C. J. and Moss, T. J. (2007) 'The trouble with the MDGs: Confronting expectations of aid and development success', *World Development*, vol 35, no 5, pp735–751.

2 The Millennium Declaration, listing these basic global objectives and more detailed targets, can be downloaded at the United Nations webpage, www.un.org/milleniumgoals. The United Nations is also publishing a yearly Millennium Development Goals Progress Report evaluating relative progress across countries and objectives.

3 For data on income poverty across and within countries, the United Nations Human Development Reports provide an excellent source, see http://hdr.undp.org/en.

4 There is a recent paper associating reduced losses from extreme weather events and disasters with income levels, educational attainments and openness to trade – see Toya, H. and Skidmore, M. (2007) 'Economic development and the impact of natural disasters', *Economic Letters*, vol 94, no 1, pp20–25.

5 This argument has been extensively used (and misused) by the US Administration in order to justify the decision to abstain from the Kyoto Protocol. The Bush Administration objected to China and India, being two of the world's top greenhouse gas emitters, being exempted from Kyoto requirements. They failed to acknowledge the special needs and characteristics of developing countries, for which priority is often given to economic development rather than environmental protection. The Americans preferred to opt out of the treaty rather than participate and actively assist developing nations in reducing their carbon emissions (by transferring greener technologies and funds).

6 The same rule of thumb can also apply to negative growth rates. In this case the calculated number of years implies the period needed for a variable to halve rather than double. Many Eastern European countries are experiencing negative growth rates in population. Countries such as Russia and Belarus have experienced a negative population growth rate of approximately 0.50 per cent annually. This suggests that their population would be expected to halve in 70/0.50 = 140 years if the growth rate stayed unchanged.

7 Jeffrey Frankel claims that the Chinese yuan may be undervalued by as much as 35 per cent against the US dollar. See Frankel, J. (2006) 'On the yuan: The choice between adjustment under a fixed exchange rate and adjustment under a flexible rate', *CESifo Economic Studies*, vol 52, no 2, pp246–275.

8 See Climate Group (2008) 'China's clean revolution', www.theclimategroup.org/assets/resources/Chinas_Clean_Revolution.pdf and Lovins, A. and Sheikh, I. (2008) *The Nuclear Illusion*, Rocky Mountain Institute, Boulder, CO.

9   See Banister, J. and Zhang, X. (2005) 'China, economic development and mortality decline', *World Development*, vol 33, no 1, pp21–41, and the World Bank Development Indicators webpage, www.worldbank.org/data. The mortality rate of children below five years of age dropped from 60 to 24 children per 1000 between 1980 and 2006. Average life expectancy also rose from 67 to 72 years in the same period.

10 See http://news.bbc.co.uk/1/hi/world/asia-pacific/6458565.stm, accessed 15 February 2009.

11 See Inglehart, R., Foa, R., Peterson, C. and Welzel, C. (2008) 'Social change, freedom and rising happiness: A global perspective (1981–2007)', *Perspectives on Psychological Science*, vol 3, no 4, pp264–285.

12 For an interesting discussion on the impacts of Chinese foreign direct investment, see Frost, S. and Ho, M. (2005) 'Going out: The growth of Chinese foreign direct investment in Southeast Asia and its implications for corporate social responsibility', *Corporate Social Responsibility and Environmental Management*, vol 12, no 3, pp157–167.

13 For instance, in 2005 only 1.4 and 1.6 per cent of the labour force was employed in the agricultural sector in the UK and the US respectively.

14 There is fear that malaria may even reappear in some of the world's richer nations that had previously eradicated the disease; see www.guardian.co.uk/environment/2007/jan/06/italy.climatechange, accessed 15 February 2009.

15 For an interesting paper on the difficulties of managing transboundary global pollution and the need for a broader institutional framework, see Dietz, T., Ostrom, E. and Stern, P. (2003) 'The struggle to govern the commons', *Science*, vol 302, no 5652, pp1907–1912.

16 See Shisanya, C. A. and Khayesi, M. (2007) 'How is climate change perceived in relation to other socioeconomic and environmental threats in Nairobi, Kenya?', *Climatic Change*, vol 85, nos 3–4, pp271–284.

17 See the special issue of *Climatic Change* in July 2006 on 'Global warming: The psychology of long-term risk', in particular Weber, E. E. (2006) 'Experience-based and description-based perceptions of long-term risk: Why global warming does not scare us (yet)', *Climatic Change*, vol 77, nos 1–2, pp103–120.

18 See Etkin, D. and Ho, E. (2007) 'Climate change: Perceptions and discourses of risk', *Journal of Risk Research*, vol 10, no 5, pp623–641, and Lorenzoni, I. and Pidgeon, N. F. (2006) 'Public views on climate change: European and USA perspectives', *Climatic Change*, vol 77, nos 1–2, pp73–95.

19 See Sachs, J. D. (2008) *Common Wealth: Economics for a Crowded Planet*, Penguin Books, London

20 Sachs, J. D., (2008) *Common Wealth: Economics for a Crowded Planet*, Penguin Books, London.

21 McKibben, B. (2005) 'Curitiba: A global model for development', CommonDreams.org, www.commondreams.org/views05/1108-33.htm, accessed 15 February 2009. See also Rabinovitch, J. (1996) 'Innovative land use and public transport policy: The case of Curitiba, Brazil', *Land Use Policy*, vol 13, no 1, pp51–67, and Rabinovitch, J. and Leitman, J. (2004) 'Urban planning in Curitiba', in S. M. Wheeler and T. Beatley (eds) *The Sustainable Urban Development Reader*, Routledge, London.

22 For an overview of the economic drivers of deforestation, see Barbier, E. B. and Burgess, J. C. (2001) 'The economics of tropical deforestation', *Journal of*

Economic Surveys, vol 15, no 3, pp413–433. For recent estimates of deforestation and the role of biofuels, see Malhi, Y., Roberts, T. J., Betts, R. A., Killeen, T. J., Li, W. and Nobre, C. A. (2008) 'Climate change, deforestation, and the fate of the Amazon', *Science*, vol 319, no 5860, pp169–172, and Fargione, J., Hill, J., Tilman, D., Polasky, S. and Hawthorne, P. (2008) 'Land clearing and the biofuel carbon debt', *Science*, vol 319, no 5867, pp1235–1238.

23 See the recent report on export-processing zones by the International Labour Organization: Boyenge, J-P. (2007) 'ILO database on export processing zones', International Labour Organization, Geneva, downloadable at www.ilo.org/public/english/dialogue/sector/themes/epz/epz-db.pdf.

24 See Levinson, A. and Taylor, M. S. (2008) 'Unmasking the pollution haven effect', *International Economic Review*, vol 49, no 1, pp223–254.

25 For a recent study on the diverging strategies of national firms and foreign multi-national corporations regarding market exit rates, see Van Beveren, I. (2007) 'Footloose multinationals in Belgium', *Review of World Economics*, vol 143, no 3, pp483–507. See also Chang, H-J. (2007) *Bad Samaritans: Rich Nations, Poor Policies and the Threat to the Developing World*, Random House Business Books.

26 See Pan, J., Phillips, J. and Chen, Y. (2008) 'China's balance of emissions embodied in trade: Approaches to measurement and allocating international responsibility', *Oxford Review of Economic Policy*, vol 24, no 2, pp354–376.

27 See Stiglitz, J. (2006) *Making Globalization Work*, Allen Lane, London (Chapters 5 and 7 in particular).

28 Trade unions of course do not always promote social interest or environmental protection. They might also oppose green policies and environmental legislation if these are expected to have an adverse effect on employment. See Fredriksson, P. G. and Gaston, N. (1999) 'The "greening" of trade unions and the demand for eco-taxes', *European Journal of Political Economy*, vol 15, no 4, pp663–686.

29 Eric Neumayer suggests that the parliamentary green/left-libertarian party strength is associated with lower pollution levels across countries. Providing evidence from 21 OECD countries, he finds that a large representation of green parties in parliament is associated with reduced carbon emissions per capita. On the other hand he found no evidence that corporatism (extent of trade union power, legal support to trade unions and nature of wage dispute resolution) results in better carbon management. See Neumayer, E. (2003) 'Are left-wing party strength and corporatism good for the environment? Evidence from panel analysis of air pollution in OECD countries', *Ecological Economics*, vol 45, no 2, pp203–220.

30 See Speth, J. G. (2008) *The Bridge at the End of the World*, Yale University Press, New Haven, CT.

31 Robert Deacon and Sarani Saha find that dictatorships reduce access to many environmental public goods (for example sanitation and safe water) by more than 30 per cent compared to democratic regimes. See Deacon, R. and Saha, S. (2006) 'Public goods provision by dictatorships: A survey', in A. F. Ott, and R. J. Cebula (eds) *The Elgar Companion to Public Economics: Empirical Public Economics*, Edward Elgar, Cheltenham.

32 The African Union drew up a convention on corruption in 2002 to bring attention to common malpractices and their repercussions for output and the most vulnerable segments of society. See the African Union Convention on Preventing and Combating Corruption, downloadable at: www.africa-union.org/root/AU/Documents/Treaties/treaties.htm.

33 See Collier, P., Conway, G. and Venables, T. (2008) 'Climate change and Africa', *Oxford Review of Economic Policy*, vol 24, no 2, pp337–353.

34 Wei, S-J. (1999) 'Corruption in economic development: Beneficial grease, minor annoyance or major obstacle?', World Bank Policy Research Working Paper No 2048, World Bank, Washington, DC.

35 See Collier, P. (2007) *The Bottom Billion: Why the Poorest Countries Are Failing and What Can Be Done About It*, Oxford University Press, Oxford.

36 See Treisman, D. (2000) 'The causes of corruption: A cross-national study', *Journal of Public Economics*, vol 76, no 3, pp399–457.

37 For an interesting discussion, see Stiglitz, J. (2006) *Making Globalization Work*, Allen Lane, London, Chapter 5, and for many further references Monbiot, G. (2008c) 'Pin-striped pirates', *The Guardian*, 16 December, www.monbiot.com/archives/2008/12/16/pin-striped-pirates.

38 See Robinson, J. A. and Torvik, R. (2005) 'White elephants', *Journal of Public Economics*, vol 89, nos 2–3, pp197–210.

39 See López, R. (2008) 'Structural adjustment and sustainable development', in R. López and M. T. Toman (eds) *Economic Development and Environmental Sustainability*, Oxford University Press, Oxford.

40 Sachs, J. D. (2008) *Common Wealth: Economics for a Crowded Planet*, Penguin Books, London, Chapter 9, pp209–212, and Barnett, J. and Adger, N. W. (2007) 'Climate change, human security and violent conflict', *Political Geography*, vol 26, no 6, pp639–655. James Lee discusses how states will increasingly face new challenges to maintain social order, as competition for scarcer natural resources in arid regions or for the exploitation of new resources in northern latitudes intensifies with climate change – see Lee R. J. (2009) *Climate Change and Armed Conflict*, Routledge, Abingdon, UK.

41 See López, R. (2008) 'Structural adjustment and sustainable development', in R. López and M. T. Toman (eds) *Economic Development and Environmental Sustainability*, Oxford University Press, Oxford.

Chapter 6: Ethics and Climate Change

1 Regional climate models show clearly the uneven distribution of expected changes in temperature and rainfall – see the 2007 IPCC Report, Intergovernmental Panel on Climate Change (2007) *Impacts, Adaptation and Vulnerability: Working Group II Contribution to the Fourth Assessment Report of the IPCC*, Cambridge University Press, Cambridge.

2 A recent pattern of gradual increases in droughts and desertification in the Chinese north-western provinces is now broadly recognized by Chinese academics themselves – see, for instance, Qian, W. and Zhu, Y. (2001) 'Climate change in China from 1880 to 1998 and its impact on the environmental condition', *Climatic Change*, vol 50, no 4, pp1480–1573, and Wu. B. and Ci, L. J. (2002) 'Landscape change and desertification development in the Mu Us Sandland, Northern China', *Journal of Arid Environments*, vol 50, no 3, pp429–444.

3 The likelihood and impact of water shortages and rising sea levels are discussed in Chapter 2. To read more on Edward Page's ideas on a 'global sufficientarian ethic', see Page, E. (2007) 'Justice between generations: Investigating a sufficientarian approach', *Journal of Global Ethics*, vol 3, no 1, pp3–20.

4   See Bentham, J. (1789) *An Introduction to the Principles of Morals and Legislation*, Kessinger Publishing (reprint 2005), Whitefish, MT and Mill, J. S. (1861) *Utilitarianism*, Oxford University Press (reprint 1998), Oxford.

5   These issues are discussed in detail in Chapter 4.

6   Princeton philosopher Peter Singer develops these ideas in his book *One World* (2001) Yale University Press, New Haven, CT. For comprehensive accounts of the evolution of morality, see Hauser, M. D. (2006) *Moral Minds: How Nature Designed Our Universal Sense of Right and Wrong*, Ecco, New York, and Joyce, R. (2006) *The Evolution of Morality (Life and Mind)*, MIT Press, Cambridge, MA.

7   See Stiglitz, J. (2006) *Making Globalization Work*, Allen Lane, London, and Barry, B. (2006) *Why Social Justice Matters*, Polity Press, Cambridge.

8   Taxes imposed on consumers of carbon-intensive products are essentially equivalent.

9   See Rawls, J. (1961) *A Theory of Justice*, Harvard University Press, Cambridge, MA. For a recent exposition of how Rawls' ethical principles relate to climate change and intergenerational ethics see Vanderheiden S. (2008) *Atmospheric Justice*, Oxford University Press, Oxford, UK.

10 The conventional economics of declining marginal utility of income or consumption also supports the welfare gains of redistribution from rich to poor, provided of course that loss of incentives, say from redistributive taxes, does not end up making everyone worse off.

11 This is often referred to as the 'maximin rule', in other words a rule that maximizes the position of the worst off (individuals, countries or generations).

12 See Sen, A. (1985) *Commodities and Capabilities*, Oxford University Press, Oxford.

13 Martha Nussbaum claims that these capabilities may be revisable over time according to changing cultural patterns; see Nussbaum, M. (2000) *Women and Human Development: The Capabilities Approach*, Cambridge University Press, Cambridge.

14 The precautionary principle is particularly relevant for environmental problems that depend on stocks of pollutants, or GHGs in the atmosphere, that accumulate over time under business as usual, rather than just on the current level of emissions. For that reason, delayed action on emissions may not be able to avert an environmental catastrophe. See Gollier, C., Jullien, B. and Treich, N. (2000) 'Scientific progress and irreversibility: An economic interpretation of the "precautionary principle"', *Journal of Public Economics*, vol 75, no 2, pp229–253.

15 See Broome, J. (2006) 'Valuing policies in response to climate change: Some ethical issues', mimeo, University of Oxford, Oxford.

16 See United Nations (1992) *Agenda 21 Earth Summit: United Nations Program of Action from Rio*, United Nations, New York.

17 See Pezzey, J. C. V. (1994) 'Concern for sustainability in a sexual world', Centre for Social and Economic Research on the Global Environment, London. There is also a summary of the main arguments in Dresner, S. (2002) *The Principles of Sustainability*, Earthscan, London.

18 The Fourth IPCC report estimates that around 20–30 per cent of known plant and animal species face a large risk of extinction if global warming exceeds 1.5–2.5°C; see Intergovernmental Panel on Climate Change (2007) *Impacts, Adaptation and Vulnerability: Working Group II Contribution to the Fourth Assessment Report of the IPCC*, Cambridge University Press, Cambridge.

19 See Alesina, A. and Glaeser, E. (2004) *Fighting Poverty in the US and Europe: A World of Difference*, Oxford University Press, Oxford.

20 See Alesina, A., Devleeschauwer, A., Easterly, W., Kurlat, S. and Wacziarg, R. (2003) 'Fractionalization', *Journal of Economic Growth*, vol 8, no 2, pp155–194.

21 See Ahuja, V. (1998) 'Land degradation, agricultural productivity, and common property: Evidence from Côte d'Ivoire', *Environment and Development Economics*, vol 3, no1, pp7–34.

22 Jackson, K. (2008) 'Why does ethnic diversity affect public good provision? An empirical analysis of water provision in Africa', mimeo, University of British Columbia, Vancouver.

23 For a recent overview of willingness to pay and willingness to accept studies, see Horowitz, J. K. and McConnell, K. E. (2002) 'A review of WTA/WTP studies', *Journal of Environmental Economics and Management*, vol 44, no 3, pp426–447.

24 See Biel, A., Johansson-Stenman, O. and Nilsson, A. (2006) 'Emotions, morality, and public goods: The WTA–WTP disparity revisited', Working Papers in Economics 193, University of Göteborg, Göteborg.

25 The Australian Human Rights and Equal Opportunity Commission has produced an excellent overview of human rights issues linked to climate change: www.humanrights.gov.au/pdf/about/media/papers/hrandclimate_change.pdf.

26 For a more in-depth discussion on the United Nations' role in international environmental law, see Birnie, P. and Boyle, A. (2002) *International Law and the Environment*, Oxford University Press, Oxford, and Cordonier Segger, M-C. and Khalfan, A. (2004) *Sustainable Development Law: Principles, Practices and Prospects*, Oxford University Press, Oxford.

27 There are two broad philosophical approaches regarding the allocation of rights. Humanist moral philosophies allocate rights exclusively to human beings. On the other hand, naturalist moral philosophies extend rights broadly to a natural system, of which human beings are part. Princeton philosopher Peter Singer pioneered the case for animal rights in his book *Animal Liberation* (1975) Random House, London; see also Singer, P. (1979) *Practical Ethics*, Cambridge University Press, Cambridge.

In a similar vein, Oxford evolutionary biologist and critic of religion Richard Dawkins wrote:

Such is the breathtaking speciesism of our Christian-inspired attitudes, the abortion of a single human zygote (most of them are destined to be spontaneously aborted anyway) can arouse more moral solicitude and righteous indignation than the vivisection of any number of intelligent adult chimpanzees! ... The only reason we can be comfortable with such a double standard is that the intermediates between humans and chimps are all dead. (Dawkins, 1986)

28 See Jenkins, T. M. (1998) 'Economics and the environment: A case of ethical neglect', *Ecological Economics*, vol 26, no 2, pp151–163.

29 For a discussion on how modern science and technologies desacralized nature, see Northcott, M. S. (2007) *A Moral Climate: The Ethics of Global Warming*, Longman, London.

30 McFague, S. (2008) A *New Climate for Theology: God, the World, and Global Warming*, Fortress Press, Minneapolis, MN.

31 Weber, M. (1904–1905) *The Protestant Ethic and the Spirit of Capitalism*, Routledge (reprint 2001), London.

32 Northcott, M. S. (2007) *A Moral Climate: The Ethics of Global Warming*, Longman, London. The distinction between 'subsistence' and 'luxury' emissions was first discussed in Shue, H. (1993) 'Subsistence emissions and luxury emissions', *Law and Policy*, vol 15, no 1, pp39–59.

33 Ricardo, D. (1817) *Principles of Political Economy and Taxation*, Dover Publications (reprint 2004), Mineola, NY.

34 These policy prescriptions advocated by the International Monetary Fund and the World Bank (which included extensive privatization, deregulation of markets and fiscal policy discipline as well as trade liberalization) are often referred to as the 'Washington Consensus', powerfully criticized by former 'insider' and Nobel economist Joseph Stiglitz; see Stiglitz, J. (2006) *Making Globalization Work*, Allen Lane, London.

35 Peter Dauvergne suggests that current global patterns of trade displace our current environmental costs of consumption away from the current rich towards distant (in time and space) ecosystems and vulnerable communities. He calls these environmental and social costs – a direct result of the current unsustainable mass-producing frenzy of powerful multinational corporations – the (ecological) shadows of consumption. See Dauvergne, P. (2008) *The Shadows of Consumption: Consequences for the Global Environment*, MIT Press, Cambridge, MA.

36 The webpage of the Fairtrade Labelling Organizations International (FLO) provides details of the scheme's certification and active projects around the world (www.fairtrade.net). For a discussion on how current trade patterns have largely failed both to alleviate poverty and to improve environmental standards, see the new book by Joseph Stiglitz and Andrew Charlton, *Fair Trade for All: How Trade Can Promote Development* (2007), Oxford University Press, Oxford.

37 Oliver, J. (2007) *Jamie at Home, Cook Your Way to the Good Life*, Penguin, London.

38 The UK supermarket chain Tesco is also planning to launch a limited two-year carbon-labelling scheme for approximately 20 of its products, ranging from potatoes to light bulbs. Consumers would be informed about carbon emissions emitted over the life of the production from its earlier stages of production to consumption.

39 For an interesting experiment on how consumers switch preferences when they associate meat with its animal origin, see Hoogland, C., de Boer, J. and Boersema, J. J. (2005) 'Transparency of the meat chain in the light of food culture and history', *Appetite*, vol 45, no 1, pp15–23.

40 For some recent estimates on the impact of meat production on carbon emissions, see McMichael, A. J., Powles, J. W., Butler, C. D. and Uauy, R. (2007) 'Food, livestock production, energy, climate change, and health, *The Lancet*, vol 370, no 9594, pp1253–1263.

Chapter 7: Kyoto and Other International Environmental Agreements

1 It is no coincidence that Fiji, Antigua and Barbuda, Tuvalu and the Maldives, with economies little dependent on carbon, were the four first countries to ratify the Kyoto Protocol in 1998.

2 Australia changed course and ratified the protocol in December 2007, shortly after Kevin Rudd's newly elected government assumed office.

3   This is often called the free-rider problem in economics.

4   This is related to the 'non-rivalry' characteristic of public goods and bads. The amount of environmental protection enjoyed by any person or country (for example in the form of climate change mitigation) does not reduce the amount of protection offered to any other party.

5   In its original form, the game deals with a situation of two partners in a crime, who are separately questioned by the police. Each of two individuals has the choice of either confessing to the crime (while implicating his/her partner) or denying participation. If only one of the two partners confesses, he/she is let free, while the other receives a maximum sentence. If both partners deny involvement, they receive the minimum sentence. Instead, if they both confess their involvement, they receive a sentence between the minimum and maximum prison terms.

6   For an interesting exposition of game-theoretical models of environmental agreements, see the two recent books by Scott Barrett: Barrett, S. (2003) *Environment and Statecraft: The Strategy of Environmental Treaty-Making*, Oxford University Press, Oxford, and Barrett, S. (2007) *Why Cooperate? The Incentive to Supply Global Public Goods*, Oxford University Press, Oxford.

7   See Bowen, M. (2007) *Censoring Science: Inside the Political Attack on Dr James Hansen and the Truth of Global Warming*, Dutton, Hialeah, FL, and Monbiot, G. (2006) *Heat*, Allen Lane, London.

8   In game theory analysis, these are often called games with multiple players.

9   In the case of the EITI, Collier makes the point that countries tend to follow strategies chosen by the majority of their neighbours in order to avoid political alienation and embarrassment. This is exactly why so many African countries successively asked to be included in such an international initiative on anti-corruption, with many more waiting to be given candidate status. See Collier, P. (2007) *The Bottom Billion: Why the Poorest Countries Are Failing and What Can Be Done About It*, Oxford University Press, Oxford.

10 In a rather perverse way, the Adaptation Fund will be financed by the proceeds from projects within the Clean Development Mechanism, rather than any taxes on environmental pollution. The two per cent tax on proceeds by CDM projects will increase the overall budget of the Adaptation Fund, but possibly at the expense of aid transfer to developing nations in the form of CDM projects. See Jarman, M. (2007) *Climate Change*, Oxfam, London, for a discussion.

11 There are plans, however, at an EU level, to impose fines between €40 and €100 per tonne of CO_2 beyond permitted targets.

12 Walker, G. and King, D. (2008) *The Hot Topic: How to Tackle Global Warming and Still Keep the Lights On*, Bloomsbury, London, p193.

13 Walker, G. and King, D., (2008) *The Hot Topic: How to Tackle Global Warming and Still Keep the Lights On*, Bloomsbury, London.

14 See Neumayer, E. (2007) 'A missed opportunity: The Stern Review of Climate Change fails to tackle the issue of non-substitutable loss of natural capital', *Global Environmental Change*, vol 17, nos 3–4, pp297–301.

15 The books by Walker and King, as well as the book by Jarman, provide a long list of recent inefficiency examples regarding CDM implementation; see Walker, G. and King, D. (2008) *The Hot Topic: How to Tackle Global Warming and Still Keep the Lights On*, Bloomsbury, London, and Jarman, M. (2007) *Climate Change*, Oxfam. See also Newell, P., Jenner, N. and Baker, L. (2009) 'Governing

clean development: A framework for analysis', Governance of Clean Development Working Paper 001, March 2009, University of East Anglia.

16 Of course, in any treaty to succeed Kyoto, emission caps should decrease over time if we want to minimize the probability of exceeding the two-degree threshold and suffering catastrophic climate change.

17 Emissions trading is often referred to as 'cap and trade' in the climate change jargon.

18 For an early discussion of the successful US experience of the SO_2 cap-and-trade scheme, see Stavins, R. N. (1998) 'What can we learn from the grand policy experiment? Lessons from SO_2 allowance trading', *The Journal of Economic Perspectives*, vol 12, no 3, pp69–88. Nevertheless, the SO_2 cap-and-trade scheme has also been criticized for failing to achieve maximum economic efficiency by grandfathering rather than auctioning SO_2 allowances; see Ellerman, D. A. (2003) 'Ex post evaluation of tradable permits: The US SO_2 cap-and-trade program', MIT-CEEPR Working Paper 0303, MIT Center for Energy and Environmental Policy Research, Cambridge, MA. Additionally, economists often favour a global environmental tax to cap-and-trade schemes, since the first is generally a less technical and complicated policy instrument to implement and can be applied more broadly across all consumers (with the latter regulating pollution in a few sectors and firms). For an interesting discussion, see the recent article by Gregory Mankiw in *The New York Times* – Mankiw, G. (2007) 'One answer to global warming: A new tax', *NY Times*, 16 September.

19 Details on the EU ETS scheme can be found at the webpage of the European Commission: http://ec.europa.eu/environment/climat/2nd_phase_ep.htm.

20 Oliver Tickell provides an excellent exposition of the four EU ETS phases; see Tickell, O. (2008) *Kyoto 2: How to Manage the Global Greenhouse*, Zed Books, London.

21 Dieter Helm discusses in detail how public revenues from auctioning permits is likely to increase rent-seeking pressure on governments; see Helm, D. (2008) 'Climate change policy: Why has so little been achieved?', *Oxford Review of Economic Policy*, vol 24, no 2, pp211–238.

22 See Stavins, R. N. (2008) 'Addressing climate change with a comprehensive US cap-and-trade system', *Oxford Review of Economic Policy*, vol 24, no 2, pp298–321.

23 See, Tickell, O. (2008) *Kyoto 2: How to Manage the Global Greenhouse*, Zed Books, London, for a discussion of a 'contraction and convergence' based cap-and-trade scheme and the political resistance it is likely to face.

24 A detailed discussion of the Montreal Protocol and its relative strengths, from which this subsection draws, can be found at Barrett, S. (2003) *Environment and statecraft: The Strategy of Environmental Treaty-Making*, Oxford University Press, Oxford, Chapter 8.

25 Details about the Montreal Protocol and its subsequent amendments can be found at the webpage of the United Nations Environment Programme: http://ozone.unep.org.

26 See Farman, J. C., Gardiner, B. G. and Shanklin, J. D. (1985) 'Large losses of total ozone in Antarctica reveal seasonal ClOx/NOx interaction', *Nature*, vol 315, pp207–210.

27 For an interesting discussion on the role of trade sanctions in international environmental agreements, see, Barrett, S. (1997) 'The strategy of trade sanctions in international environmental agreements', *Resource and Energy Economics*, vol 19, no 4, pp345–361, and Werksman, J. W. (1992) 'Trade sanctions under the Montreal Protocol', *Review of European Community and International Environmental Law*, vol 1, no 1, pp69–72.

28 James Garvey makes this point at his new book on climate change; see Garvey, J. (2008) *The Ethics of Climate Change: Right and Wrong in a Warming Planet*, Continuum, London.

29 Helm, D. (2008) 'Climate change policy: Why has so little been achieved?', *Oxford Review of Economic Policy*, vol 24, no 2, pp211–238.

30 The Global Commons Institute (GCI) in the UK claims that what the world has experienced so far instead is a growing trend of 'expansion and divergence'. For more information on 'contraction and convergence', visit the institute's webpage at www.gci.org.uk.

31 See Barrett, S. (2008) 'Climate treaties and the imperative of enforcement', *Oxford Review of Economic Policy*, vol 24, no 2, pp239–258.

Chapter 8: Incentives for Mitigation – Carbon Taxes and Emissions Trading

1 Tickell, O. (2008) *Kyoto 2*, Zed Books, discusses the institutional background and how energy-saving initiatives in the US have been effective and profitable. Such policies in California have helped to reduce electricity consumption there to almost half the US per capita average.

2 Sunstein, C. and Thaler, R. (2008) *Nudge*, Yale University Press, discusses recent advances in behavioural economics that explain these reactions.

3 A prominent epidemiologist, Devra Davis, provides a gripping account of these campaigns in her book *When Smoke Ran Like Water: Tales of Environmental Deception and the Battle Against Pollution* (2002), Basic Books.

4 Stavins, R. (2008) 'Addressing climate change with a comprehensive US cap-and-trade system', *Oxford Review of Economic Policy*, vol 24, no 2, pp298–321.

Chapter 9: The Costs of Climate Change and the Benefits of Mitigation

1 See Nordhaus, W. (2008) *A Question of Balance: Weighing the Options on Global Warming Policies*, Yale University Press. In grim contrast, one famous scientist, James Lovelock, predicts only around a billion survivors by the end of the century; see Lovelock, J. (2009a) *The Vanishing Face of Gaia*, Allen Lane, and Lovelock, J. (2009b) 'We're doomed but it's not all bad', *New Scientist*, 24 January.

2 See Nordhaus, W. (2007) 'A review of the *Stern Review on the Economics of Climate Change*', *Journal of Economic Literature*, vol XLV, September. Nordhaus's quite outdated view of climate science leads him to the conclusion that Stern's implausible model destroys his much more general arguments for a substantial carbon price or tax, and hence justifies Nordhaus's own 'do-nothing-now' conclusion. A more perceptive critic is Weitzman, M. (2007) 'A review of the *Stern Review on the Economics of Climate Change*', *Journal of Economic*

Literature, vol XLV, September, who agrees with Stern on the urgency of substantial carbon taxes, though also rejecting his formal modelling of almost equal weighting of all future lives. Instead, Weitzman suggests that insurance against the risk of unlikely but disastrous long-term effects of global warming could justify the carbon tax and perhaps other mitigation policies, though in the end he qualifies this with the usual call for more research before taking drastic action for mitigation. Like most economists, all these critics seem to be unaware that current climate science predicts very high risks of runaway warming with disastrous outcomes – rather than a very low probability of catastrophic events – unless a major mitigation effort is initiated soon. Ackerman, F. (2008) *Can We Afford the Future?*, Zed Books, uniquely among critics, offers sensible policy alternatives based on the precautionary principle, discussed below. See also Jeroen van den Bergh (2009) 'Safe climate policy is affordable' mimeo, ICREA, Barcelona, for similar arguments and Worldwatch Institute (2009) *State of the World 2009: Into a Warming World*.

3   Stern, N. (2008) 'The economics of climate change', *American Economic Review: Papers and Proceedings*, vol 98, no 2, pp1–37; Stern, N. (2009) *A Blueprint for a Safer Planet*, Bodley Head.

4   For example, Eby, M., Montenegro, A., Weaver, A. J. and Zickfeld K. (2007) 'Long term climate implications of 2050 emission reduction targets', *Geophysical Letters*, vol 34, L19703, doi:10.1029/2007GL031018.

5   Stern, N. (2007) *The Economics of Climate Change*, Cambridge University Press, p221. Stern has often been criticized by economists with little knowledge of the science for producing a political document and exaggerating the likely costs of climate change. In fact, he seriously underestimates the risks of catastrophic climate change, even in his latest *Blueprint*, and does not even consider the possibility of large-scale loss of life from agricultural collapse under his weak targets. See also Van den Borgh, J. C. J. M. (2004) 'Optimal climate policy is a utopia: from quantitative and qualitative cost-benefit analysis', *Ecological Economics*, vol 48, no 4, pp385–393.

6   See Neumayer, E. (2007) 'A missed opportunity: The Stern Review of Climate Change fails to tackle the issue of non-substitutable loss of natural capital', *Global Environmental Change*, vol 17, nos 3–4, pp297–301.

7   This point is developed in the general context of environmental resources that cannot be replaced or easily substituted by Persson, M. and Sterner, T. (2007) 'An even Sterner Review', World Resources Institute.

8   The negative carbon balance of currently heavily subsidized biofuels is discussed below.

9   GEO 4, published by the United Nations Environment Programme (UNEP) in October 2007 is the most comprehensive report on the whole global environment since the path-breaking report *Our Common Future* appeared in 1987 (UNEP 2007 *GEO4: Global Environmental Outlook*, United Nations Environment Programme, Nairobi). See also Pearce, F. (2007) 'IPCC hardens stance on climate change', *New Scientist*, 24 November.

10   See Wilkinson, R. and Pickett, K. (2009) *The Spirit Level*, Allen Lane; Barry, B. (2005) *Why Social Justice Matters*, Polity Press; Irvin, G. (2008) *Super Rich: The Rise of Inequality in Britain and the United States*, Polity. The most striking example of inequality in a developed economy comes from the traditionally deprived Calton ward in central Glasgow, where male life expectancy has been

estimated at 54 years, less than in many very poor countries. In the nearby, prosperous small town of Lenzie, male life expectancy is 82 years, no less than 28 years more.

11 See Sachs, J. (2005) *The End of Poverty*, Penguin, London, and his *Common Wealth* (2008), Penguin, London. Sachs is Director of the Earth Institute, Columbia University, and was Reith Lecturer in Britain in 2007. These problems are discussed in much more detail in Chapter 5.

12 See the detailed discussion in Chapter 6.

13 See Campbell, K. M., Gulledge, J., McNeill, J. R., Podesta, J., Ogden, P., Fuerth, L., Woolsey, R. J., Lennon, A. T. J., Smith, J., Weitz, R. and Mix, D. (2007) *The Age of Consequences: The Foreign Policy and National Security Implications of Global Climate Change*, Center for Strategic and International Studies – Center for a New American Security, November. In their executive summary (p7), the authors note that:
The catastrophic scenario, with average global temperatures increasing by 5.6°C by 2100, finds strong and surprising intersections between the two great security threats of the day – global climate change and international terrorism waged by Islamist extremists. This catastrophic scenario would pose almost inconceivable challenges as human society struggled to adapt.

14 Though the complaint is often justified in particular cases that receive extensive publicity, there is generally little discussion of the disastrous overall effects of Western policies on the development of the 'Third World', as documented in detail by Stiglitz, J. (2006) *Making Globalization Work*, Allen Lane, and many others.

15 Ackerman, F. (2008) *Can We Afford the Future?*, Zed Books, and Weitzman, M. L. (2009) 'On modelling and interpreting the costs of catastrophic climate change', *Review of Economics and Statistics*, vol 91, no 1, pp1–19. Weitzman's main concern is that the probabilities of catastrophic climate events are unknown, so that traditional cost-benefit analysis breaks down. He does not recognize the more fundamental problem that large-scale loss of life cannot be evaluated in money terms as a percentage of future GDP, so climate catastrophe has an inescapable ethical dimension. Stern does emphasize the ethical component, while also almost completely neglecting loss of human life in a future catastrophic collapse of food production.

16 Helm, D. (2008) 'Climate-change policy: Why has so little been achieved?', *Oxford Review of Economic Policy*, vol 24, no 2, pp211–238.

17 Wooster, M. (2007) 'Progress in quantifying biomass burning contributions to the global carbon cycle', Royal Geographical Society Annual International Conference, Climate Change Research Group, Imperial College, London, August.

18 As described in Chapter 3, and further discussed below, biowaste can be cheaply converted by anaerobic heating into 'biochar', a form of active charcoal that remains stable in the soil when used as an effective fertilizer, and clean-burning biofuel. See also Scherr, S. J. and Sthapit, S. (2009) *Mitigating Climate Change through Food and Land Use*, Worldwatch Report 179, Washington DC.

19 This is discussed in more detail, and references are given, in Chapter 3. Briefly, to give an idea of the magnitudes involved, we can add the long-term (though not permanent) annual sequestration of about one tonne of carbon per hectare (observed by the Rodale Institute) in much of the world's 1.5 billion hectares of arable land, plus the major reduction of energy inputs and other GHG emissions from a switch to no-till agriculture. Application of composted biowaste can

substantially raise the rate of carbon sequestration. This could probably reduce net carbon emissions by 2–3 billion tonnes per year or more, in addition to greatly reduced direct and indirect energy inputs in conservation agriculture. Stopping deforestation and replacing biomass burning with cheap solar cookers could effect a similar reduction, as could really large-scale reforestation and systematic invest-ment in energy saving and efficiency. There is thus the potential to cut current emissions of 10Gt by more than half, at very low net financial cost, though requir-ing some redistribution, even before switching to alternative energy. See Hunt, C. A. G. (2009) *Carbon Sinks and Climate Change*, Edward Elgar, Cheltenham.

20 Eby, M., Montenegro, A., Weaver, A. J. and Zickfeld K. (2007) 'Long-term climate implications of 2050 emission reduction targets', *Geophysical Letters*, vol 34, L19703, doi:10.1029/2007GL031018. The authors' abstract summarizes their findings in more detail as follows:

A coupled atmosphere–ocean carbon-cycle model is used to examine the long-term climate implications of various 2050 greenhouse gas emission reduction targets. All emission targets considered with less than 60 per cent global reduction by 2050 break the 2°C threshold warming this century, a number that some have argued represents an upper bound on manageable climate warming. Even when emissions are stabilized at 90 per cent below present levels at 2050, this 2°C threshold is eventually broken. Our results suggest that if a 2°C warming is to be avoided, direct CO_2 capture from the air, together with subsequent sequestration, would eventually have to be introduced in addition to sustained 90 per cent global carbon emissions reductions by 2050.

21 The production of biofuels is discussed in detail below.

22 Foresight (2007) Tackling Obesities: Future Choices Project, Foresight, October, www.dh.gov.uk/en/Publichealth/Healthimprovement/Obesity/DH_079713.

23 CAFE (2005) 'Baseline Scenarios for the Clean Air for Europe (CAFE) Programme, Clean Air for Europe, IIASA, Laxenburg, Austria. Available at www.iiasa.ac.at/rains/CAFE-Lot1_Final(Oct).pdf.

24 Brown, L. (2008b), 'Plan B update', Earth Policy Institute, 11 December, www.earthpolicy.org/Updates/2008/Update80.htm.

25 See Walker, G. and King, D. (2008) *The Hot Topic*, Bloomsbury, which is enthusi-astic about new (but untested) nuclear technology, ignoring the evidence that nuclear is currently the most expensive low-carbon alternative. Similarly, the chief scientific advisor to the Department of Energy and Climate Change, David MacKay, offers a far too optimistic estimate for the cost of new nuclear power stations, apparently based on Olkiluoto 3, the long-overdue Finnish nuclear power station, which has been plagued by cost overruns, delays and safety problems, which he does not mention. The latest cost projection for Olkiluoto 3, now only due for completion in 2012, is more than twice the original estimate, which seems to be what MacKay is using. See MacKay, D. J. C. (2009) *Sustainable Energy – Without the Hot Air*, UIT, Cambridge, p216. Detailed discussion of comparative energy costs is given by Flavin, C. (2009) *Low-Carbon Energy: A Roadmap*, Worldwatch Report 178, Worldwatch Institute, and Lovins, A. and Sheikh, I. (2008) *The Nuclear Illusion*, Rocky Mountain Institute, Boulder, CO, and authors cited in note 28 below.

26 The Energy Watch Group (Berlin) published detailed studies of oil and coal reserves and output prospects in 2007, and concluded that both have been system-atically overestimated by the International Energy Authority (Paris). The recession

that started in 2008 has, of course, brought a dramatic fall in prices that had risen steadily for a decade. Rising prices had begun to encourage efficiency and alternative energy development, similar to the effect of carbon taxes, but were much more disruptive to the global economy, especially poor countries, by transferring wealth to the energy producers, mainly OPEC and Russia. Fossil fuel prices will doubtless begin to rise again when the global economy recovers. See also Strahan, D. (2008) 'The great coal hole', *New Scientist*, 19 January, and www.energywatchgroup.org/fileadmin/global/pdf/EWG_Oilreport_Summary_10-2007.pdf.

27 See Walker, G. and King, D. (2008) *The Hot Topic*, Bloomsbury, Note 19, and Brown, L. (2009) *Plan B 4.0: Mobilizing to Save Civilization*, Norton.

28 See Viebahn, P. (2008) 'Comparison of carbon capture and storage with renewable energy technologies regarding structural, economic, and ecological aspects', German Aerospace Center, ACCSEPT Workshop, 10-11 May, Bonn; Pearce, F. (2008) 'Can coal live up to its clean promise?', *New Scientist*, 27 March; Sachs, J. (2008) *Common Wealth*, Penguin, London; Jacobson, M. (2008) 'Review of solutions to global warming, air pollution and energy security', draft ms, Department of Civil and Environmental Engineering, Stanford University, Stanford, CA, September.

29 See Pacala S. and Socolow, R. (2004) 'Stabilization wedges: Solving the climate problem for the next 50 years with current technologies', *Science*, 13 August, vol 305, no 5686, pp968–972. They summarize their arguments in the following abstract:
Humanity already possesses the fundamental scientific, technical and industrial know-how to solve the carbon and climate problem for the next half century. A portfolio of technologies now exists to meet the world's energy needs over the next 50 years and limit atmospheric CO_2 to a trajectory that avoids a doubling of the pre-industrial concentration. Every element in this portfolio has passed beyond the laboratory bench and demonstration project [stage]; many are already implemented somewhere at full industrial scale. Although no element is a credible candidate for doing the entire job (or even half the job) by itself, the portfolio as a whole is large enough that not every element has to be used.

30 Brown, L. (2008a) *Plan B 3.0*, Norton, suggests the use of wind power to charge electric cars in the US. Surprisingly, neither he nor Monbiot, G. (2006) *Heat*, Allen Lane, London, consider this idea for heating buildings, although this is one of the largest components of energy use in northern latitudes.

31 Nowak, R. (2008) 'Who needs coal when you can have deep heat', *New Scientist*, 19 July.

32 'Biofuels – At what cost?', Global Subsidies Initiative, www.globalsubsidies.org.

33 Fargione, J., Hill, J., Tilman, D., Polasky, S. and Hawthorne, P. (2008) 'Land clearing and the biofuel carbon debt', *Science*, 7 February, vol 319, no 5867, pp1235–1238. This and other related work is discussed by Monbiot, G. (2008d) 'The last straw: A new generation of biofuels turns out to be another environmental disaster', *The Guardian*, 12 February. However there are errors and omissions in Monbiot's general rejection of biofuels which are discussed in Note 38 below.

34 Crutzen, P. J., Mosier, A. R., Smith, K. A. and Winiwarter, W. (2007) 'N_2O release from agro-biofuel production negates global warming reduction by replacing fossil fuels', *Atmospheric Chemistry and Physics Discussions*, vol 7, 1 August, pp11,191–11,205, and *Physics Discussions*, vol 8, no 2, pp389–395, www.atmos-chem-phys-discuss.net/7/11191/2007/acpd-7-11191-2007.pdf.

35 Smith, J. and Hughes, J. (2007) 'Less waste, more speed', *Ecologist Online*, 29 March.

36 The reasons for this positive effect on soil fertility are not well understood, and research is ongoing to better understand the properties of biochar, their dependence on the type of feedstock used and on the details of the pyrolysis process. See Lehmann, J. (2007b) 'Bio-energy in the black', *Ecology and Environment*, vol 5, no 7, pp381–387, and Lehmann, J. and Joseph, S. (eds) (2009) *Biochar for Environmental Management*, Earthscan.

37 This assumes about half the dry yield by weight is carbon, and that half the carbon content is left as biochar residue. The other half is captured in the resulting biofuels.

38 George Monbiot's claim that 'there is no such thing as a sustainable biofuel' (Monbiot, G., 2008d, 'The last straw: A new generation of biofuels turns out to be another environmental disaster', *The Guardian*, 12 February) is wrong, and is actually contradicted by Fargione et al's paper (Fargione, J., Hill, J., Tilman, D., Polasky, S. and Hawthorne, P., 2008, 'Land clearing and the biofuel carbon debt' *Science*, vol 319, no 5867, pp1235–1238) that he cites. These authors point out that, in contrast to conventional cultivation or conversion of rainforest or grassland, 'biofuels made from waste biomass or from biomass grown on abandoned agricultural lands planted with perennials incur little or no carbon debt and offer immediate and sustained GHG advantages'.

39 Environmental author Monbiot, G. (2007) 'Agricultural crimes against humanity', *The Guardian*, 7 November, and Monbiot, G. (2008d) 'The last straw: A new generation of biofuels turns out to be another environmental disaster', *The Guardian,* 12 February, rightly criticizes current policies, but fails to mention or recognize the real potential for biochar, and perennial cultivation on wasteland.

40 Walker, G. and King, D. (2008) *The Hot Topic*, Bloomsbury, p147.

41 Daviss, B. (2007) 'Our solar future', *New Scientist*, 8 December.

42 See Ackerman, F. (2008), *Can We Afford the Future?*, Zed Books.

43 See the research summarized in the IPCC Synthesis Report, 2007 (Intergovernmental Panel on Climate Change (2007) *Impacts, Adaptation and Vulnerability: Working Group II Contribution to the Fourth Assessment Report of the IPCC*, Cambridge University Press, Cambridge, UK), and regular reports on www.realclimate.org. Monbiot, G. (2008a) 'One shot left', *The Guardian*, 25 November, and Pearce, F. (2009) 'Arctic meltdown is a threat to humanity', *New Scientist,* 28 March, summarize recent evidence that Arctic sea ice is disappearing far faster than predicted. The reduced reflectivity or albedo effect will accelerate warming throughout the northern permafrost regions, and the resulting release of GHGs, particularly methane, from thawing peat deposits.

Chapter 10: From Economic Crisis to Mobilization for Mitigation

1 Grayling, A.C. (2009) 'Commentary: The World needs a Slogan for Climate Change', *New Scientist,* 11 February

2 Hansen, J.E. (2009) 'Coal-fired power stations are death factories. Close them', *Observer,* 15 February

References

Ackerman, F. (2008) *Can We Afford the Future? Economics for a Warming World*, Zed Books, London

Adamchak, R. and Ronald, P. (2008) *Tomorrow's Table: Organic Farming, Genetics, and the Future of Food*, Oxford University Press, New York

Ahuja, V. (1998) 'Land degradation, agricultural productivity, and common property: Evidence from Côte d'Ivoire', *Environment and Development Economics*, vol 3, no 1, pp7–34

Albritton, R. (2009) *Let Them Eat Junk,* Pluto Press, London

Aldred, J. (2009) *The Skeptical Economist*, Earthscan, London

Alesina, A. and Glaeser, E. (2004) *Fighting Poverty in the US and Europe: A World of Difference*, Oxford University Press, Oxford

Alesina, A., Devleeschauwer, A., Easterly, W., Kurlat, S. and Wacziarg, R. (2003) 'Fractionalization', *Journal of Economic Growth*, vol 8, no 2, pp155–194

Andersons (2008) 'The impact of rising oil prices on organic and non-organic farm profitability', August, www.soilassociationscotland.org

Archer, D. (2008) *The Long Thaw: How Humans Are Changing the Next 100,000 Years of Earth's Climate,* Princeton University Press, Princeton, NJ

Baer, P. and Mastrandrea, M. (2006) *High Stakes*, Institute for Public Policy Research, London

Banister, J. and Zhang, X. (2005) 'China, economic development and mortality decline', *World Development*, vol 33, no 1, pp21–41

Barbier, E. B. and Burgess, J. C. (2001) 'The economics of tropical deforestation', *Journal of Economic Surveys*, vol 15, no 3, pp413–433

Barnett, J. and Adger, N. W. (2007) 'Climate change, human security and violent conflict', *Political Geography*, vol 26, no 6, pp639–655

Barrett, S. (1997) 'The strategy of trade sanctions in international environmental agreements', *Resource and Energy Economics*, vol 19, no 4, pp345–361

Barrett, S. (2003) *Environment and Statecraft: The Strategy of Environmental Treaty-Making*, Oxford University Press, Oxford, UK

Barrett, S. (2007) *Why Cooperate? The Incentive to Supply Global Public Goods*, Oxford University Press, Oxford, UK

Barrett, S. (2008) 'Climate treaties and the imperative of enforcement', *Oxford Review of Economic Policy*, vol 24, no 2, pp239–258

Barry, B. (2006) *Why Social Justice Matters*, Polity Press, Cambridge, UK

Bazerman, M. H. (2006) 'Climate change as a predictable surprise', *Climatic Change*, vol 77, nos 1–2, pp179–193

Beath, J. and FitzRoy, F. (2008) 'Public economics of relative income', Mansholt Lecture, University of Wageningen, The Netherlands, September

Benjamin, A. and McCallum, B. (2008) *A World without Bees,* Guardian Books, London

Bentham, J. (1789) *An Introduction to the Principles of Morals and Legislation,* Kessinger Publishing, reprint2005, Whitefish, MT

Biel, A., Johansson-Stenman, O. and Nilsson, A. (2006) 'Emotions, morality, and public goods: The WTA–WTP disparity revisited', Working Papers in Economics 193, University of Göteborg, Göteborg, Sweden

Birnie, P. and Boyle, A. (2002) *International Law and the Environment,* Oxford University Press, Oxford, UK

Blanchflower, D. G. (2007) 'Is unemployment more costly than inflation?', Working Paper 13505, National Bureau of Economic Research, Cambridge, MA

Blythman, J. (2004) *Shopped: The Shocking Power of British Supermarkets,* Fourth Estate, London

Boulding, K. (1966) 'The economics of the coming spaceship Earth', in H. Jarrett (ed) *Environmental Quality in a Growing Economy,* John Hopkins Press, Baltimore, MD

Bowen, M. (2007) *Censoring Science: Inside the Political Attack on Dr James Hansen and the Truth of Global Warming,* Dutton, Hialeah, FL

Boyenge, J-P. (2007) 'ILO database on export processing zones', International Labour Organization, Geneva, downloadable at www.ilo.org/public/english/dialogue/sector/themes/epz/epz-db.pdf

Brockmann, H., Delhey, J., Welzel, C. and Yuan, H. (2008) 'The China puzzle: Falling happiness in a rising economy', *Journal of Happiness Studies,* doi: 10.1007/s10902-008-9095-4

Broome, J. (2006) 'Valuing policies in response to climate change: Some ethical issues', mimeo, University of Oxford, Oxford, UK

Brown, L. (2005) *Outgrowing the Earth: The Food Security Challenge in an Age of Falling Water Tables and Rising Temperatures,* Earthscan, London

Brown, L. (2008a) *Plan B 3.0,* W. W. Norton, London

Brown, L. (2008b) 'Plan B update', Earth Policy Institute, 11 December

Brown, L. (2009) *Plan B 4.0: Mobilizing to Save Civilization,* Norton, London

Burke, J. E., Brown, J. S. and Christidis, N. (2006) 'Modeling the recent evolution of global drought and projections for the twenty-first century with the Hadley Centre climate model', *Journal of Hydrometeorology,* vol 7, no 5, pp1113–1125

Buttal, F. H., Foster, J. B. and Magdoff, F. (eds) (2000) *Hungry for Profit: The Agribusiness Threat to Farmers, Food, and the Environment,* Monthly Review Press, New York

CAFE (2005) 'Baseline Scenarios for the Clean Air for Europe (CAFE) Programme, Clean Air for Europe, IIASA, Laxenburg, Austria. Available at: www.iiasa.ac.at/rains/CAFE_files/Cafe-Lot1_FINAL(Oct).pdf.

Calvin, W. (2008) *Global Fever,* University of Chicago Press, Chicago, IL

Campbell, K. M., Gulledge, J., McNeill, J. R., Podesta, J., Ogden, P., Fuerth, L., Woolsey, R. J., Lennon, A. T. J., Smith, J., Weitz, R. and Mix, D. (2007) 'The age of consequences: The foreign policy and national security implications of global climate change', Center for Strategic and International Studies – Center for a New American Security, Washington, DC, November

Carson, R. (1962) *Silent Spring,* Houghton Mifflin, New York

Chang, H-J. (2007) *Bad Samaritans: Rich Nations, Poor Policies and the Threat to the Developing World,* Random House Business Books, London

Chertow, M. R. (2008) 'The IPAT equation and its variants', *Journal of Industrial Ecology*, vol 4, no 4, pp 13–29

Clemens, M. A., Kenny, C. J. and Moss, T. J. (2007) 'The trouble with the MDGs: Confronting expectations of aid and development success', *World Development*, vol 35, no 5, pp735–751

Climate Group (2008) 'China's clean revolution', www.theclimategroup.org/assets/resources/Chinas_Clean_Revolution.pdf

Cline, W. (2007) *Global Warming and Agriculture*, Center for Global Development, Washington, DC

Collier, P. (2007) *The Bottom Billion: Why the Poorest Countries Are Failing and What Can Be Done About It*, Oxford University Press, Oxford, UK

Collier, P., Conway, G. and Venables, T. (2008) 'Climate change and Africa', *Oxford Review of Economic Policy*, vol 24, no 2, pp337–353

Connolley, W. and Schmidt, G. (2007) 'Swindled', *RealClimate*, 7 March

Connolley, W. and Schmidt, G. (2008) 'Climate swindlers excused', *New Scientist*, 26 July

Cordonier Segger, M-C. and Khalfan, A. (2004) *Sustainable Development Law: Principles, Practices and Prospects*, Oxford University Press, Oxford, UK

Costanza, R., Erickson, J., Fligger, K., Adams, A., Adams, C., Altschuler, B., Balter, S., Fisher, B., Hike, J., Kelly, J., Kerr, T., McCauley, M., Montone, K., Rauch, M., Schmiedeskamp, K., Saxton, D., Sparacino, L., Tusinski, W. and Williams, L. (2004) 'Estimates of the Genuine Progress Indicator (GPI) for Vermont, Chittenden County and Burlington, from 1950 to 2000', *Ecological Economics*, vol 51, nos 1–2, pp139–155

Crutzen, P. J., Mosier, A. R., Smith, K. A. and Winiwarter, W. (2007) 'N_2O release from agro-biofuel production negates global warming reduction by replacing fossil fuels', *Atmospheric Chemistry and Physics Discussions*, vol 7, 1 August, pp11,191–11,205 and *Physics Discussions*, vol 8, no 2, pp389–395

Daly, H. E. and Cobb, J. (1989) *For the Common Good: Redirecting the Economy towards Community, the Environment and a Sustainable Future*, Beacon Press, Boston, MA

Dauvergne, P. (2008) *The Shadows of Consumption: Consequences for the Global Environment*, MIT Press, Cambridge, MA

Davis, D. (2002) *When Smoke Ran Like Water: Tales of Environmental Deception and the Battle Against Pollution*, Basic Books, New York

Daviss, B. (2007) 'Our solar future', *New Scientist*, 8 December

Dawkins, R. (1986) *The Blind Watchmaker*, Norton, New York

Deacon, R. and Saha, S. (2006) 'Public goods provision by dictatorships: A survey', in A. F. Ott, and R. J. Cebula (eds) *The Elgar Companion to Public Economics: Empirical Public Economics*, Edward Elgar, Cheltenham, UK

Dietz, T., Ostrom, E. and Stern, P. (2003) 'The struggle to govern the commons', *Science*, vol 302, no 5652, pp1907–1912

Douds, D., Hanson, J., Hepperly, P., Pimentel, D. and Seidel. R. (2005) 'Environment, energy, and economic comparisons of organic and conventional farming systems', *Bioscience*, vol 55, no 7, pp573–582

Dresner, S. (2002) *The Principles of Sustainability*, Earthscan, London

Earley, J., Niggli, U. and Ogorzalek, K. (2007) 'Issues paper: Organic agriculture and environmental stability of the food supply', International Conference on Organic Agriculture and Food Security, FAO, Rome, Italy, May

Easterlin, R. A. (1974) 'Does economic growth improve the human lot?', in P. A. David and M. W. Reder (eds) *Nations and Households in Economic Growth: Essays in Honour of Moses Abramowitz*, Academic Press, New York

Easterlin, R. A. (2005) 'Building a better theory of well-being', in L. Bruni and P. L. Porter (eds) *Economics and Happiness*, Oxford University Press, Oxford, UK

Easterlin, R. A. and Angelescu, L. (2009) 'Happiness and growth the world over: Time series evidence on the happiness–income paradox', IZA, Bonn, DP 4060

Eby, M., Montenegro, A., Weaver, A. J. and Zickfeld, K. (2007) 'Long term climate implications of 2050 emission reduction targets', *Geophysical Letters*, vol 34, L19703, doi:10.1029/2007GL031018

Ehrlich, P. and Holdren, J. (1972) 'One-dimensional ecology', *Bulletin of the Atomic Scientists*, vol 28, no 5, pp16–27

Ellerman, D. A. (2003) 'Ex-post evaluation of tradable permits: The US SO_2 cap-and-trade program', MIT-CEEPR Working Paper 0303, MIT Center for Energy and Environmental Policy Research, Cambridge, MA

Ernsting, A. and Rughani, D. (2008) 'Climate geo-engineering with "carbon negative" bioenergy', www.biofuelwatch.org.uk

Etkin, D. and Ho, E. (2007) 'Climate change: Perceptions and discourses of risk', *Journal of Risk Research*, vol 10, no 5, pp623–641

Evans, A. (2009) *The Feeding of the Nine Billion: Global Food Security for the 21st Century*, Chatham House, London, UK

Fargione, J., Hill, J., Tilman, D., Polasky, S. and Hawthorne, P. (2008) 'Land clearing and the biofuel carbon debt', *Science*, vol 319, no 5867, pp1235–1238

Farman, J. C., Gardiner, B. G. and Shanklin, J. D. (1985) 'Large losses of total ozone in Antarctica reveal seasonal ClOx/NOx interaction', *Nature*, vol 315, pp207–210

Flavin, C. (2008) *Low-Carbon Energy: A Roadmap*, Worldwatch Report 178, Worldwatch Institute, Washington, DC

Foresight (2007) *Tackling Obesities: Future Choices Project*, Foresight, October, www.dh.gov.uk/en/Publichealth/Healthimprovement/Obesity/DH_079713

Franco, M., Ordunez, P., Cabillaro, B., Tapia Granados, J. A., Lazo, M., Bernal, J. L., Guallar, E., and Cooper R. S. (2007) 'Impact of energy intake, physical activity, and population-wide weight loss on cardiovascular disease and diabetes mortality in Cuba, 1980–2005', *American Journal of Epidemiology*, vol 166, no 12, pp1374–1380

Frankel, J. (2006) 'On the Yuan: The choice between adjustment under a fixed exchange rate and adjustment under a flexible rate', *CESifo Economic Studies*, vol 52, no 2, pp246–275

Franz, J. and FitzRoy, F. (2007) 'Desertification and climate change: Global and regional impacts of degradation in the Aral Sea basin', paper presented at Royal Geographical Society Conference, London, August

Fredriksson, P. G. and Gaston, N. (1999) 'The "greening" of trade unions and the demand for eco-taxes', *European Journal of Political Economy*, vol 15, no 4, pp663–686

Frey, B. S. (2008) *Happiness: A Revolution in Economics*, MIT Press, Cambridge, MA

Friends of the Earth and New Economics Foundation (2006) 'The Happy Planet Index', www.neweconomics.org/gen/uploads/dl44k145g5scuy453044 gqbu11072006194758.pdf, accessed 15 February 2009, p8

Frost, S. and Ho, M. (2005) 'Going out: The growth of Chinese foreign direct investment in Southeast Asia and its implications for corporate social responsibility', *Corporate Social Responsibility and Environmental Management*, vol 12, no 3, pp157–167

Garvey, J. (2008) *The Ethics of Climate Change: Right and Wrong in a Warming Planet*, Continuum, London

Gollier, C., Jullien, B. and Treich, N. (2000) 'Scientific progress and irreversibility: An economic interpretation of the "precautionary principle"', *Journal of Public Economics*, vol 75, no 2, pp229–253

Grayling, A. C. (2009) 'Commentary: The world needs a slogan for climate change', *New Scientist*, 11 February

Hanley, N., Moffatt, I., Faichney, R. and Wilson, M. (1999) 'Measuring sustainability: A time series of indicators for Scotland', *Ecological Economics*, vol 28, no 1, pp53–73

Hansen, J. (2007) 'Special Report Earth', *New Scientist*, 25 July

Hansen, J. (2009) 'Coal-fired power stations are death factories. Close them', *The Observer*, 15 February

Hansen, J., Sato, M., Kharecha, P., Beerling, D., Masson-Delmotte, V., Pagani, M., Raymo, M., Royer, L. D. and Zachos, C. (2008) 'Target atmospheric CO_2: Where should humanity aim?', *Open Atmospheric Science Journal*, vol 2, pp217–231

Hartwick, J. M. (1977) 'Intergenerational equity and the investing of rents from exhaustible resources', *American Economic Review*, vol 67, no 5, pp972–974

Harvey, G. (2006) *We Want Real Food*, Constable, London

Harvey, G. (2008) *The Carbon Fields: How our Countryside can Save Britain*, Grass Roots, Bridgewater, Somerset

Hauser, M. D. (2006) *Moral Minds: How Nature Designed our Universal Sense of Right and Wrong*, Ecco, New York

Helliwell, J. F. (2006) 'Well-being, social capital and public policy: What's new?', *The Economic Journal*, vol 116, no 510, pp34–46

Helliwell, J. F. and Huang, H. (2005) 'How's the job? Well-being and social capital in the workplace', Working Paper 11759, National Bureau of Economic Research, Washington, DC

Helm, D. (2008) 'Climate change policy: Why has so little been achieved?', *Oxford Review of Economic Policy*, vol 24, no 2, pp211–238

Ho, M. W., Burcher, S., Lim, L. C. et al (2008) *Food Futures Now, Organic, Sustainable and Fossil-Free*, Institute for Science in Society/Third World Network, London/Penang, Malaysia

Hoogland, C., de Boer, J. and Boersema, J. J. (2005) 'Transparency of the meat chain in the light of food culture and history', *Appetite*, vol 45, no 1, pp15–23

Horowitz, J. K. and McConnell, K. E. (2002) 'A review of WTA/WTP studies', *Journal of Environmental Economics and Management*, vol 44, no 3, pp426–447

Hughes, M. K. and H. F. Diaz (1994) 'Was there a "Medieval Warm Period", and if so, where and when?' *Climatic Change*, vol 26, pp109–142

Hunt, C. A. G. (2009) *Carbon Sinks and Climate Change*, Edward Elgar, Cheltenham

Inglehart, R., Foa, R., Peterson, C. and Welzel, C. (2008) 'Social change, freedom and rising happiness: A global perspective (1981–2007)', *Perspectives on Psychological Science*, vol 3, no 4, pp264–285

Intergovernmental Panel on Climate Change (2007) *Impacts, Adaptation and Vulnerability: Working Group II Contribution to the Fourth Assessment Report of the IPCC*, Cambridge University Press, Cambridge, UK

Irvin, G. (2008) *Super Rich: The Rise of Inequality in Britain and the United States*, Polity, Cambridge, UK

Jackson, K. (2008) 'Why does ethnic diversity affect public good provision? An empirical analysis of water provision in Africa', mimeo, University of British Columbia, Vancouver, Canada

Jackson, T. (2009) *Prosperity without Growth*, Earthscan, London

Jacobsen, R. (2008) *Fruitless Fall: The Collapse of the Honey Bee and the Coming Agricultural Crisis*, Bloomsbury, New York

Jacobson, M. (2008) 'Review of solutions to global warming, air pollution and energy security', draft ms, Department of Civil and Environmental Engineering, Stanford University, Stanford, CA, September

Jarman, M. (2007) *Climate Change*, Oxfam, London

Jenkins, T. M. (1998) 'Economics and the environment: A case of ethical neglect', *Ecological Economics*, vol 26, no 2, pp151–163

Jones, C. I. (2002) *Introduction to Economic Growth*, Norton, New York

Joyce, R. (2006) *The Evolution of Morality (Life and Mind)*, MIT Press, Cambridge, MA

Konow, J. and Earley, J. (2008) 'The hedonistic paradox: Is *Homo economicus* happier?', *Journal of Public Economics*, vol 92, nos 1–2, pp1–33

Lane, R. E. (2001) *The Loss of Happiness in Market Economies*, Yale University Press, New Haven, CT

Lange, G. M. (2004) 'Wealth, natural capital and sustainable development: Contrasting examples from Botswana and Namibia', *Environmental and Resource Economics*, vol 29, no 3, pp257–283

LaSalle, T. J. and Hepperly, P. (2008) 'Regenerative organic farming: A solution to global warming', Rodale Research Paper 5-28-08, Rodale Institute, PA

LaSalle, T. J., Hepperly, P. and Diop, A. (2008) 'The organic green revolution', Rodale Institute, PA

Lawrence, F. (2008) *Eat Your Heart Out*, Penguin, London

Layard, R., Mayraz, G. and Nickell, S. (2009) 'Does relative income matter? Are the critics right?', SOEP papers on multidisciplinary panel data research, DIW Berlin

Lee, R. J. (2009) *Climate Change and Armed Conflict*, Routledge, Abingdon, UK

Lehmann, J. (2007a) 'A handful of carbon', *Nature*, 10 May

Lehmann, J. (2007b) 'Bio-energy in the black', *Ecology and Environment*, vol 5, no 7, pp381–387

Lehmann, J. and Joseph, S. (eds) (2009) *Biochar for Environmental Management*, Earthscan, London

Levinson, A. and Taylor, M. S. (2008) 'Unmasking the pollution haven effect', *International Economic Review*, vol 49, no 1, pp223–254

Lockwood, M. and Fröhlich, C. (2007) 'Recent oppositely directed trends in solar climate forcings and the global mean surface air temperature', *Proceedings of the Royal Society A*, vol 463, pp2447–2460

López, R. (2008) 'Structural adjustment and sustainable development', in R. López and M. T. Toman (eds) *Economic Development and Environmental Sustainability*, Oxford University Press, Oxford, UK

Lorenzoni, I. and Pidgeon, N. F. (2006) 'Public views on climate change: European and USA perspectives', *Climatic Change*, vol 77, nos 1–2, pp73–95

Lovelock, J. (2009a) *The Vanishing Face of Gaia*, Allen Lane, London

Lovelock, J. (2009b) 'We're doomed but it's not all bad', interview in *New Scientist*, 24 January

Lovins, A. and Sheikh, I. (2008) *The Nuclear Illusion*, Rocky Mountain Institute, Boulder, CO

Luttmer, R. F. P. (2005) 'Neighbors as negatives: Relative earnings and well-being', *Quarterly Journal of Economics*, vol 120, no 3, pp963–1002

Lynas, M. (2007a) *Six Degrees*, Fourth Estate, London

Lynas, M. (2007b) 'Neutrality is cowardice', *New Statesman*, 3 September, p21

MacKay, D. J. C. (2009) *Sustainable Energy – Without the Hot Air*, UIT, Cambridge, UK

MacKenzie, D. (2008) 'Let them eat spuds', *New Scientist*, 2 August

MacKenzie, D. (2009) 'Resistant wheat to tackle destructive fungus', *New Scientist*, 20 March

Malhi, Y., Roberts, T. J., Betts, R. A., Killeen, T. J., Li, W. and Nobre, C. A. (2008) 'Climate change, deforestation, and the fate of the Amazon', *Science*, vol 319, no 5860, pp169–172

Malthus, T. (1798) *An Essay on the Principle of Population*, Oxford University Press (reprint 1993), Oxford, UK

Mankiw, G. (2007) 'One answer to global warming: A new tax', *New York Times*, 16 September

Mann, C. (2008) 'The future rests on soil. Can we protect it?', *National Geographic*, September

Mann, M. and Schmidt, G. (2007) 'Lindzen in *Newsweek*', *RealClimate*, 17 April

Mason, T. and Singer, P. (2006) *The Way We Eat: Why our Food Choices Matter*, Rodale, New York

McFague, S. (2008) A *New Climate for Theology: God, the World, and Global Warming*, Fortress Press, Minneapolis, MN

McKibben, B. (2005) 'Curitiba: A global model for development', CommonDreams.org, www.commondreams.org/views05/1108-33.htm, accessed 15 February 2009

McMichael, A. J., Powles, J. W., Butler, C. D. and Uauy, R. (2007) 'Food, livestock production, energy, climate change, and health, *The Lancet*, vol 370, no 9594, pp1253–1263

Michaelson, J. (2009) 'National accounts of well-being: A new measure of success', New Economics Foundation, 26 January, www.neftriplecrunch.wordpress.com/ 2009/01/26/national-accounts-of-well-being-a-new-measure-of-success, accessed 15 February 2009

Mill, J. S. (1861) *Utilitarianism*, Oxford University Press, reprint 1998, Oxford, UK

Monbiot, G. (2006) *Heat*, Allen Lane, London

Monbiot, G. (2007) 'Agricultural crimes against humanity', *The Guardian*, 7 November

Monbiot, G. (2008a) 'One shot left', *The Guardian*, 25 November

Monbiot, G. (2008b) 'Small is bountiful', *The Guardian*, 10 June

Monbiot, G. (2008c) 'Pin-striped pirates', *The Guardian*, 16 December; www.monbiot.com/archives/2008/12/16/pin-striped-pirates

Monbiot, G. (2008d) 'The last straw: A new generation of biofuels turns out to be another environmental disaster', *The Guardian*, 12 February

Montgomery, D. (2007) *Dirt: The Erosion of Civilizations*, University of California Press, Berkeley, CA

Morton, O. (2007) *Eating the Sun*, Fourth Estate, London

Nestle, M. (2007) *Food Politics: How the Food Industry Influences Nutrition and Health*, University of California Press, Berkeley, CA

Neumayer, E. (2003) 'Are left-wing party strength and corporatism good for the environment? Evidence from panel analysis of air pollution in OECD countries', *Ecological Economics*, vol 45, no 2, pp203–220

Neumayer, E. (2007) 'A missed opportunity: The Stern Review of Climate Change fails to tackle the issue of non-substitutable loss of natural capital', Global Environmental Change, vol 17, nos 3–4, pp297–301

New Economics Foundation (2008) *A Green New Deal*, New Economics Foundation, London

Newell, P., Jenner, N. and Baker, L. (2009) 'Governing clean development: A framework for analysis', Governance of Clean Development Working Paper 001, March 2009, University of East Anglia, Norwich, UK

Nordhaus, W. (2007) 'A review of the *Stern Review on the Economics of Climate Change*', *Journal of Economic Literature*, vol XLV, September

Nordhaus, W. (2008) *A Question of Balance: Weighing the Options on Global Warming Policies*, Yale University Press, New Haven, CT

Northcott, M. S. (2007) *A Moral Climate: The Ethics of Global Warming*, Longman, London

Nowak, R. (2008) 'Who needs coal when you can have deep heat', *New Scientist*, 19 July

Nussbaum, M. (2000) *Women and Human Development: The Capabilities Approach*, Cambridge University Press, Cambridge, UK

Offer, A. (2001) *The Challenge of Affluence*, Oxford University Press, Oxford, UK

Oliver, J. (2007) *Jamie at Home, Cook Your Way to the Good Life*, Penguin, London

Pacala, S. and Socolow, R. (2004) 'Stabilization wedges: Solving the climate problem for the next 50 years with current technologies', *Science*, vol 305, no 5686, pp968–972

Pachauri, R. (2008) 'Global warning: The impact of meat production and consumption on climate change', Peter Roberts Memorial Lecture, Compassion in World Farming, London, September

Page, E. (2007) 'Justice between generations: Investigating a sufficientarian approach', *Journal of Global Ethics*, vol 3, no 1, pp3–20

Pan, J., Phillips, J. and Chen, Y. (2008) 'China's balance of emissions embodied in trade: Approaches to measurement and allocating international responsibility', *Oxford Review of Economic Policy*, vol 24, no 2, pp354–376

Patel, R. (2007) *Stuffed and Starved*, Portobello Books, London

Pearce, F. (2006) *The Last Generation*, Eden Project Books, London

Pearce, F. (2007) 'IPCC hardens stance on climate change', *New Scientist*, 24 November

Pearce, F. (2008) 'Can coal live up to its clean promise?', *New Scientist*, 27 March

Pearce, F. (2009) 'Arctic meltdown is a threat to humanity', *New Scientist*, 28 March

Persson, M. and Sterner, T. (2007) *An Even Sterner Review*, World Resources Institute, Washington, DC

Pezzey, J. C. V. (1994) 'Concern for sustainability in a sexual world', Centre for Social and Economic Research on the Global Environment, London

Pezzey, J. C. V. (1997) 'Sustainability constraints versus optimality versus intertemporal concern, and axioms versus data', *Land Economics*, vol 73, no 2, pp448–466

Pittock, B. (2009) *Climate Change: Turning up the Heat*, Earthscan, London

Pollan, M. (2007) *The Omnivore's Dilemma: A History of Four Meals*, Penguin, London

Pollan, M. (2008) *In Defence of Food*, Penguin, London

Qian, W. and Zhu, Y. (2001) 'Climate change in China from 1880 to 1998 and its impact on the environmental condition', *Climatic Change*, vol 50, no 4, pp1480–1573

Quah, D. (1996) 'Twin peaks: Growth and convergence in models of distribution dynamics', *Economic Journal*, vol 106, no 437, pp1045–1055

Rabinovitch, J. (1996) 'Innovative land use and public transport policy: The case of Curitiba, Brazil', *Land Use Policy*, vol 13, no 1, pp51–67

Rabinovitch, J. and Leitman, J. (2004) 'Urban planning in Curitiba', in S. M. Wheeler and T. Beatley (eds) *The Sustainable Urban Development Reader*, Routledge, London

Rajotte, T. and Tansey, G. (eds) (2008) *The Future Control of Food*, Earthscan, London

Ravilious, K. (2007) 'Asia's brown clouds heat the Himalayas', *New Scientist*, 1 August

Rawls, J. (1961) *A Theory of Justice*, Harvard University Press, Cambridge, MA

Ricardo, D. (1817) *Principles of Political Economy and Taxation*, Dover Publications (reprint 2004), Mineola, NY

Roberts, J. T. and Grimes, P. E. (1997) 'Carbon intensity and economic development 1962–1991: A brief exploration of the Environmental Kuznets Curve', *World Development*, vol 25, no 2, pp191–198

Roberts, M. and Schlenker, W. (2008) 'Estimating the impact of climate change on crop yields: The importance of non-linear temperature effects', Working Paper No 13799, NBER, Cambridge, MA

Robinson, J. A. and Torvik, R. (2005) 'White elephants', *Journal of Public Economics*, vol 89, nos 2–3, pp197–210

Rosset, P. M. (2000) 'Cuba: A successful case study of alternative agriculture', in F. Magdoff (ed) *Hungry for Profit: The Agribusiness Threat to Farmers, Food, and the Environment*, Monthly Review Press, New York, NY

Rowe, J. (2003) 'Grossly distorting perception', *The Ecologist*, 1 February, www.theecologist.org/pages/archive_detail.asp?content_id=400, accessed 15 February 2009

Sachs, J. D. (2005) *The End of Poverty*, Penguin, London

Sachs, J. D. (2008) *Common Wealth: Economics for a Crowded Planet*, Penguin Books, London

Sahn, D. E. and Stifel, D. C. (2003) 'Progress toward the Millennium Development Goals in Africa', *World Development*, vol 31, no 1, pp23–52

Scherr, S. J. and Sthapit, S. (2009) *Mitigating Climate Change through Food and Land Use*, Worldwatch Report 179, Washington, DC

Schlosser, E. (2001) *Fast Food Nation*, Allen Lane/Penguin, London

Seinfeld, J. (2008) 'Atmospheric science: Black carbon and brown clouds', *Nature Geoscience*, vol 1, pp15–16

Sen, A. (1985) *Commodities and Capabilities*, Oxford University Press, Oxford, UK

Shisanya, C. A. and Khayesi, M. (2007) 'How is climate change perceived in relation to other socioeconomic and environmental threats in Nairobi, Kenya?', *Climatic Change*, vol 85, nos 3–4, pp271–284

Shue, H. (1993) 'Subsistence emissions and luxury emissions', *Law and Policy*, vol 15, no 1, pp39–59

Singer, P. (1975) *Animal Liberation: A New Ethics for our Treatment of Animals*, Random House, New York

Singer, P. (1979) *Practical Ethics*, Cambridge University Press, Cambridge, UK

Singer, P. (2001) *One World*, Yale University Press, New Haven, CT

Smith, J. and Hughes, J. (2007) 'Less waste, more speed', *Ecologist Online*, 29 March

Smyth, R., Mishra, V. and Qian, X. (2008) 'The environment and well-being in urban China', *Ecological Economics*, vol 68, nos 1–2, pp547–555

Speth, J. G. (2008) *The Bridge at the End of the World*, Yale University Press, New Haven, CT

Stavins, R. N. (1998) 'What can we learn from the grand policy experiment? Lessons from SO_2 allowance trading', *The Journal of Economic Perspectives*, vol 12, no 3, pp69–88

Stavins, R. N. (2008) 'Addressing climate change with a comprehensive US cap-and-trade system', *Oxford Review of Economic Policy*, vol 24, no 2, pp298–321

Stern, N. (2007) *The Economics of Climate Change*, Cambridge University Press, Cambridge, UK

Stern, N. (2008) 'The economics of climate change', Richard Ely Lecture, *American Economic Review: Papers and Proceedings*, vol 98, no 2, pp1–37

Stern, N. (2009a) *A Blueprint for a Safer Planet: How to Manage Climate Change and Create a New Era of Progress and Prosperity*, Bodley Head, London

Stern, N. (2009b) 'Decision time', *New Scientist*, 24 January

Stevenson, B. and Wolfers, J. (2008) 'Economic growth and subjective well-being: Reassessing the Easterlin Paradox', Papers on Economic Activity No 1, Brookings Institution, Washington, DC, pp1–87

Stiglitz, J. (2006) *Making Globalization Work*, Allen Lane, London

Stiglitz, J. and Charlton, A. (2007) *Fair Trade for All: How Trade Can Promote Development*, Oxford University Press, Oxford, UK

Strahan, D. (2008) 'The great coal hole', *New Scientist,* 19 January

Strom, R. (2007) *Hot House: Global Climate Change and the Human Condition*, Praxis-Springer-Copernicus, New York

Sunstein, C. and Thaler, R. (2008) *Nudge: Improving Decisions about Health, Wealth, and Happiness*, Yale University Press, New Haven, CT

Tansey, G. (2008) 'For good or for greed', *The Ecologist,* November

Tickell, O. (2008) *Kyoto 2: How to Manage the Global Greenhouse*, Zed Books, London

Toya, H. and Skidmore, M. (2007) 'Economic development and the impact of natural disasters', *Economics Letters*, vol 94, no 1, pp20–25

Treisman, D. (2000) 'The causes of corruption: A cross-national study', *Journal of Public Economics*, vol 76, no 3, pp399–457

UCS News (2007) 'Smoke, mirrors and hot air: How ExxonMobil uses big tobacco's tactics to "manufacture uncertainty"', www.ucsusa.org/news/press_release/ExxonMobil-GlobalWarming-tobacco.html, 3 January

UNEP (2007) *GEO 4: Global Environment Outlook*, United Nations Environment Programme, Nairobi

UNFPA (2007) 'State of world population 2007: Unleashing the potential of urban growth', www.unfpa.org/swp

UN-Habitat (2003) *The Challenge of Slums*, Earthscan, London

United Nations (1992) *Agenda 21 Earth Summit: United Nations Program of Action from Rio*, United Nations, New York

Van Beveren, I. (2007) 'Footloose multinationals in Belgium', *Review of World Economics*, vol 143, no 3, pp483–507

Van den Bergh, J.C.J.M. (2004) 'Optimal climate policy is a utopia: from quantitative to qualitative cost-benefit analysis', *Ecological Economics*, vol 48, no 4, pp385–393

Van den Bergh, J.C.J.M. (2009) 'Safe climate policy is affordable', mimeo, ICREA, Barcelona

Vanderheiden S. (2008) *Atmospheric Justice*, Oxford University Press, Oxford, UK

Viebahn, P. (2008) 'Comparison of carbon capture and storage with renewable energy technologies regarding structural, economic, and ecological aspects', ACCSEPT Workshop, German Aerospace Center, 10–11 May, Bonn

Wackernagel, M. and Rees, W. E. (1996) *Our Ecological Footprint: Reducing the Human Impact on the Earth*, New Society Publishers, Gabriola Island, British Columbia, Canada

Walker, G. and King, D. (2008) *The Hot Topic: How to Tackle Global Warming and Still Keep the Lights On*, Bloomsbury, London

Weber, C. L. and Matthews, S. H. (2008) 'Quantifying the global and distributional aspects of American household carbon footprint', *Ecological Economics*, vol 66, nos 2–3, pp379–391

Weber, E. E. (2006) 'Experience-based and description-based perceptions of long-term risk: Why global warming does not scare us (yet)', *Climatic Change*, vol 77, nos 1–2, pp103–120

Weber, M. (1904–1905) *The Protestant Ethic and the Spirit of Capitalism*, Routledge (reprint 2001), London

Wei, S-J. (1999) 'Corruption in economic development: Beneficial grease, minor annoyance or major obstacle?', World Bank Policy Research Working Paper No 2048, The World Bank, Washington, DC

Weis, T. (2007) *The Global Food Economy: The Battle for the Future of Farming*, Zed Books, London

Weitzman, M. (2007) 'A review of the *Stern Review on the Economics of Climate Change*', *Journal of Economic Literature*, vol XLV, September

Weitzman, M. (2009) 'On modelling and interpreting the costs of catastrophic climate change', Review of Economics and Statistics, vol 19, no 1, pp1–9

Werksman, J. W. (1992) 'Trade sanctions under the Montreal Protocol', *Review of European Community and International Environmental Law*, vol 1, no 1, pp69–72

Wilkinson, R. and Pickett, K. (2009) *The Spirit Level: Why More Equal Socieites Almost Always Do Better*, Allen Lane, London

Wooster, M. (2007) 'Progress in quantifying biomass burning contributions to the global carbon cycle', presented at Royal Geographical Society Annual International Conference, Climate Change Research Group, Imperial College, London, London, 29–31 August

World Commission on Environment and Development (1987) *Our Common Future*, Oxford University Press, Oxford, UK

Worldwatch Institute (2009) *State of the World 2009: Into a Warming World*, Worldwatch Institute, Washington, DC

Wright, J. (2008) *Sustainable Agriculture and Food Security in an Era of Oil Scarcity*, Earthscan, London

Wu, B. and Ci, L. J. (2002) 'Landscape change and desertification development in the Mu Us Sandland, Northern China', *Journal of Arid Environments*, vol 50, no 3, pp429–444

List of Abbreviations

ABC	atmospheric brown cloud
AOSIS	Alliance of Small Island States
BIC	Brazil, India and China
BSE	bovine spongiform encephalopathy
CAFE	Clean Air for Europe
CAFO	concentrated animal feeding operation
CAP	Common Agricultural Policy
CCS	carbon capture and storage
CDM	Clean Development Mechanism
CFCs	chlorofluorocarbons
CHP	combined heat and power
CO_2	carbon dioxide
CSR	corporate social responsibility
CVM	Contingent Valuation Method
DC	direct current
EGS	engineered geothermal systems
EITI	Extractive Industry Transparency Initiative
ETS	emissions trading system
FDI	foreign direct investment
GDP	gross domestic product
GEO 4	Fourth Global Environment Outlook
gha	global hectares
GHG	greenhouse gas
GPI	Genuine Progress Indicator
HDI	Human Development Index
HIV/AIDS	human immunodeficiency virus/ acquired immune deficiency syndrome
HPI	Happy Planet Index
HVDC	high-voltage direct current
IMF	International Monetary Fund
IPAT	impacts, population, affluence and technology
IPCC	Intergovernmental Panel on Climate Change
IPPUC	Urban Planning Institute of Curitiba
ISEW	Index of Sustainable Economic Welfare

LDC	less developed country
MDGs	Millennium Development Goals
MIT	Massachusetts Institute of Technology
MRSA	methicillin-resistant *Staphylococcus aureus*
MW	megawatt
NNP	net national product
OECD	Organisation for Economic Co-operation and Development
OPEC	Organization of the Petroleum Exporting Countries
PETM	Palaeocene–Eocene thermal maximum
PFCs	perfluorocarbons
ppm	parts per million
ppme	parts per million equivalent
PPP	polluter pays principle
PV	photovoltaic
R&D	research and development
REACH	Registration, Evaluation, Authorization and Restriction of Chemical Substances (EU)
RGGI	Regional Greenhouse Gas Initiative
SEEA	System of Integrated Environmental and Economic Accounting
SWB	subjective wellbeing
UN	United Nations
UNEP	United Nations Environment Programme
UV	ultraviolet
VAT	value added tax
WTA	willingness to accept
WTO	World Trade Organization
WTP	willingness to pay

Index